CULLEN BUNN

BONE PARISH ™

JONAS SCHARF   ALEX GUIMARÃES

VOLUME ONE

BOOM!
STUDIOS

BONE PARISH Volume One, May 2019. Published by BOOM! Studios, a division of Boom
Entertainment, Inc. Bone Parish is ™ & © 2019 Cullen Bunn. Originally published in single
magazine form as BONE PARISH No. 1-4. ™ & © 2018 Cullen Bunn. All rights reserved.
BOOM! Studios™ and the BOOM! Studios logo are trademarks of Boom Entertainment,
Inc., registered in various countries and categories. All characters, events, and institutions
depicted herein are fictional. Any similarity between any of the names, characters, persons, events, and/or institutions in this
publication to actual names, characters, and persons, whether living or dead, events, and/or institutions is unintended and
purely coincidental. BOOM! Studios does not read or accept unsolicited submissions of ideas, stories, or artwork.

For information regarding the CPSIA on this printed material, call: (203) 595-3636 and provide reference #RICH - 837714.

BOOM! Studios, 5670 Wilshire Boulevard, Suite 400, Los Angeles, CA 90036-5679. Printed in USA. First Printing.

ISBN: 978-1-68415-354-1, eISBN: 978-1-64144-337-1

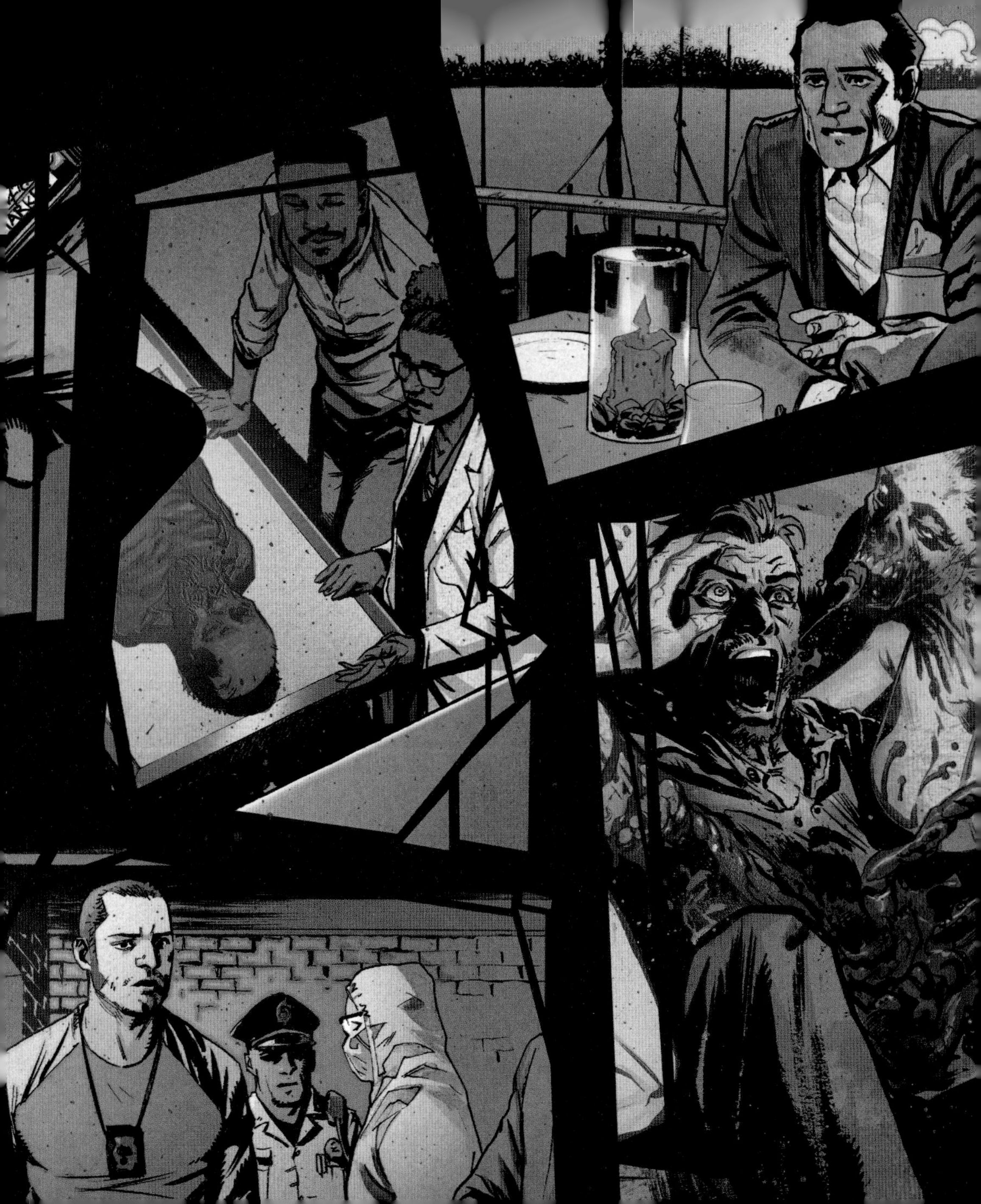

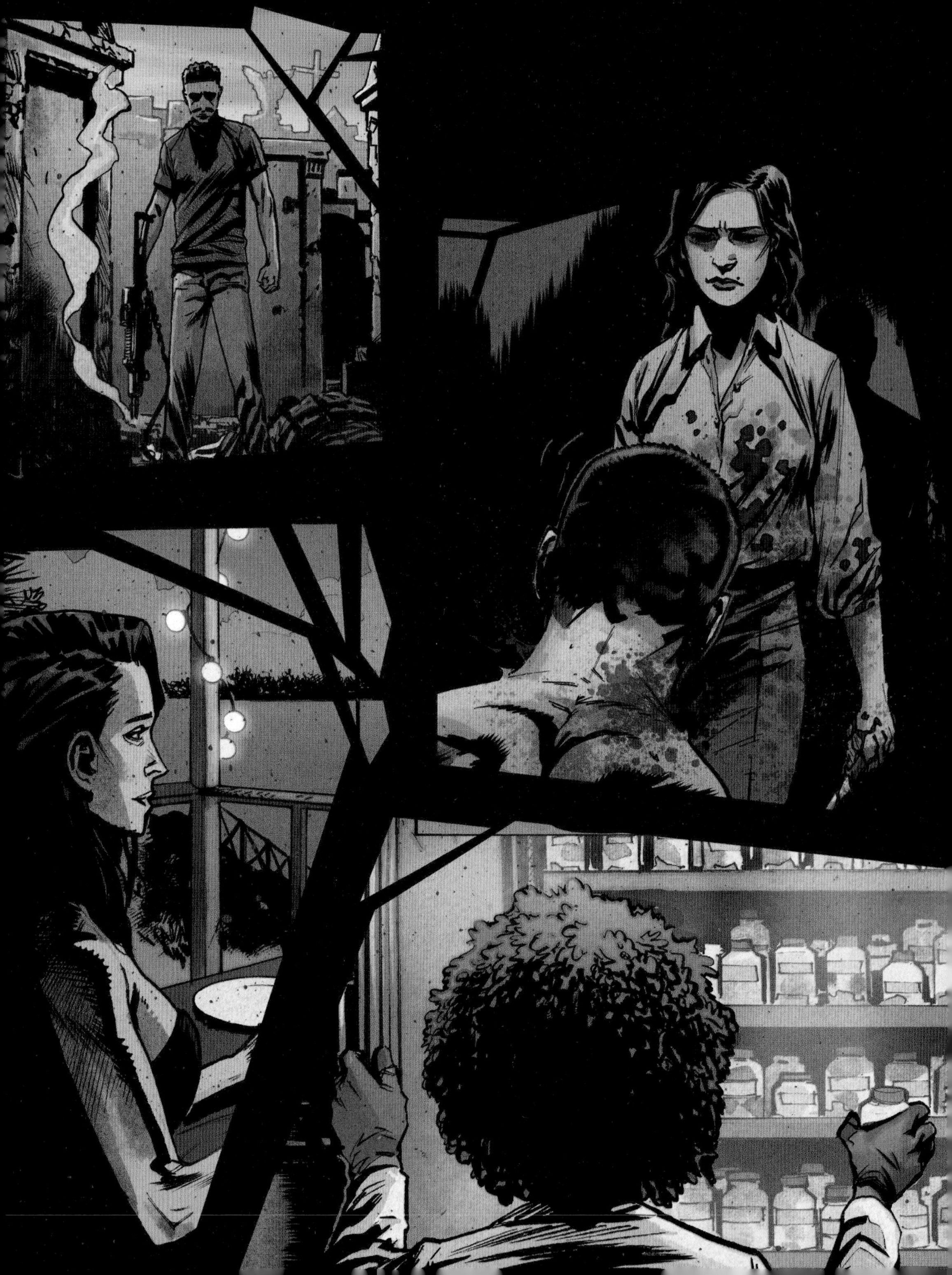

Written by
CULLEN BUNN

Illustrated by
JONAS SCHARF

Colored by
ALEX GUIMARÃES

Lettered by
ED DUKESHIRE

Cover by
LEE GARBETT

Series Designer
MICHELLE ANKLEY

Collection Designer
JILLIAN CRAB

Editor
ERIC HARBURN

BONE PARISH Created by
CULLEN BUNN & JONAS SCHARF

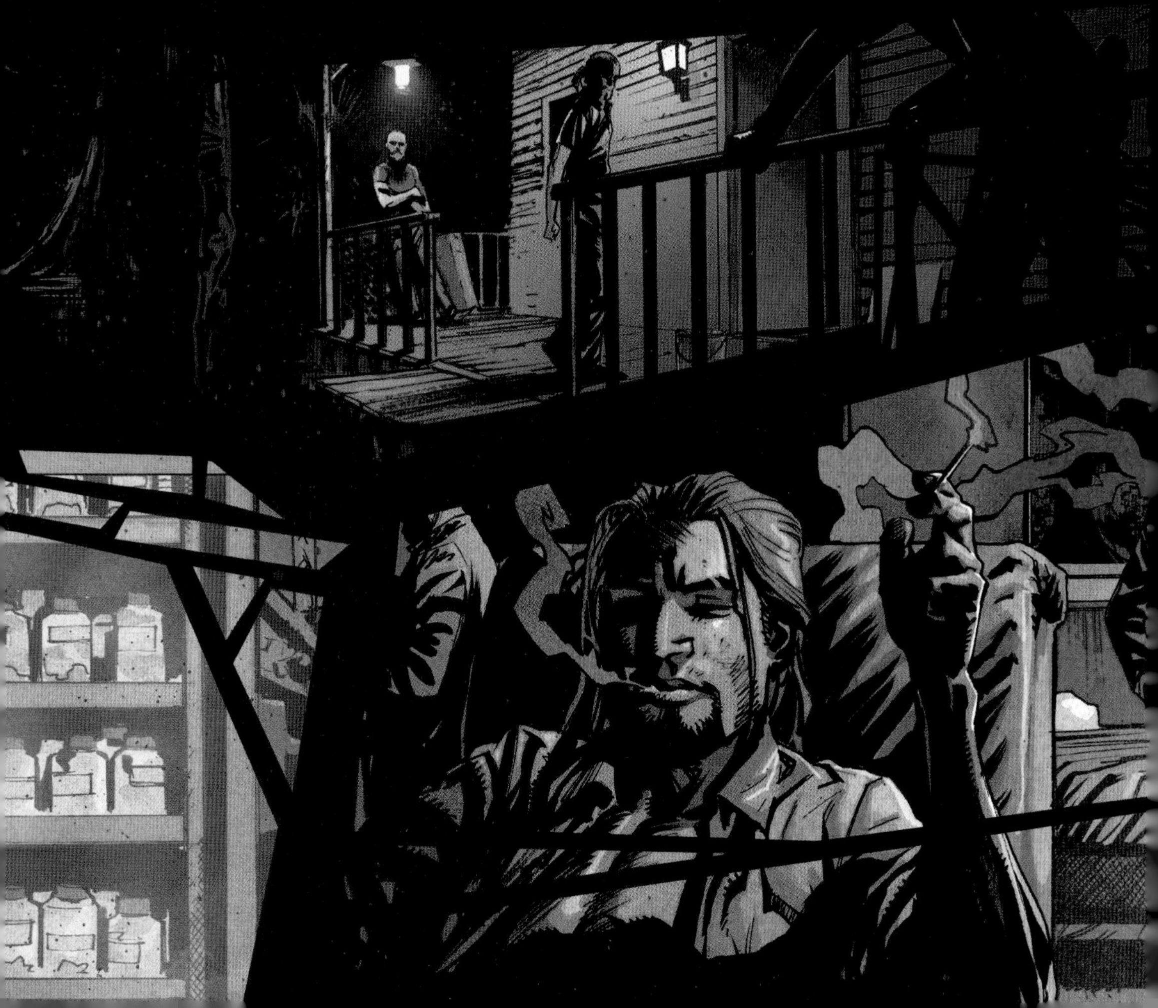

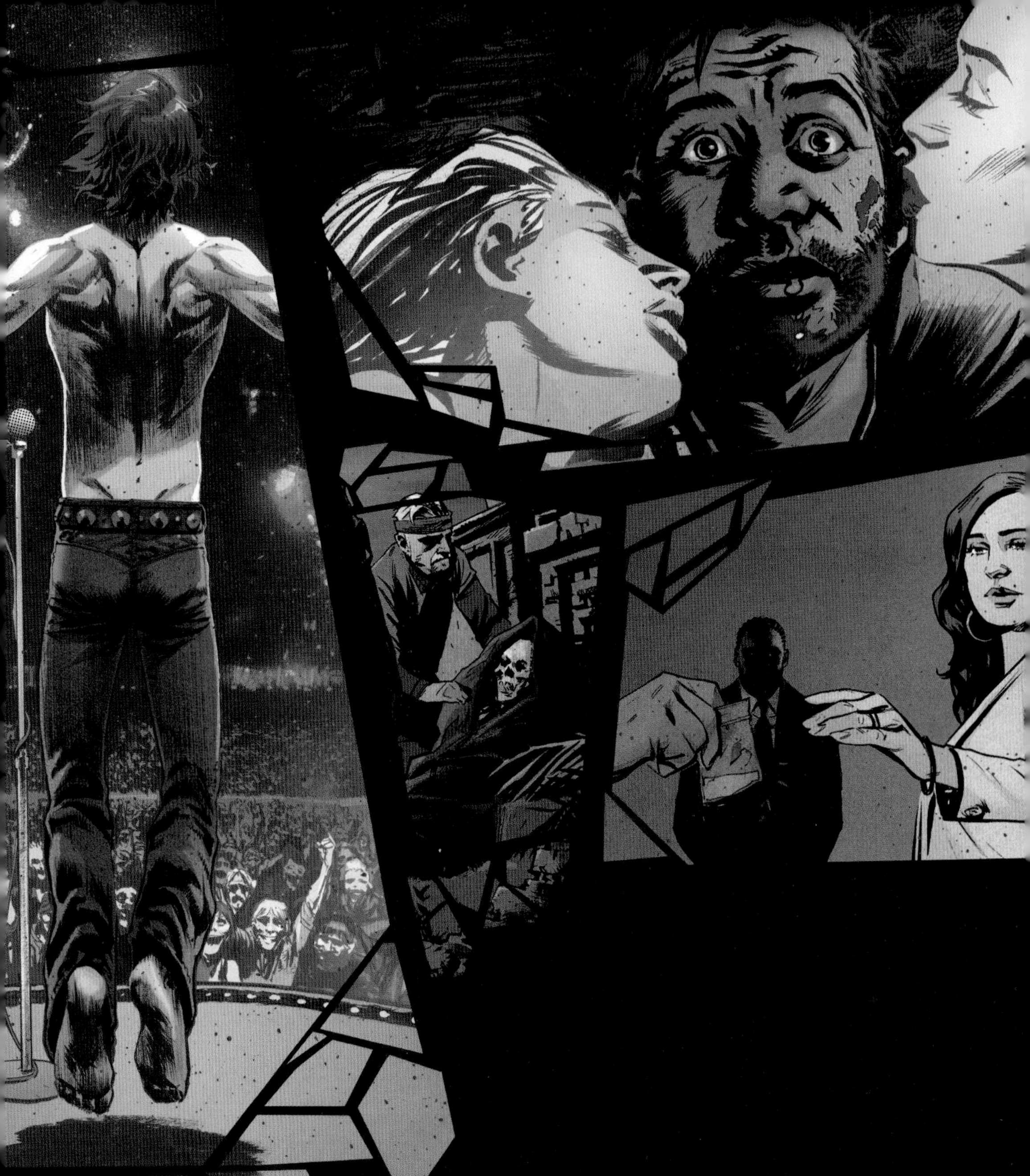

Chapter One

BE NOT PROUD

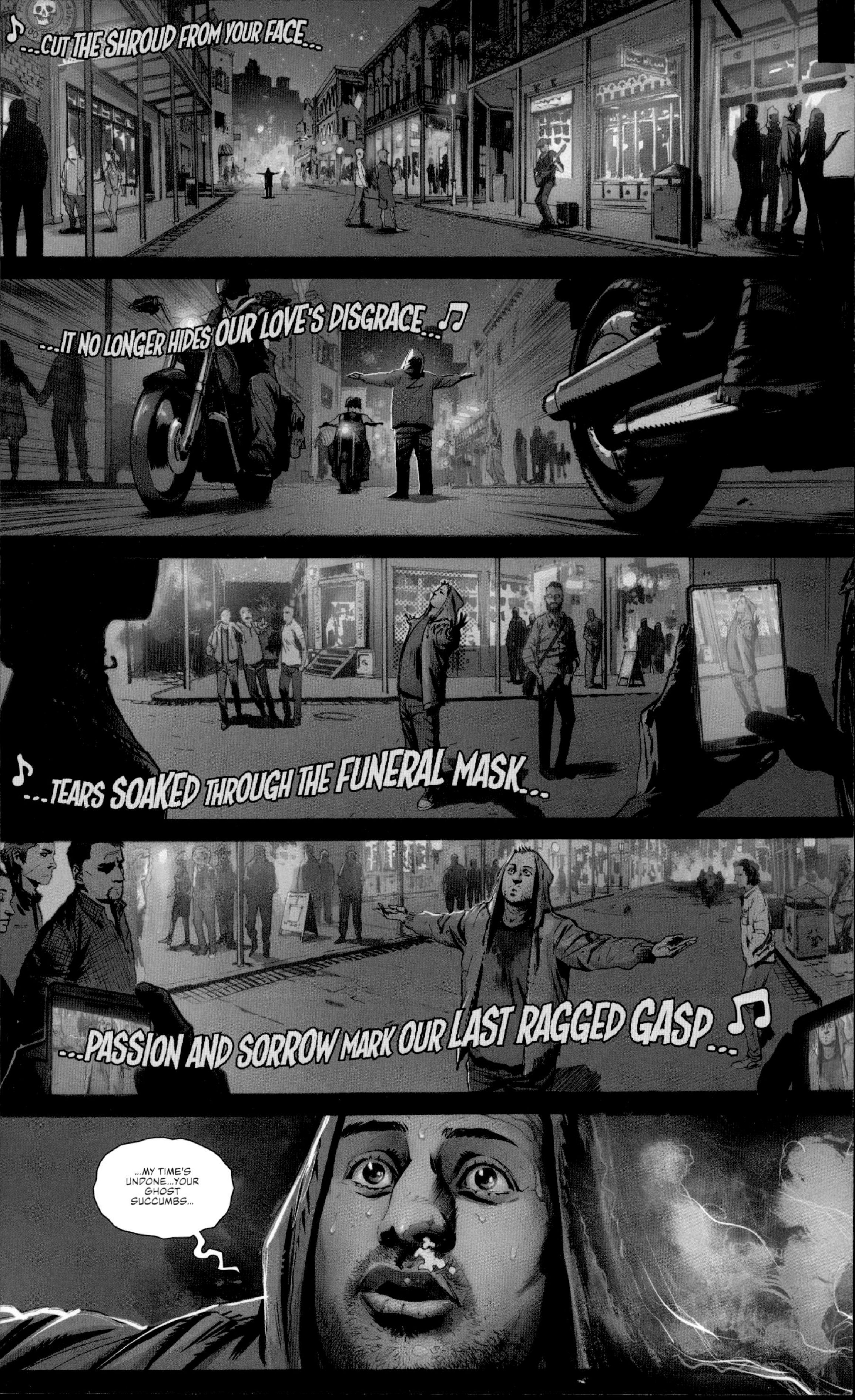
...CUT THE SHROUD FROM YOUR FACE...
...IT NO LONGER HIDES OUR LOVE'S DISGRACE...
...TEARS SOAKED THROUGH THE FUNERAL MASK...
...PASSION AND SORROW MARK OUR LAST RAGGED GASP...
...MY TIME'S UNDONE...YOUR GHOST SUCCUMBS...

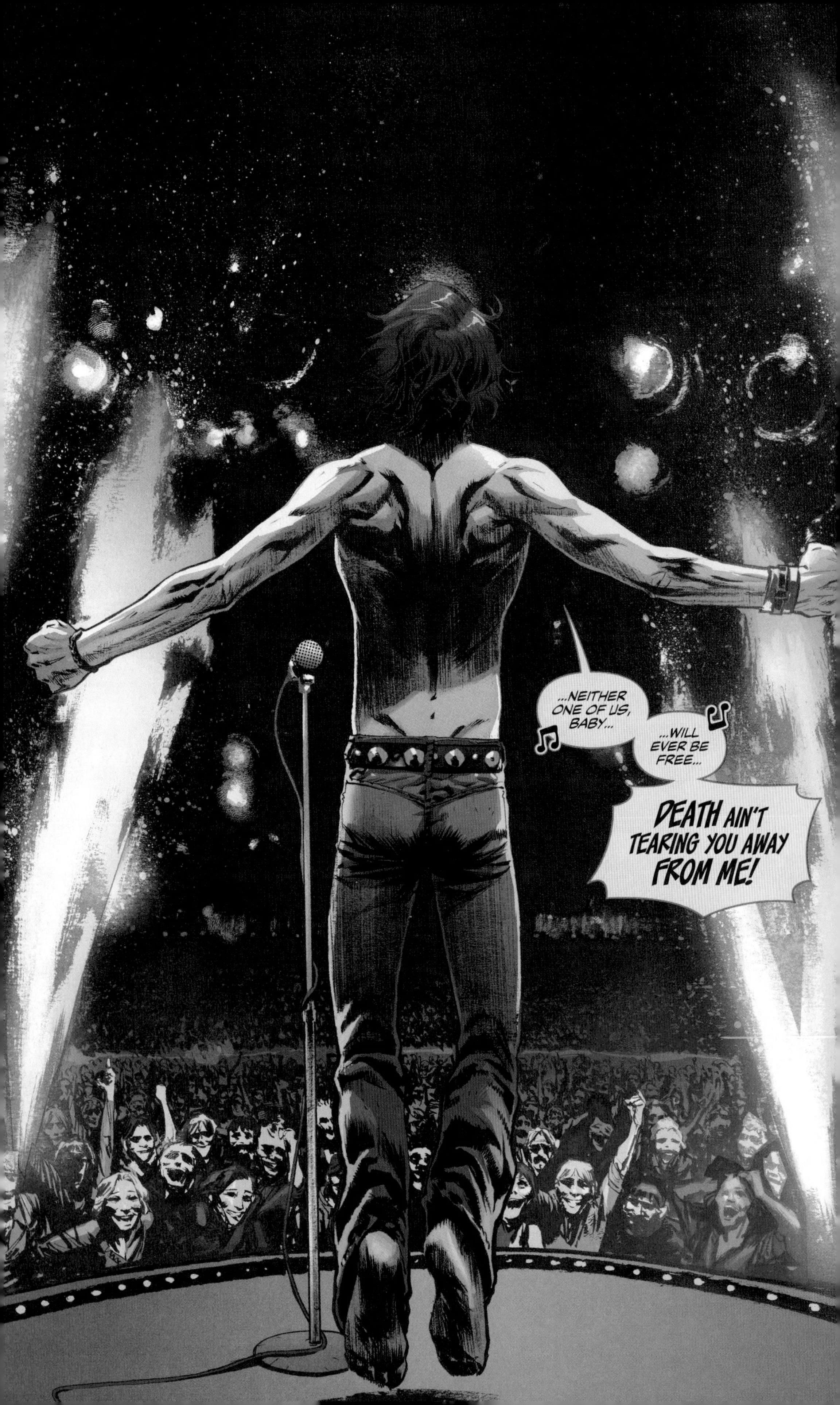
...NEITHER ONE OF US, BABY...
...WILL EVER BE FREE...
DEATH AIN'T TEARING YOU AWAY FROM ME!

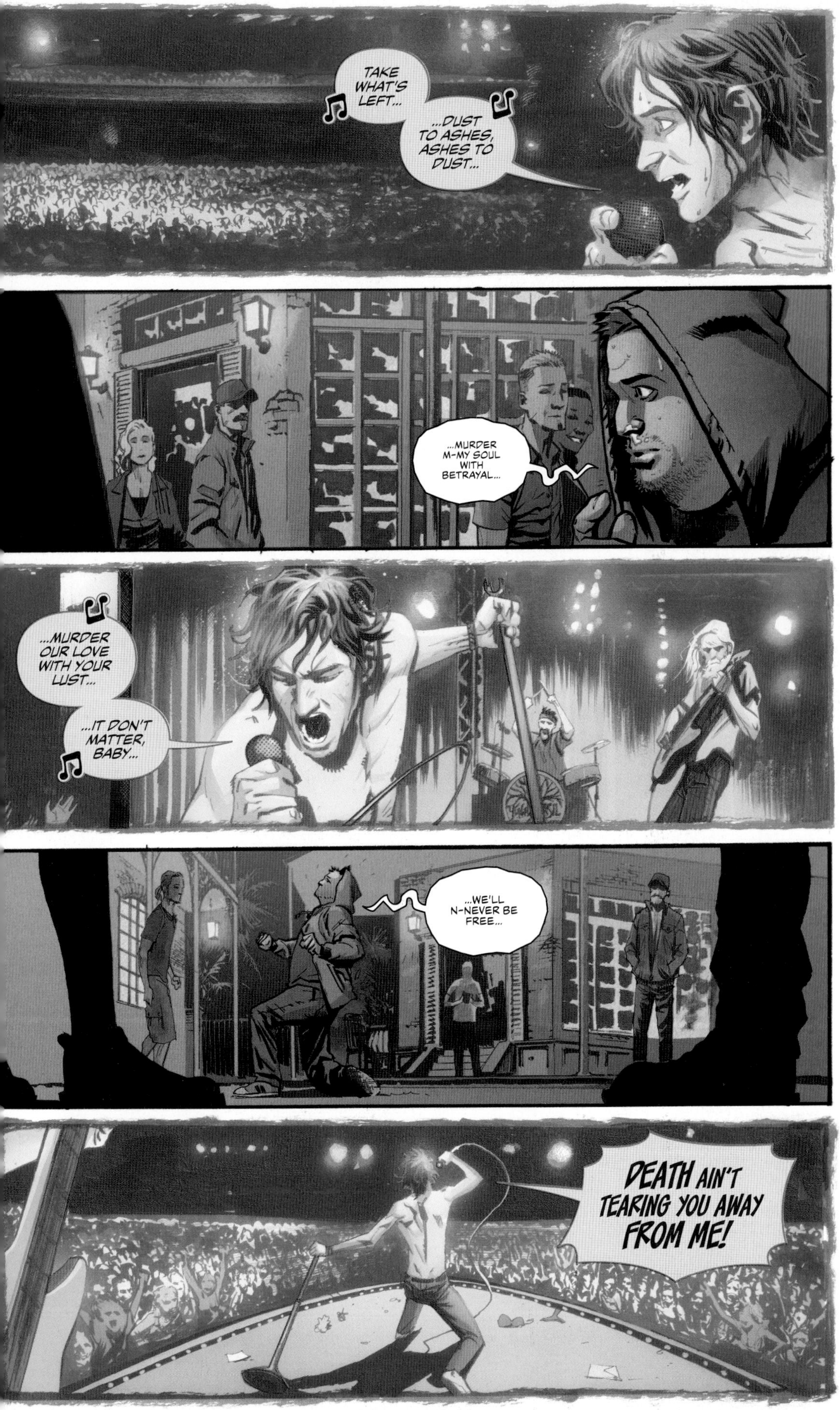
TAKE WHAT'S LEFT...
...DUST TO ASHES, ASHES TO DUST...
...MURDER M-MY SOUL WITH BETRAYAL...
...MURDER OUR LOVE WITH YOUR LUST...
...IT DON'T MATTER, BABY...
...WE'LL N-NEVER BE FREE...
DEATH AIN'T TEARING YOU AWAY FROM ME!

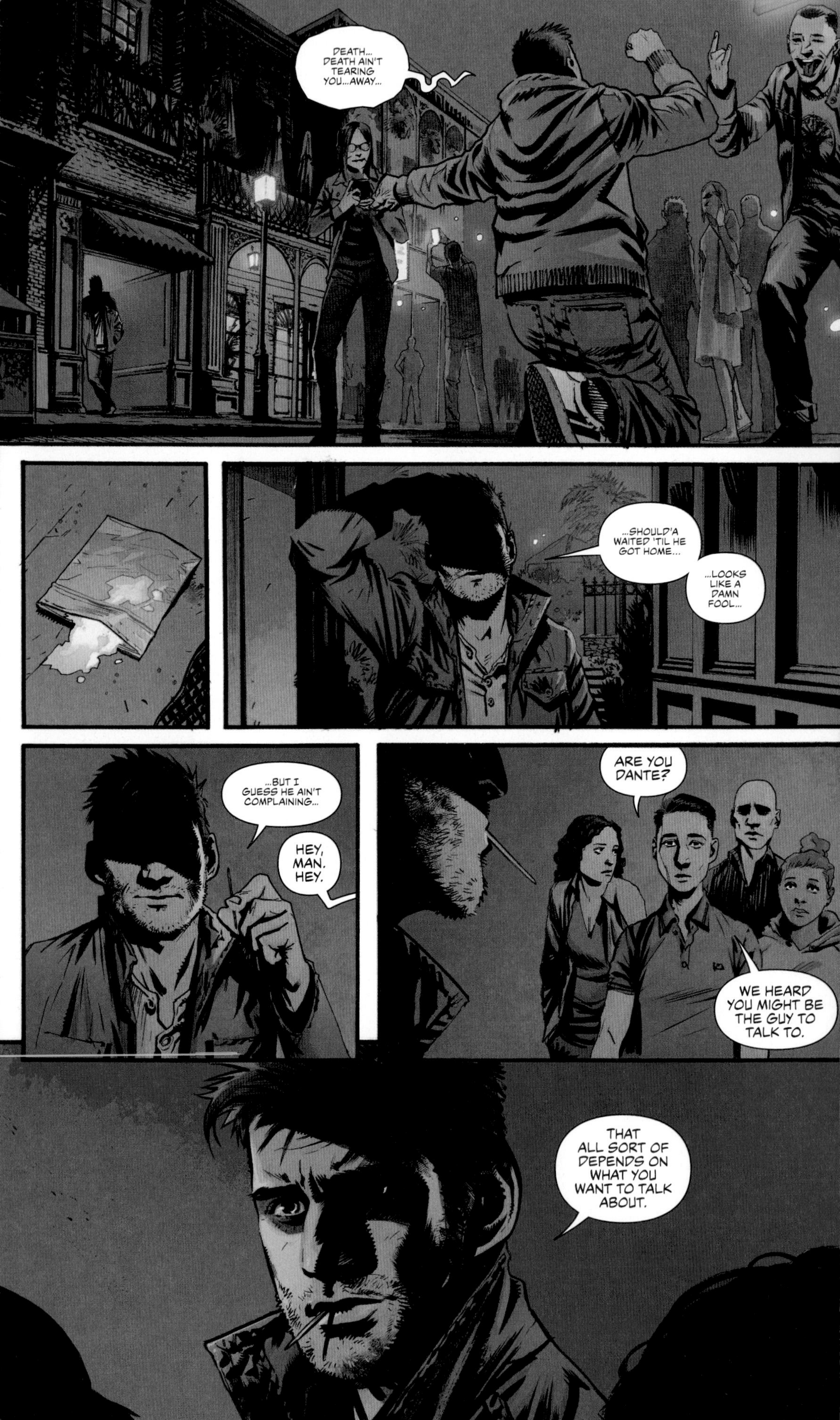
DEATH... DEATH AIN'T TEARING YOU...AWAY...
...SHOULD'A WAITED 'TIL HE GOT HOME...
...LOOKS LIKE A DAMN FOOL...
...BUT I GUESS HE AIN'T COMPLAINING...
HEY, MAN. HEY.
ARE YOU DANTE?
WE HEARD YOU MIGHT BE THE GUY TO TALK TO.
THAT ALL SORT OF DEPENDS ON WHAT YOU WANT TO TALK ABOUT.

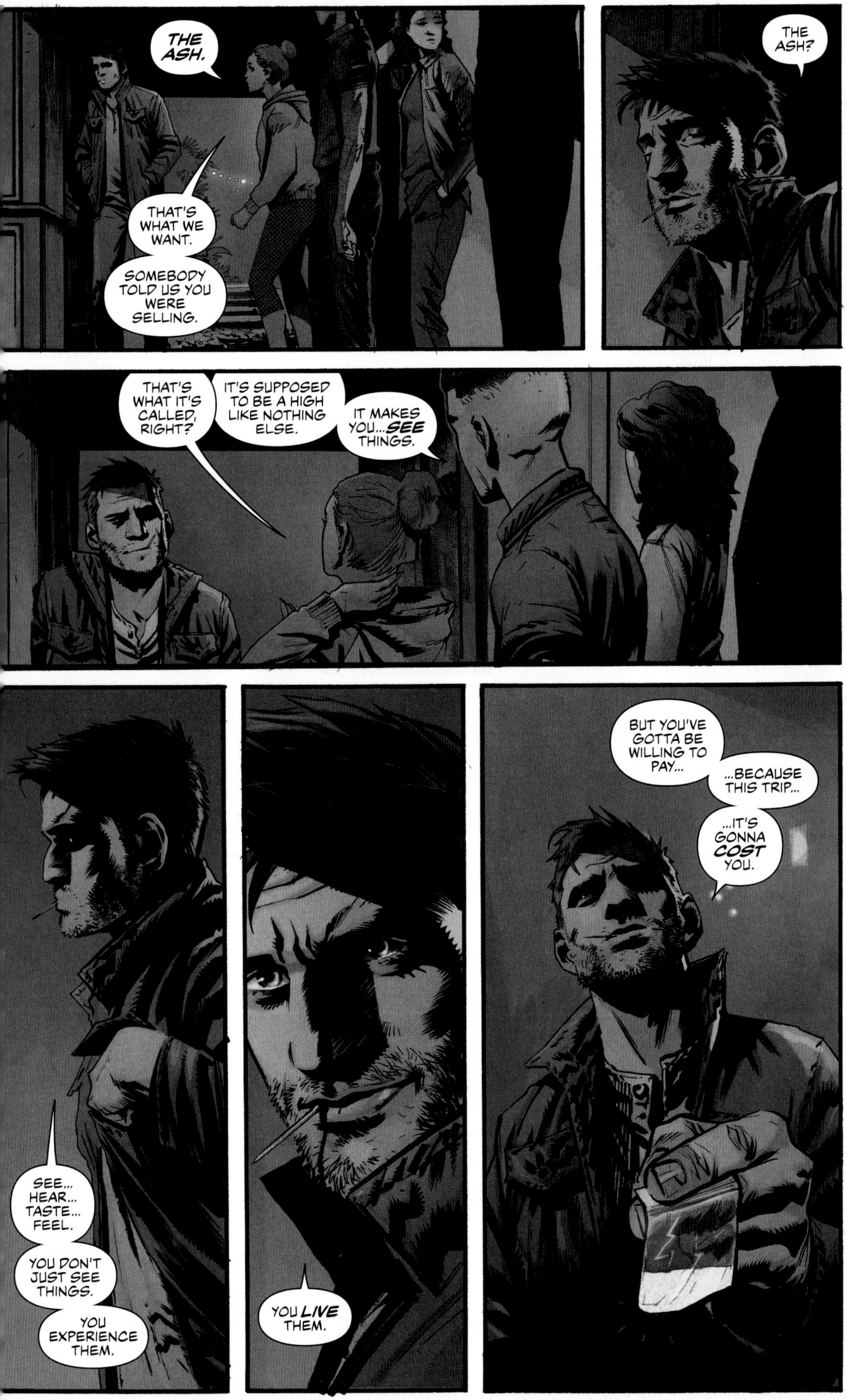

THE ASH.
THAT'S WHAT WE WANT.
SOMEBODY TOLD US YOU WERE SELLING.
THE ASH?
THAT'S WHAT IT'S CALLED, RIGHT?
IT'S SUPPOSED TO BE A HIGH LIKE NOTHING ELSE.
IT MAKES YOU...SEE THINGS.
SEE... HEAR... TASTE... FEEL.
YOU DON'T JUST SEE THINGS.
YOU EXPERIENCE THEM.
YOU LIVE THEM.
BUT YOU'VE GOTTA BE WILLING TO PAY...
...BECAUSE THIS TRIP...
...IT'S GONNA COST YOU.

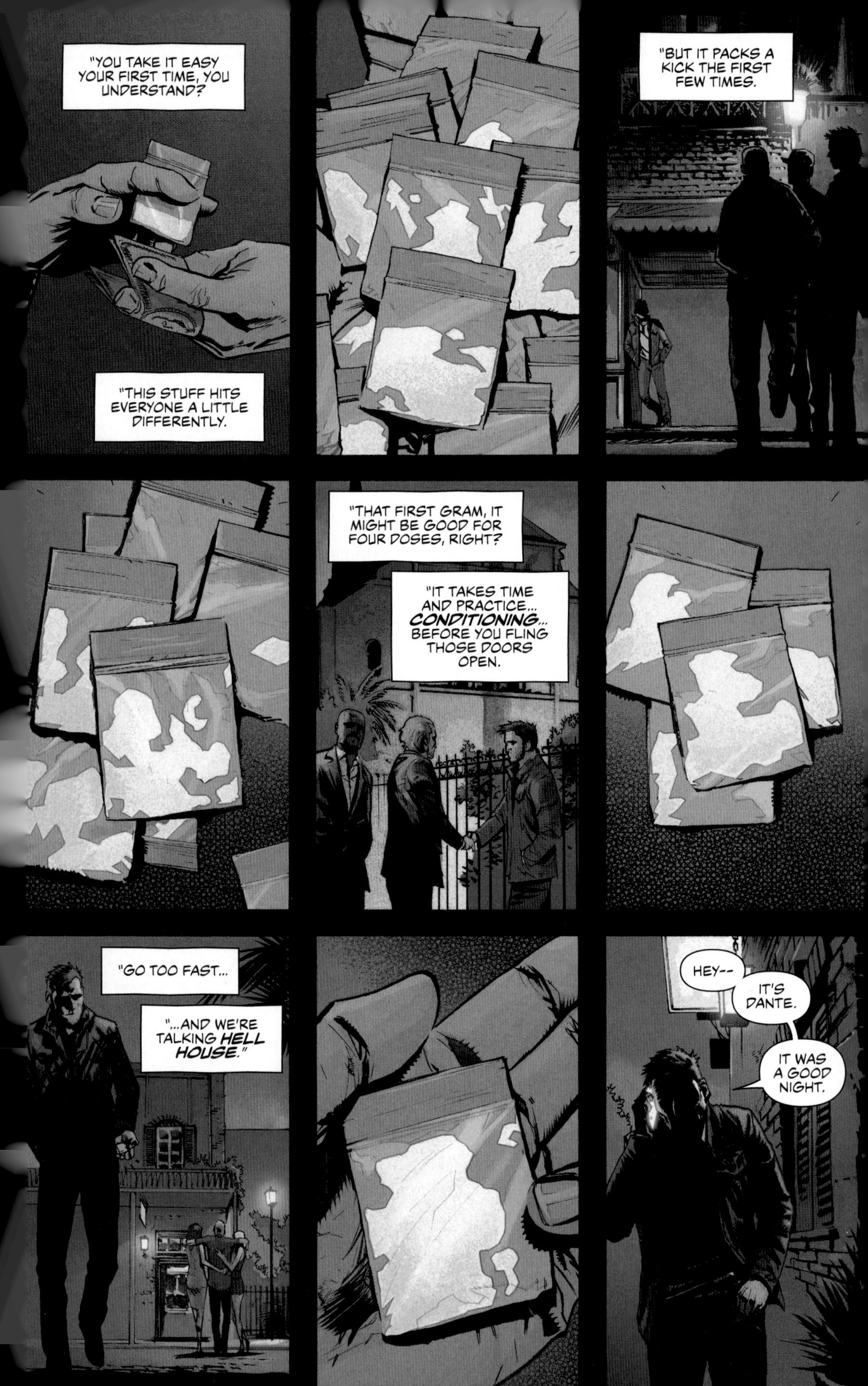
"YOU TAKE IT EASY YOUR FIRST TIME, YOU UNDERSTAND?
"THIS STUFF HITS EVERYONE A LITTLE DIFFERENTLY.
"BUT IT PACKS A KICK THE FIRST FEW TIMES.
"THAT FIRST GRAM, IT MIGHT BE GOOD FOR FOUR DOSES, RIGHT?
"IT TAKES TIME AND PRACTICE... CONDITIONING... BEFORE YOU FLING THOSE DOORS OPEN.
"GO TOO FAST...
"...AND WE'RE TALKING HELL HOUSE."
HEY--
IT'S DANTE.
IT WAS A GOOD NIGHT.

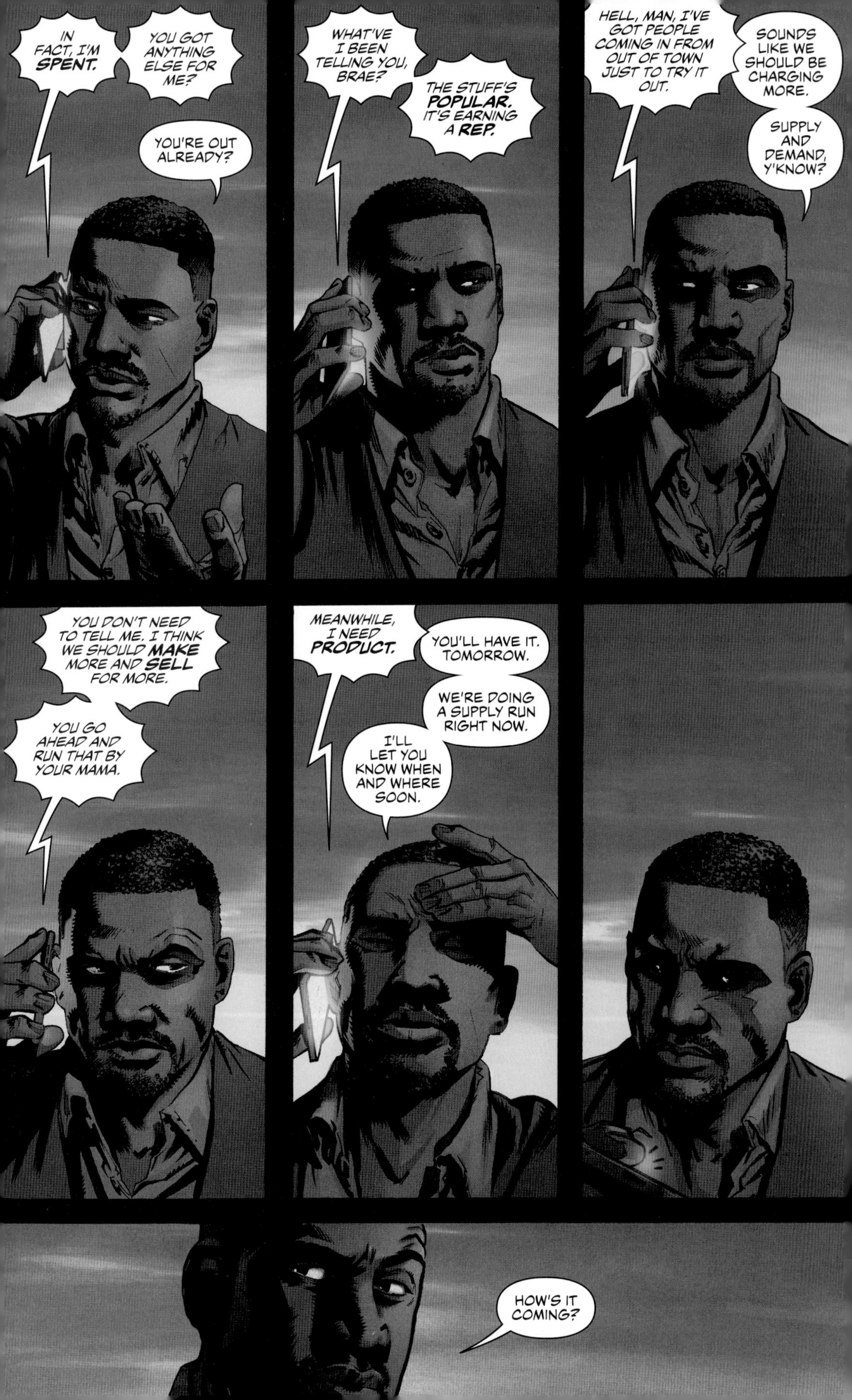
IN FACT, I'M SPENT.
YOU GOT ANYTHING ELSE FOR ME?
YOU'RE OUT ALREADY?
WHAT'VE I BEEN TELLING YOU, BRAE?
THE STUFF'S POPULAR. IT'S EARNING A REP.
HELL, MAN, I'VE GOT PEOPLE COMING IN FROM OUT OF TOWN JUST TO TRY IT OUT.
SOUNDS LIKE WE SHOULD BE CHARGING MORE.
SUPPLY AND DEMAND, Y'KNOW?
YOU DON'T NEED TO TELL ME. I THINK WE SHOULD MAKE MORE AND SELL FOR MORE.
YOU GO AHEAD AND RUN THAT BY YOUR MAMA.
MEANWHILE, I NEED PRODUCT.
YOU'LL HAVE IT. TOMORROW.
WE'RE DOING A SUPPLY RUN RIGHT NOW.
I'LL LET YOU KNOW WHEN AND WHERE SOON.
HOW'S IT COMING?

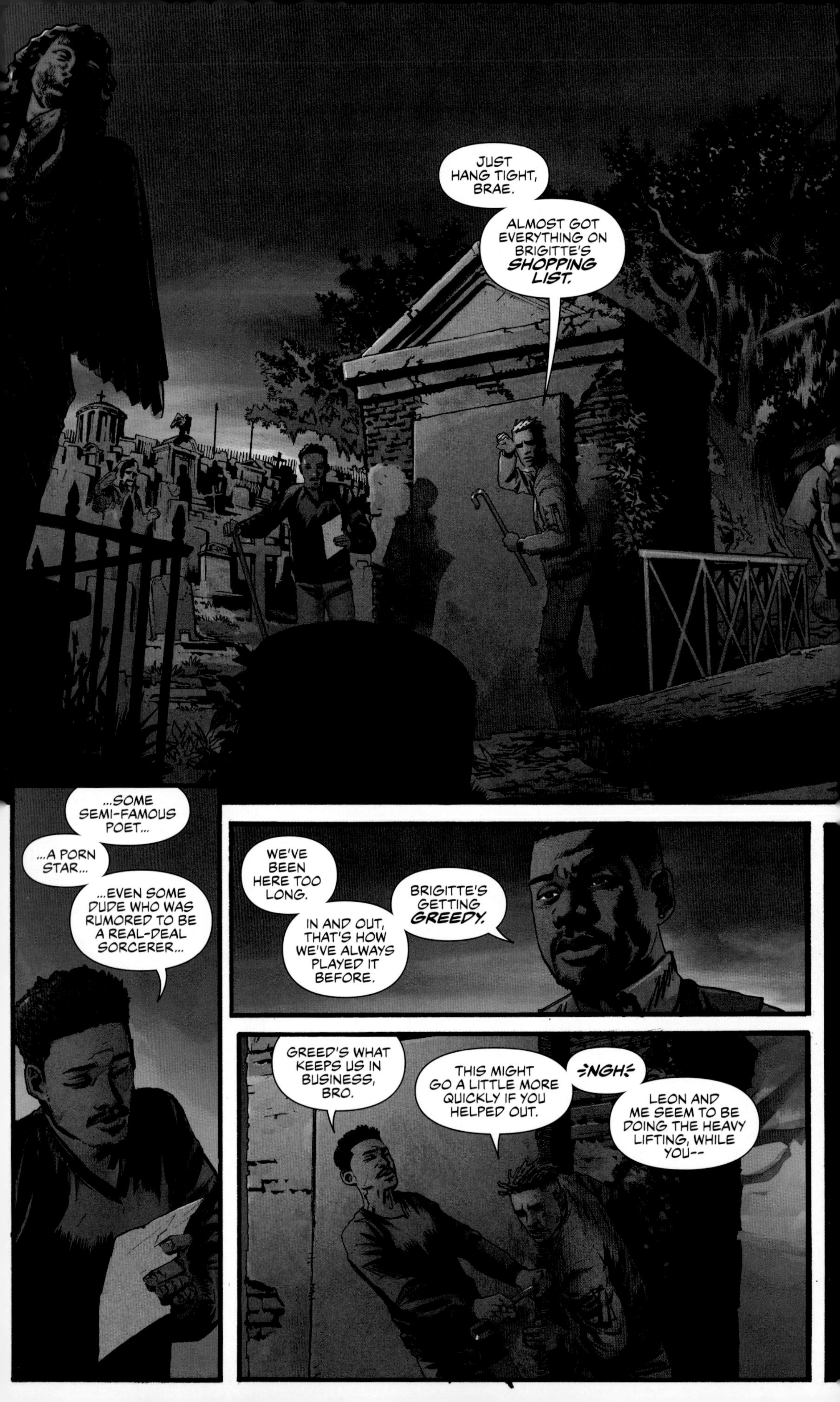

JUST HANG TIGHT, BRAE.
ALMOST GOT EVERYTHING ON BRIGITTE'S *SHOPPING LIST.*
...SOME SEMI-FAMOUS POET...
...A PORN STAR...
...EVEN SOME DUDE WHO WAS RUMORED TO BE A REAL-DEAL SORCERER...
WE'VE BEEN HERE TOO LONG.
IN AND OUT, THAT'S HOW WE'VE ALWAYS PLAYED IT BEFORE.
BRIGITTE'S GETTING *GREEDY.*
GREED'S WHAT KEEPS US IN BUSINESS, BRO.
THIS MIGHT GO A LITTLE MORE QUICKLY IF YOU HELPED OUT.
NGH
LEON AND ME SEEM TO BE DOING THE HEAVY LIFTING, WHILE YOU--

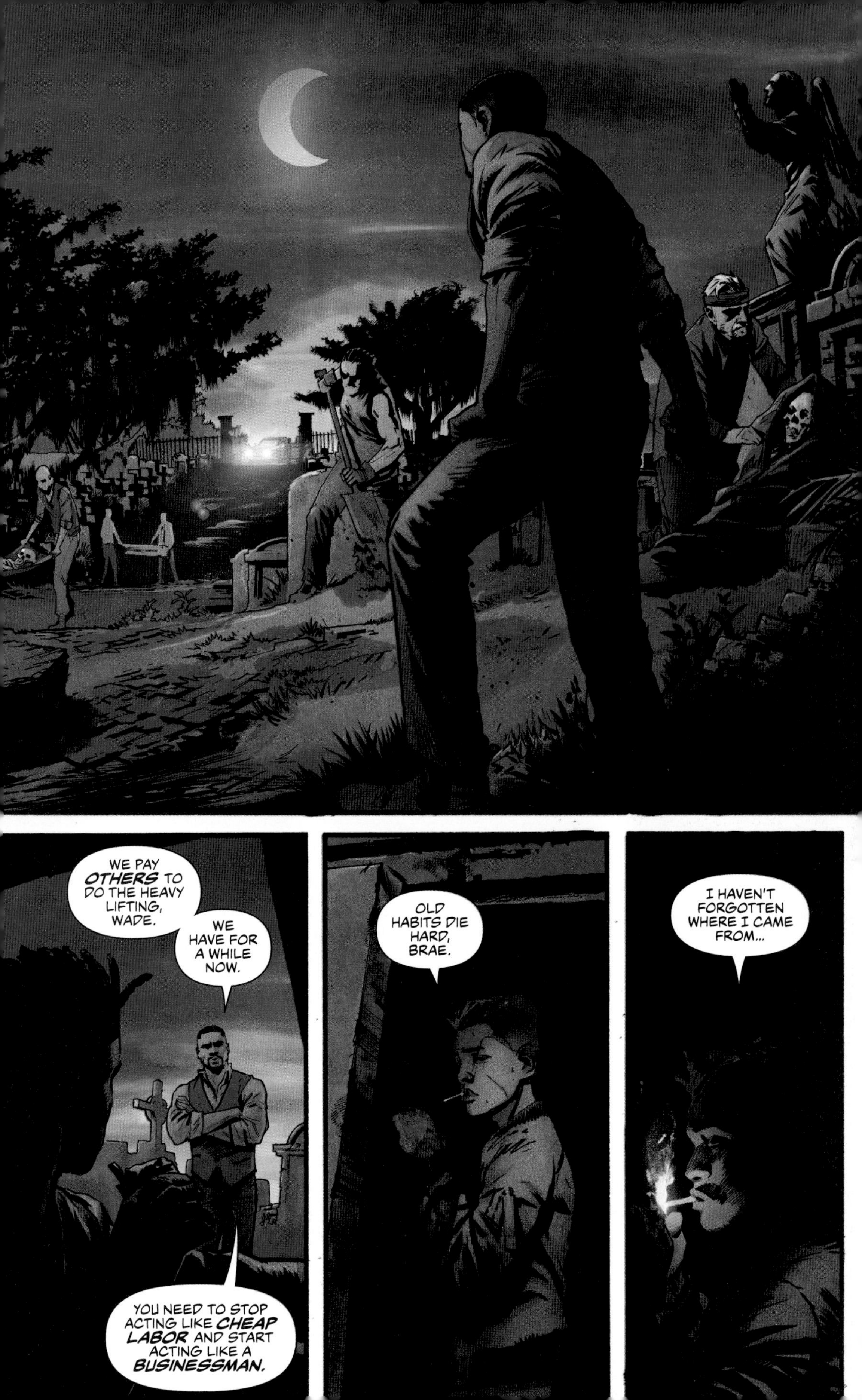
WE PAY OTHERS TO DO THE HEAVY LIFTING, WADE.
WE HAVE FOR A WHILE NOW.
YOU NEED TO STOP ACTING LIKE CHEAP LABOR AND START ACTING LIKE A BUSINESSMAN.
OLD HABITS DIE HARD, BRAE.
I HAVEN'T FORGOTTEN WHERE I CAME FROM...

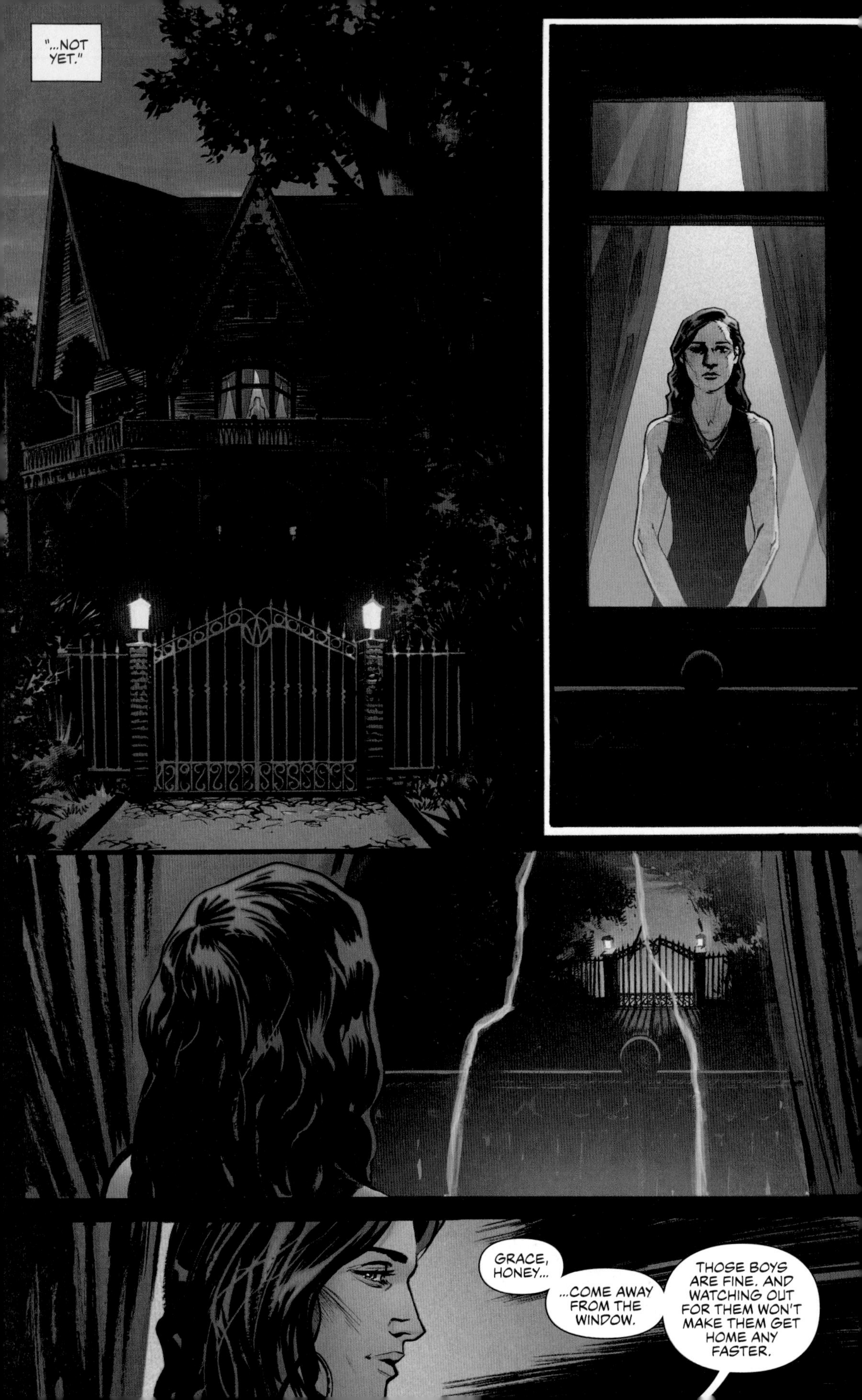
"...NOT YET."
GRACE, HONEY...
...COME AWAY FROM THE WINDOW.
THOSE BOYS ARE FINE. AND WATCHING OUT FOR THEM WON'T MAKE THEM GET HOME ANY FASTER.

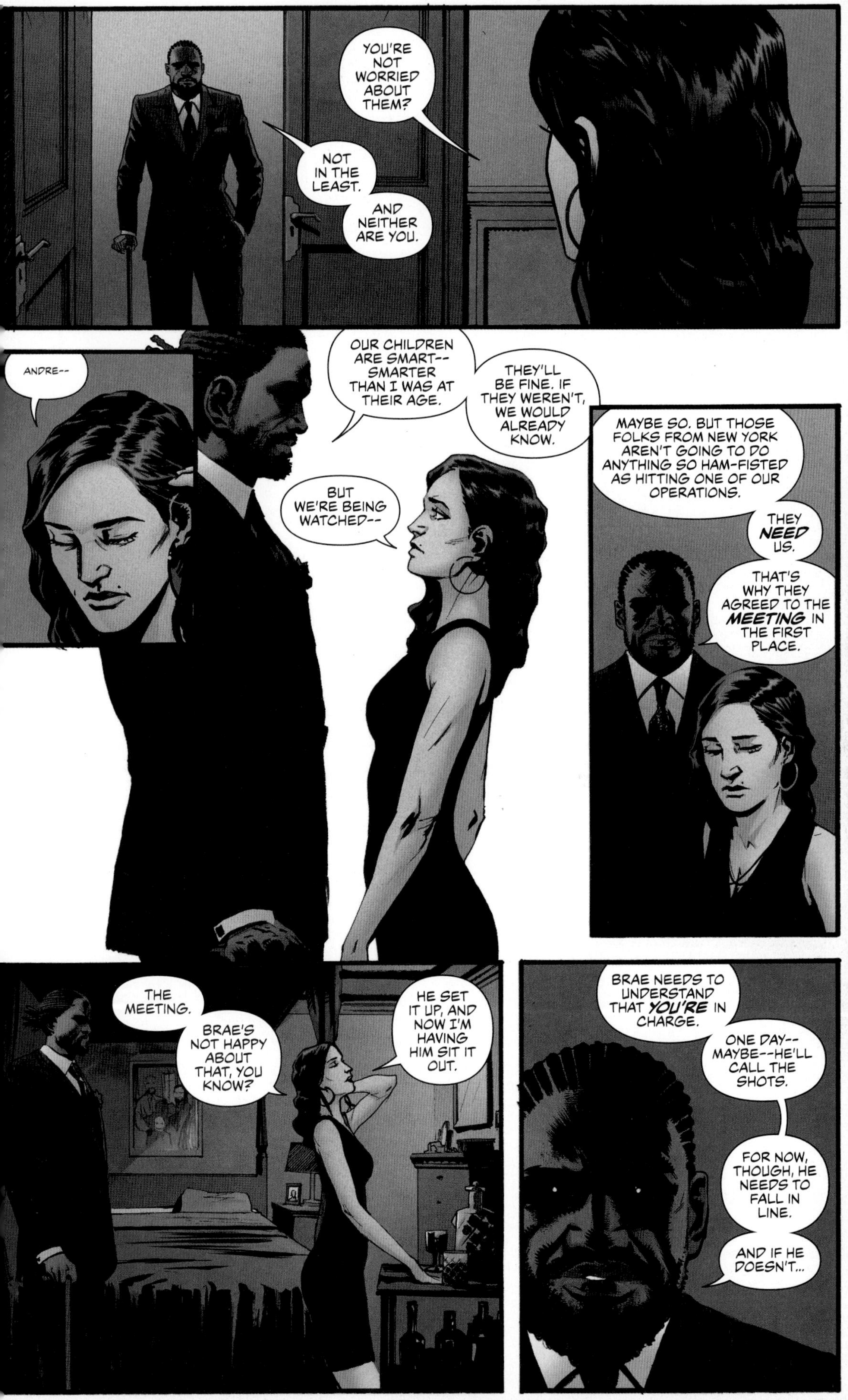
YOU'RE NOT WORRIED ABOUT THEM?
NOT IN THE LEAST.
AND NEITHER ARE YOU.
ANDRE--
OUR CHILDREN ARE SMART-- SMARTER THAN I WAS AT THEIR AGE.
THEY'LL BE FINE. IF THEY WEREN'T, WE WOULD ALREADY KNOW.
BUT WE'RE BEING WATCHED--
MAYBE SO. BUT THOSE FOLKS FROM NEW YORK AREN'T GOING TO DO ANYTHING SO HAM-FISTED AS HITTING ONE OF OUR OPERATIONS.
THEY NEED US.
THAT'S WHY THEY AGREED TO THE MEETING IN THE FIRST PLACE.
THE MEETING.
BRAE'S NOT HAPPY ABOUT THAT, YOU KNOW?
HE SET IT UP, AND NOW I'M HAVING HIM SIT IT OUT.
BRAE NEEDS TO UNDERSTAND THAT YOU'RE IN CHARGE.
ONE DAY-- MAYBE--HE'LL CALL THE SHOTS.
FOR NOW, THOUGH, HE NEEDS TO FALL IN LINE.
AND IF HE DOESN'T...

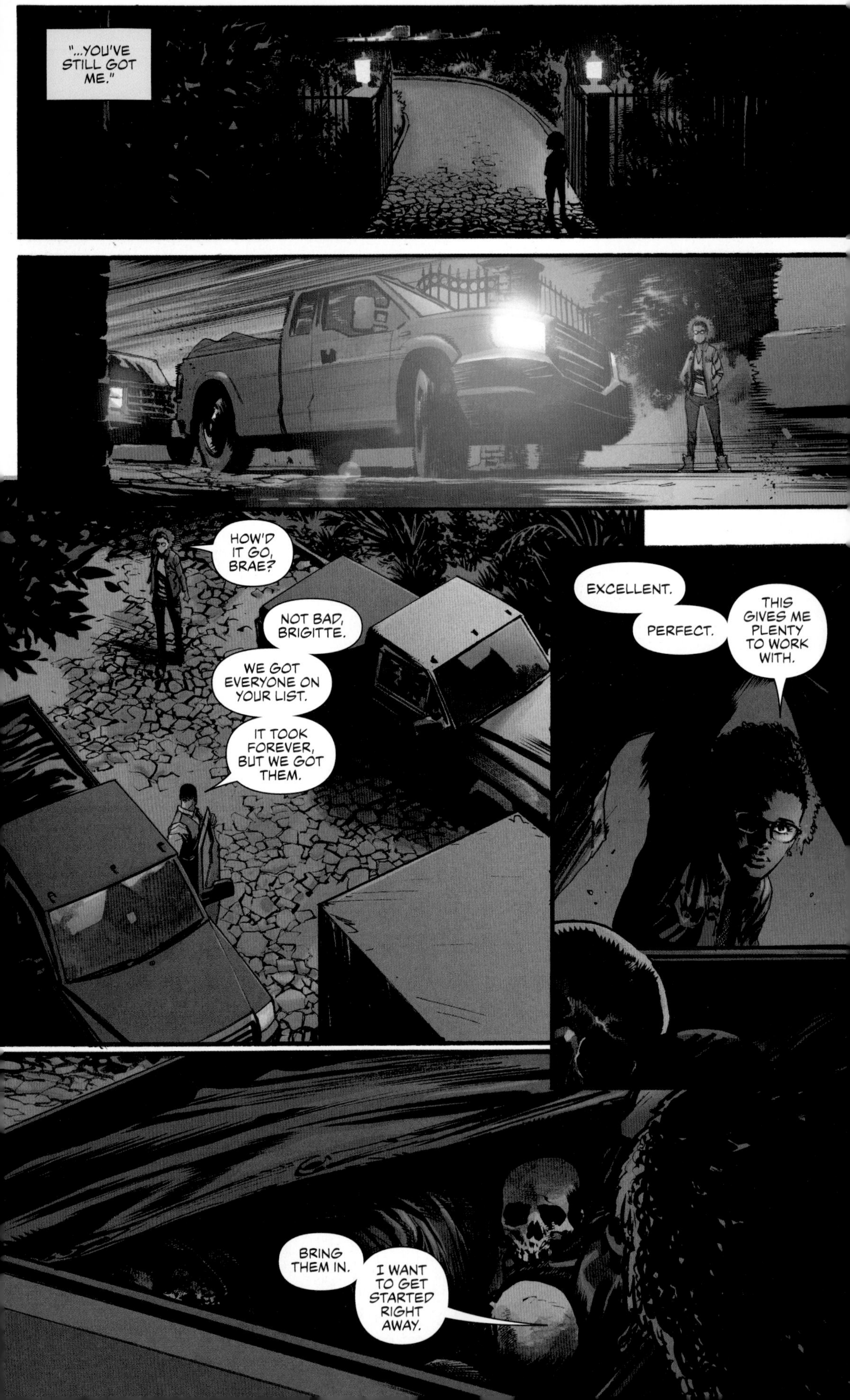

"...YOU'VE STILL GOT ME."
HOW'D IT GO, BRAE?
NOT BAD, BRIGITTE.
WE GOT EVERYONE ON YOUR LIST.
IT TOOK FOREVER, BUT WE GOT THEM.
EXCELLENT.
PERFECT.
THIS GIVES ME PLENTY TO WORK WITH.
BRING THEM IN.
I WANT TO GET STARTED RIGHT AWAY.

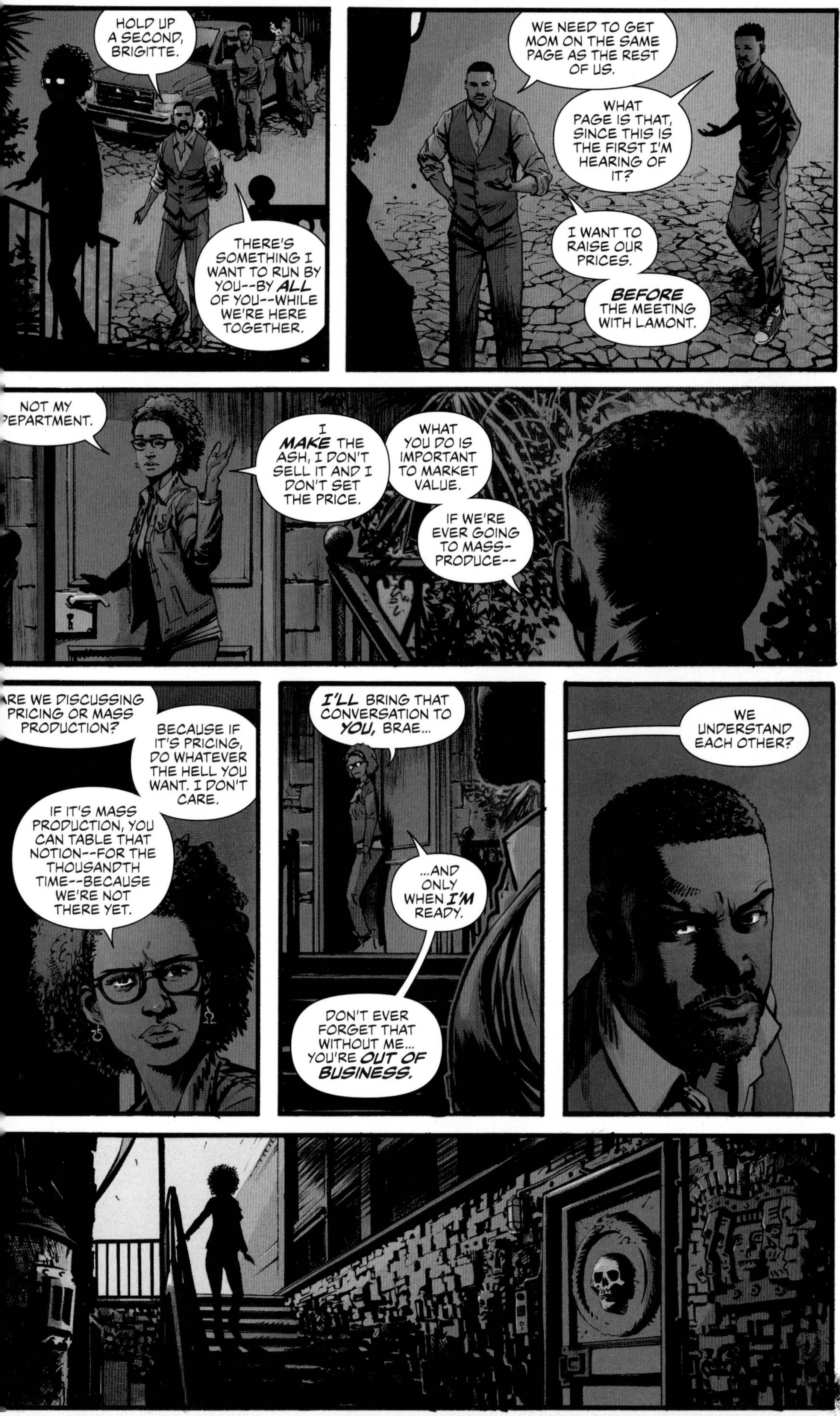
HOLD UP A SECOND, BRIGITTE.
THERE'S SOMETHING I WANT TO RUN BY YOU--BY ALL OF YOU--WHILE WE'RE HERE TOGETHER.
WE NEED TO GET MOM ON THE SAME PAGE AS THE REST OF US.
WHAT PAGE IS THAT, SINCE THIS IS THE FIRST I'M HEARING OF IT?
I WANT TO RAISE OUR PRICES.
BEFORE THE MEETING WITH LAMONT.
NOT MY DEPARTMENT.
I MAKE THE ASH, I DON'T SELL IT AND I DON'T SET THE PRICE.
WHAT YOU DO IS IMPORTANT TO MARKET VALUE.
IF WE'RE EVER GOING TO MASS-PRODUCE--
ARE WE DISCUSSING PRICING OR MASS PRODUCTION?
BECAUSE IF IT'S PRICING, DO WHATEVER THE HELL YOU WANT. I DON'T CARE.
IF IT'S MASS PRODUCTION, YOU CAN TABLE THAT NOTION--FOR THE THOUSANDTH TIME--BECAUSE WE'RE NOT THERE YET.
I'LL BRING THAT CONVERSATION TO YOU, BRAE...
...AND ONLY WHEN I'M READY.
DON'T EVER FORGET THAT WITHOUT ME... YOU'RE OUT OF BUSINESS.
WE UNDERSTAND EACH OTHER?

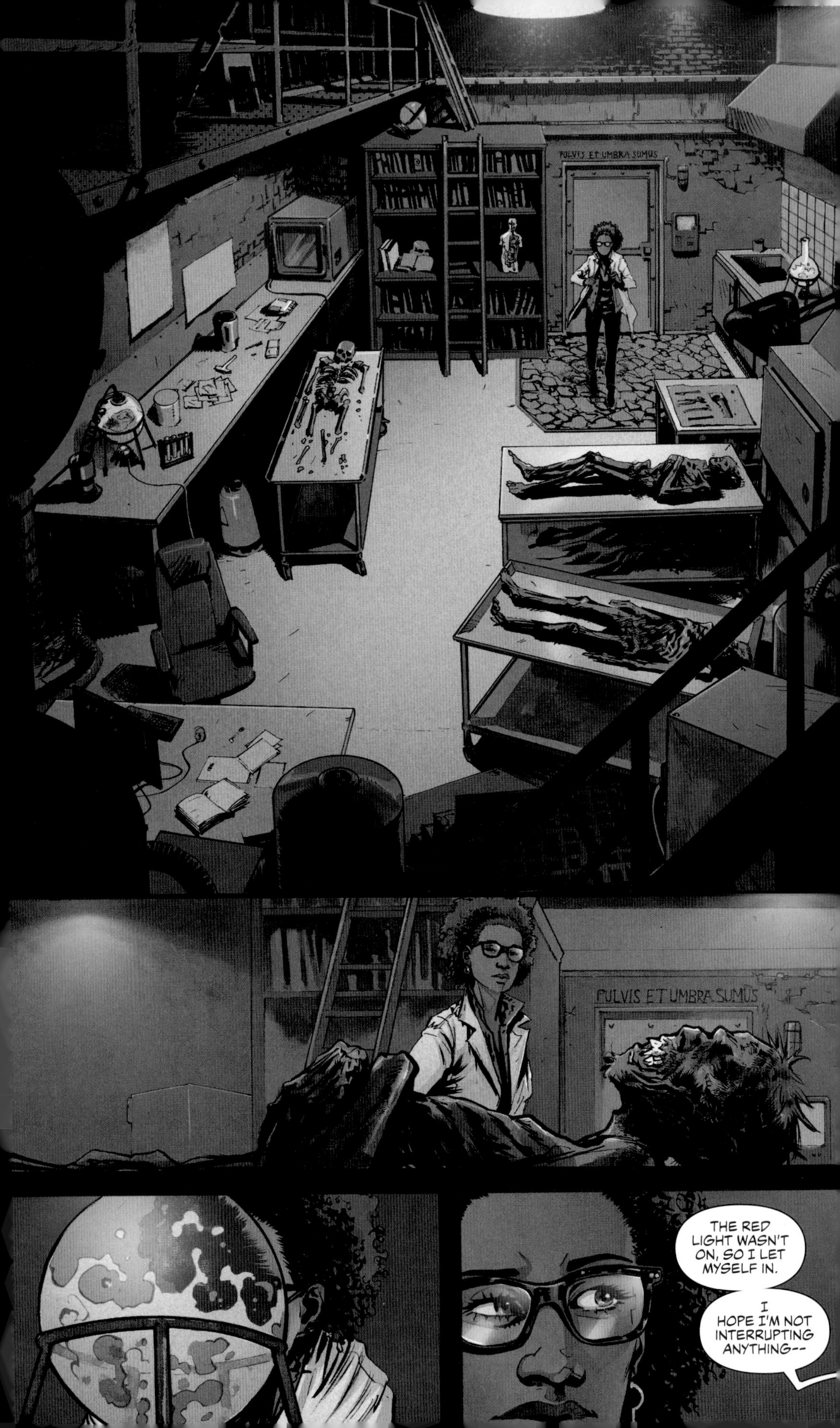
PULVIS ET UMBRA SUMUS
PULVIS ET UMBRA SUMUS
THE RED LIGHT WASN'T ON, SO I LET MYSELF IN.
I HOPE I'M NOT INTERRUPTING ANYTHING--

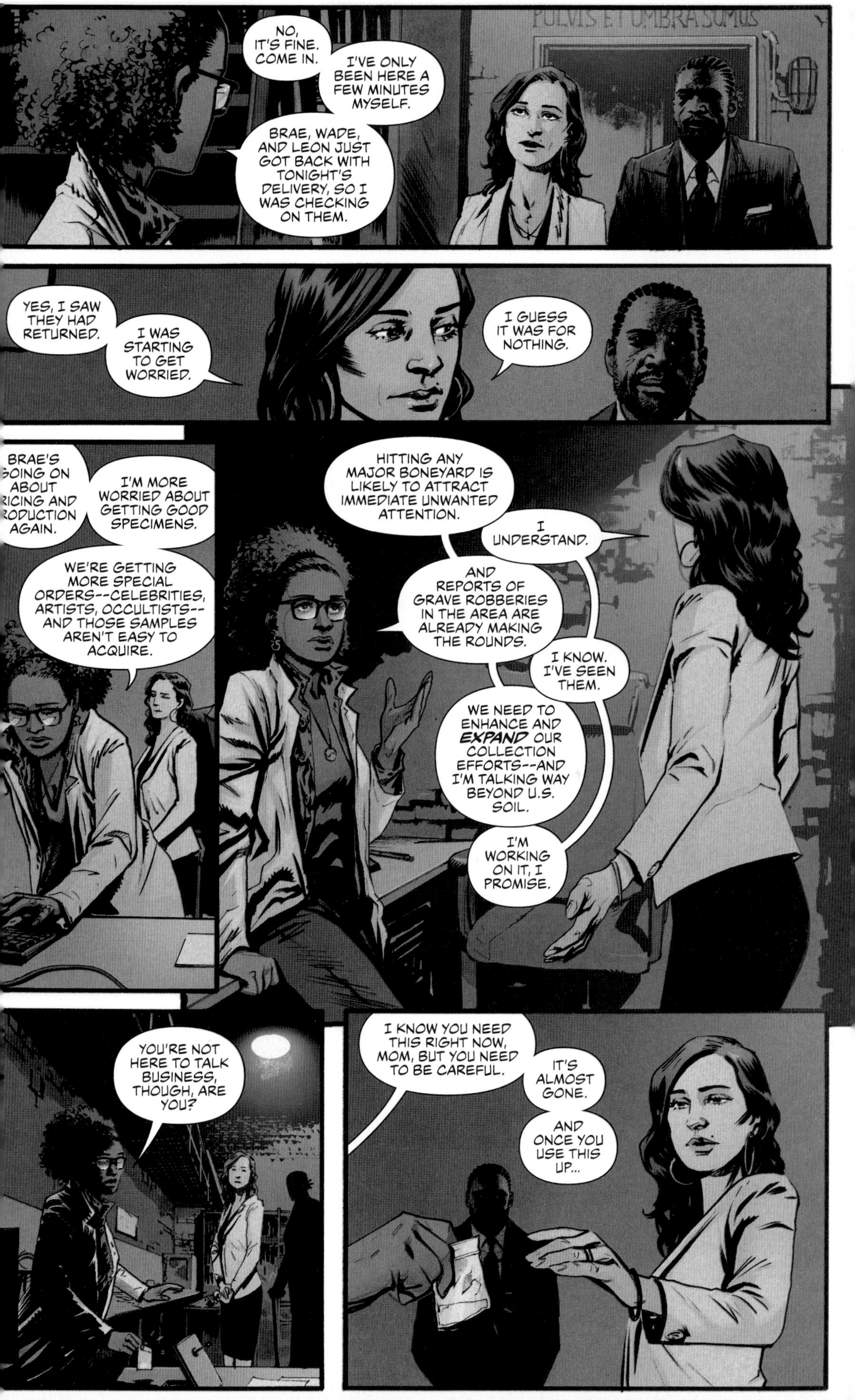

PULVIS ET UMBRA SUMUS
NO, IT'S FINE. COME IN.
I'VE ONLY BEEN HERE A FEW MINUTES MYSELF.
BRAE, WADE, AND LEON JUST GOT BACK WITH TONIGHT'S DELIVERY, SO I WAS CHECKING ON THEM.
YES, I SAW THEY HAD RETURNED.
I WAS STARTING TO GET WORRIED.
I GUESS IT WAS FOR NOTHING.
BRAE'S GOING ON ABOUT RICING AND RODUCTION AGAIN.
I'M MORE WORRIED ABOUT GETTING GOOD SPECIMENS.
WE'RE GETTING MORE SPECIAL ORDERS--CELEBRITIES, ARTISTS, OCCULTISTS--AND THOSE SAMPLES AREN'T EASY TO ACQUIRE.
HITTING ANY MAJOR BONEYARD IS LIKELY TO ATTRACT IMMEDIATE UNWANTED ATTENTION.
I UNDERSTAND.
AND REPORTS OF GRAVE ROBBERIES IN THE AREA ARE ALREADY MAKING THE ROUNDS.
I KNOW. I'VE SEEN THEM.
WE NEED TO ENHANCE AND *EXPAND* OUR COLLECTION EFFORTS--AND I'M TALKING WAY BEYOND U.S. SOIL.
I'M WORKING ON IT, I PROMISE.
YOU'RE NOT HERE TO TALK BUSINESS, THOUGH, ARE YOU?
I KNOW YOU NEED THIS RIGHT NOW, MOM, BUT YOU NEED TO BE CAREFUL.
IT'S ALMOST GONE.
AND ONCE YOU USE THIS UP...

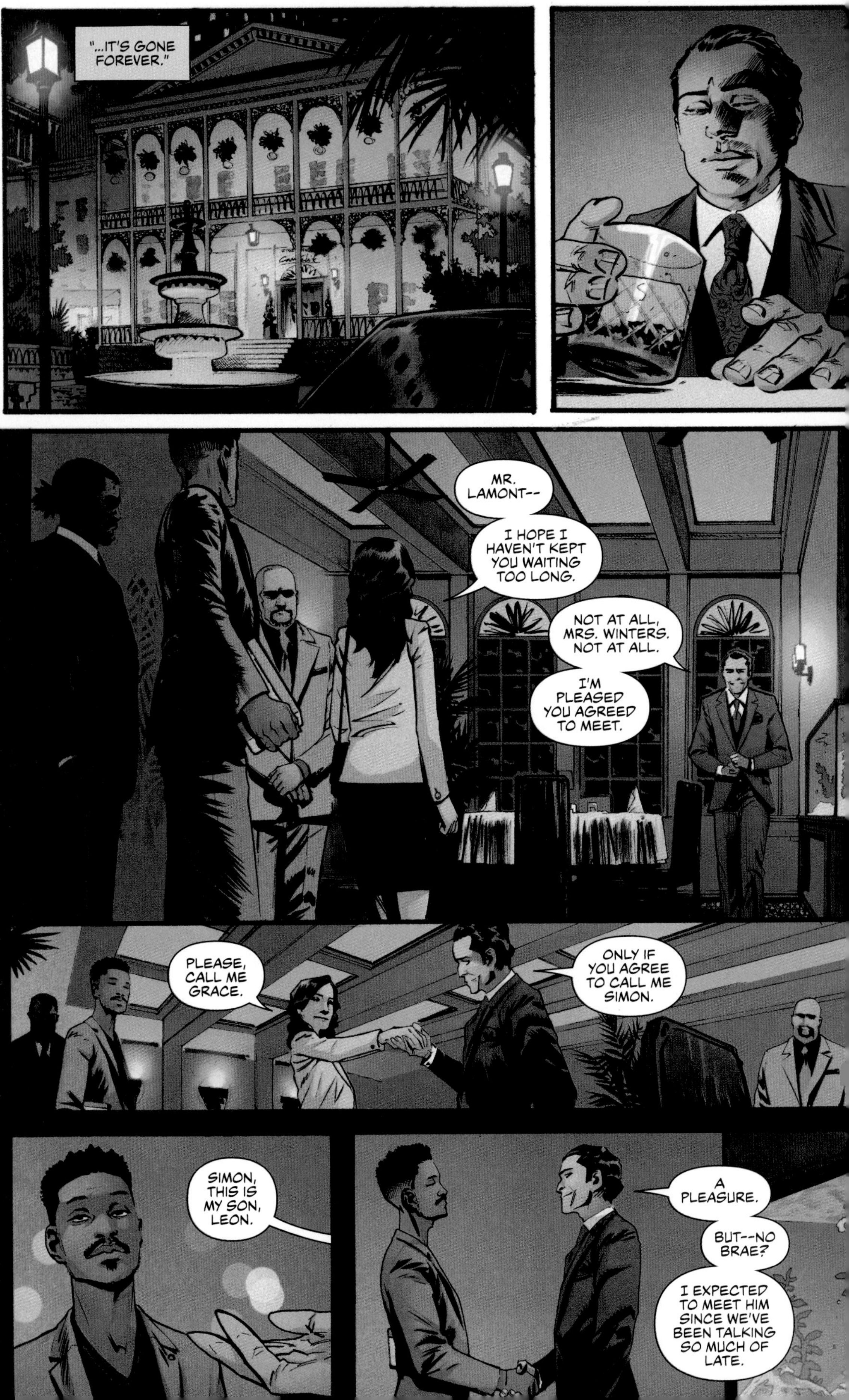
"...IT'S GONE FOREVER."
MR. LAMONT--
I HOPE I HAVEN'T KEPT YOU WAITING TOO LONG.
NOT AT ALL, MRS. WINTERS. NOT AT ALL.
I'M PLEASED YOU AGREED TO MEET.
PLEASE, CALL ME GRACE.
ONLY IF YOU AGREE TO CALL ME SIMON.
SIMON, THIS IS MY SON, LEON.
A PLEASURE.
BUT--NO BRAE?
I EXPECTED TO MEET HIM SINCE WE'VE BEEN TALKING SO MUCH OF LATE.

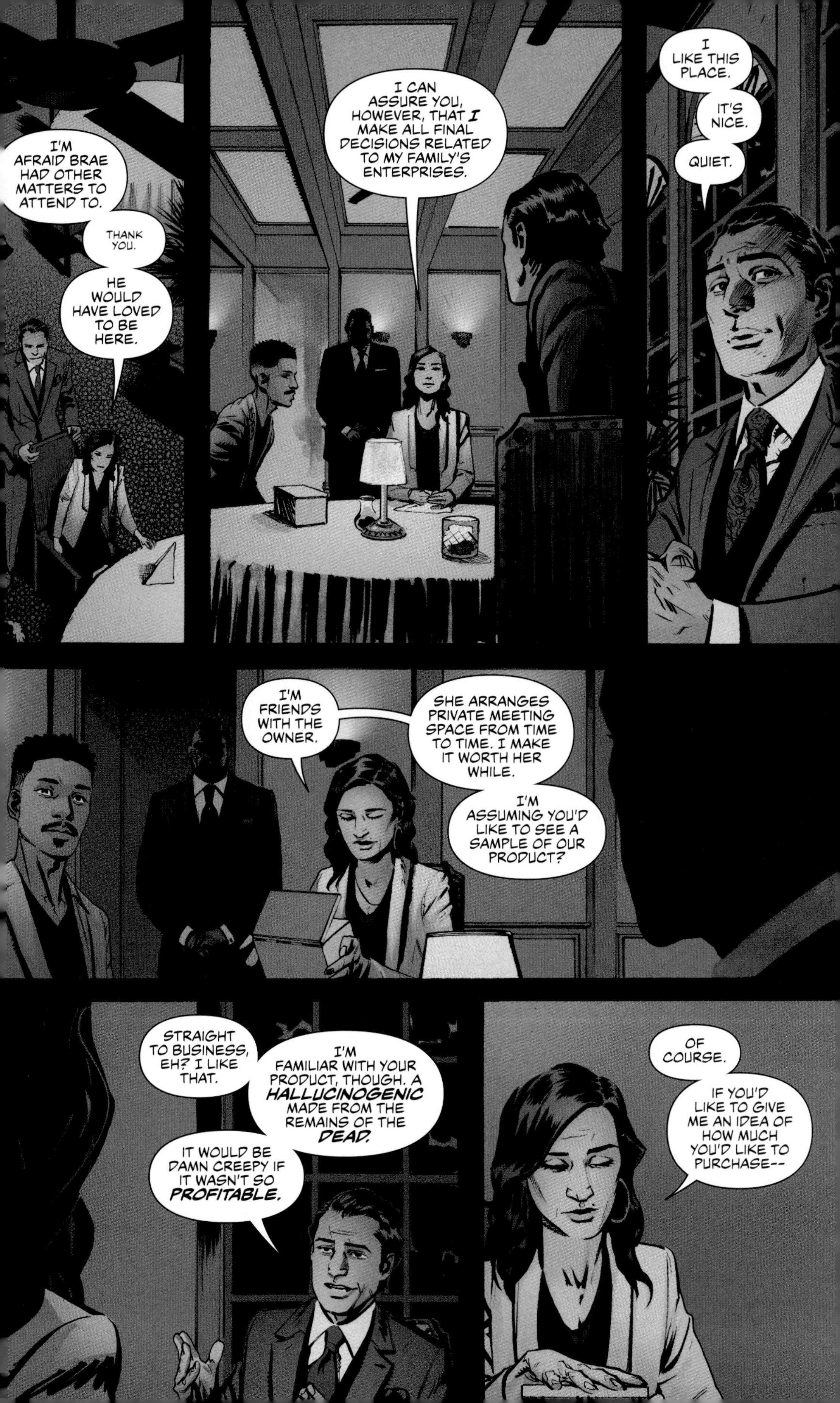

I'M AFRAID BRAE HAD OTHER MATTERS TO ATTEND TO.
THANK YOU.
HE WOULD HAVE LOVED TO BE HERE.
I CAN ASSURE YOU, HOWEVER, THAT *I* MAKE ALL FINAL DECISIONS RELATED TO MY FAMILY'S ENTERPRISES.
I LIKE THIS PLACE.
IT'S NICE.
QUIET.
I'M FRIENDS WITH THE OWNER.
SHE ARRANGES PRIVATE MEETING SPACE FROM TIME TO TIME. I MAKE IT WORTH HER WHILE.
I'M ASSUMING YOU'D LIKE TO SEE A SAMPLE OF OUR PRODUCT?
STRAIGHT TO BUSINESS, EH? I LIKE THAT.
I'M FAMILIAR WITH YOUR PRODUCT, THOUGH. A ***HALLUCINOGENIC*** MADE FROM THE REMAINS OF THE ***DEAD.***
IT WOULD BE DAMN CREEPY IF IT WASN'T SO ***PROFITABLE.***
OF COURSE.
IF YOU'D LIKE TO GIVE ME AN IDEA OF HOW MUCH YOU'D LIKE TO PURCHASE--

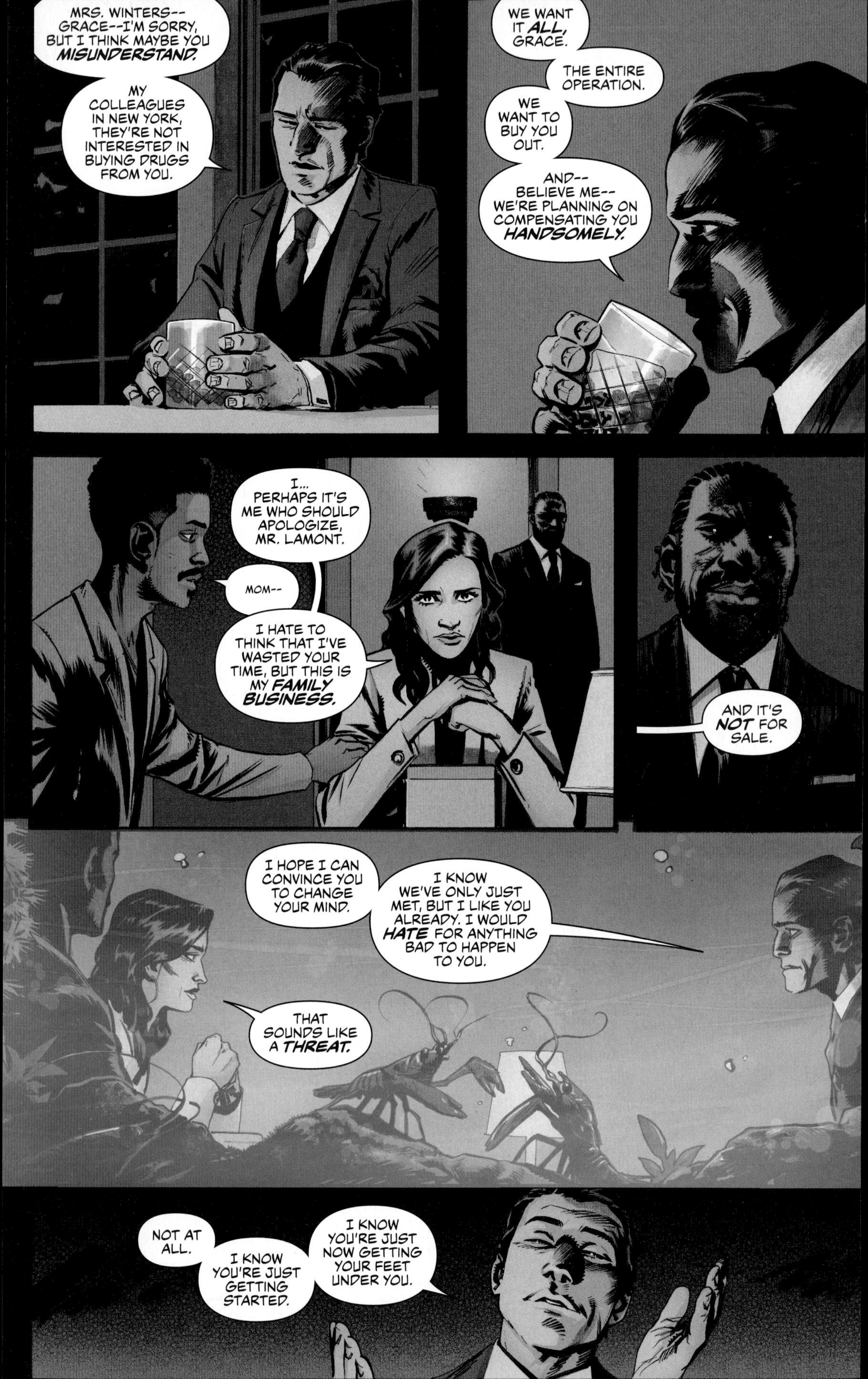

MRS. WINTERS-- GRACE--I'M SORRY, BUT I THINK MAYBE YOU *MISUNDERSTAND.*
MY COLLEAGUES IN NEW YORK, THEY'RE NOT INTERESTED IN BUYING DRUGS FROM YOU.
WE WANT IT *ALL,* GRACE.
THE ENTIRE OPERATION.
WE WANT TO BUY YOU OUT.
AND-- BELIEVE ME-- WE'RE PLANNING ON COMPENSATING YOU *HANDSOMELY.*
I... PERHAPS IT'S ME WHO SHOULD APOLOGIZE, MR. LAMONT.
MOM--
I HATE TO THINK THAT I'VE WASTED YOUR TIME, BUT THIS IS MY *FAMILY BUSINESS.*
AND IT'S *NOT* FOR SALE.
I HOPE I CAN CONVINCE YOU TO CHANGE YOUR MIND.
I KNOW WE'VE ONLY JUST MET, BUT I LIKE YOU ALREADY. I WOULD *HATE* FOR ANYTHING BAD TO HAPPEN TO YOU.
THAT SOUNDS LIKE A *THREAT.*
NOT AT ALL.
I KNOW YOU'RE JUST GETTING STARTED.
I KNOW YOU'RE JUST NOW GETTING YOUR FEET UNDER YOU.

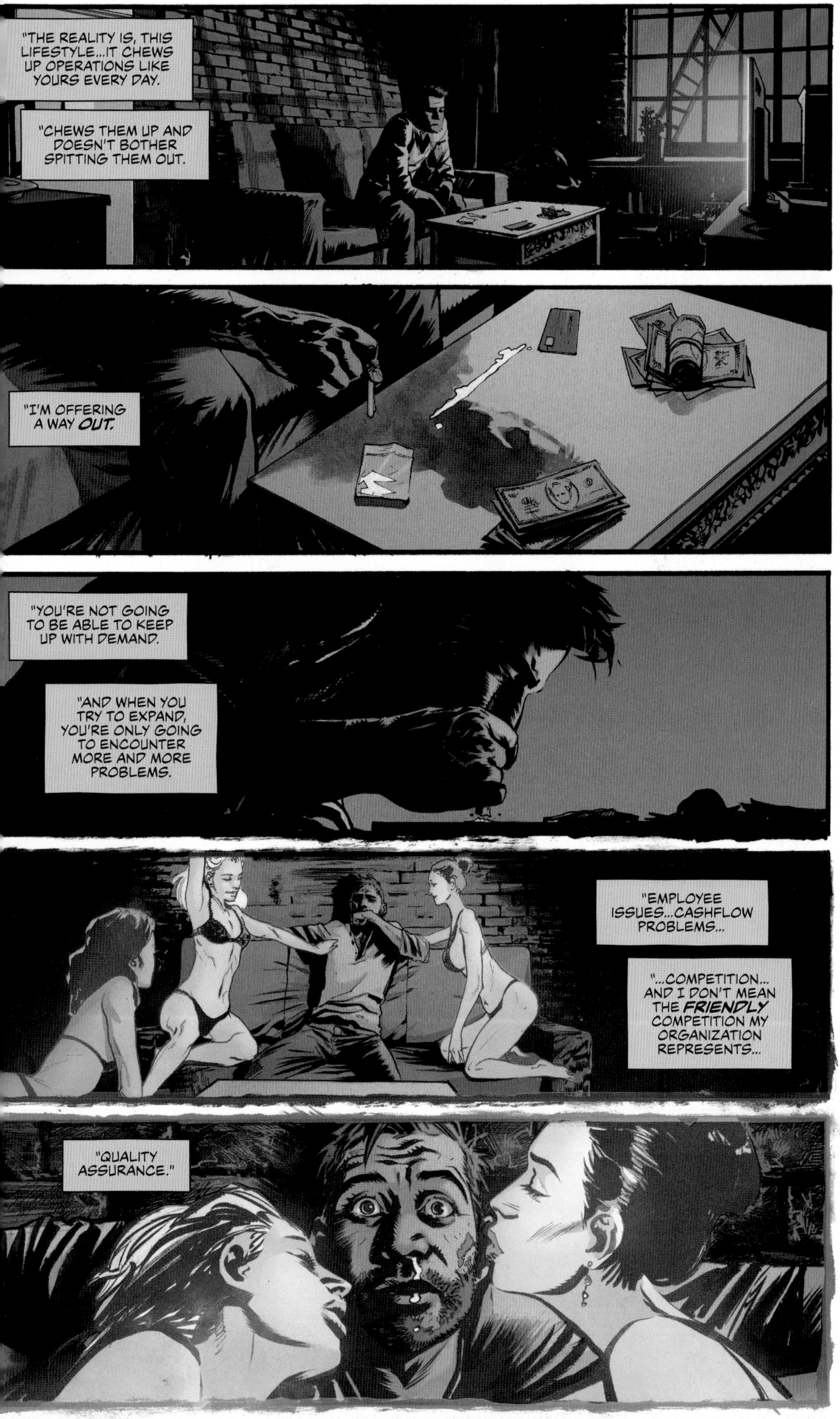
"THE REALITY IS, THIS LIFESTYLE...IT CHEWS UP OPERATIONS LIKE YOURS EVERY DAY.
"CHEWS THEM UP AND DOESN'T BOTHER SPITTING THEM OUT.
"I'M OFFERING A WAY *OUT.*
"YOU'RE NOT GOING TO BE ABLE TO KEEP UP WITH DEMAND.
"AND WHEN YOU TRY TO EXPAND, YOU'RE ONLY GOING TO ENCOUNTER MORE AND MORE PROBLEMS.
"EMPLOYEE ISSUES...CASHFLOW PROBLEMS...
"...COMPETITION... AND I DON'T MEAN THE *FRIENDLY* COMPETITION MY ORGANIZATION REPRESENTS...
"QUALITY ASSURANCE."

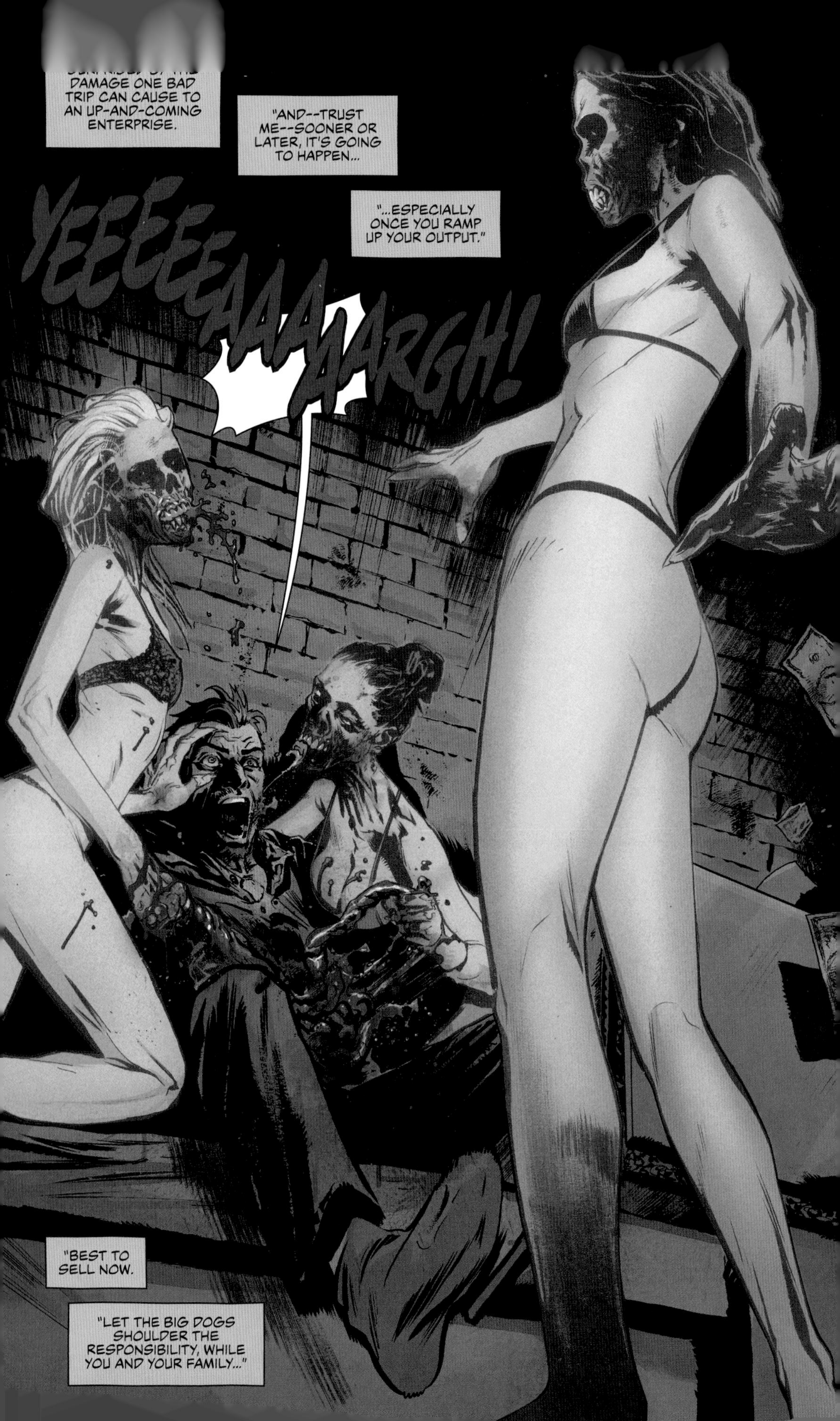
DAMAGE ONE BAD TRIP CAN CAUSE TO AN UP-AND-COMING ENTERPRISE.
"AND--TRUST ME--SOONER OR LATER, IT'S GOING TO HAPPEN...
"...ESPECIALLY ONCE YOU RAMP UP YOUR OUTPUT."
YEEEEEAAAAAARGH!
"BEST TO SELL NOW.
"LET THE BIG DOGS SHOULDER THE RESPONSIBILITY, WHILE YOU AND YOUR FAMILY..."

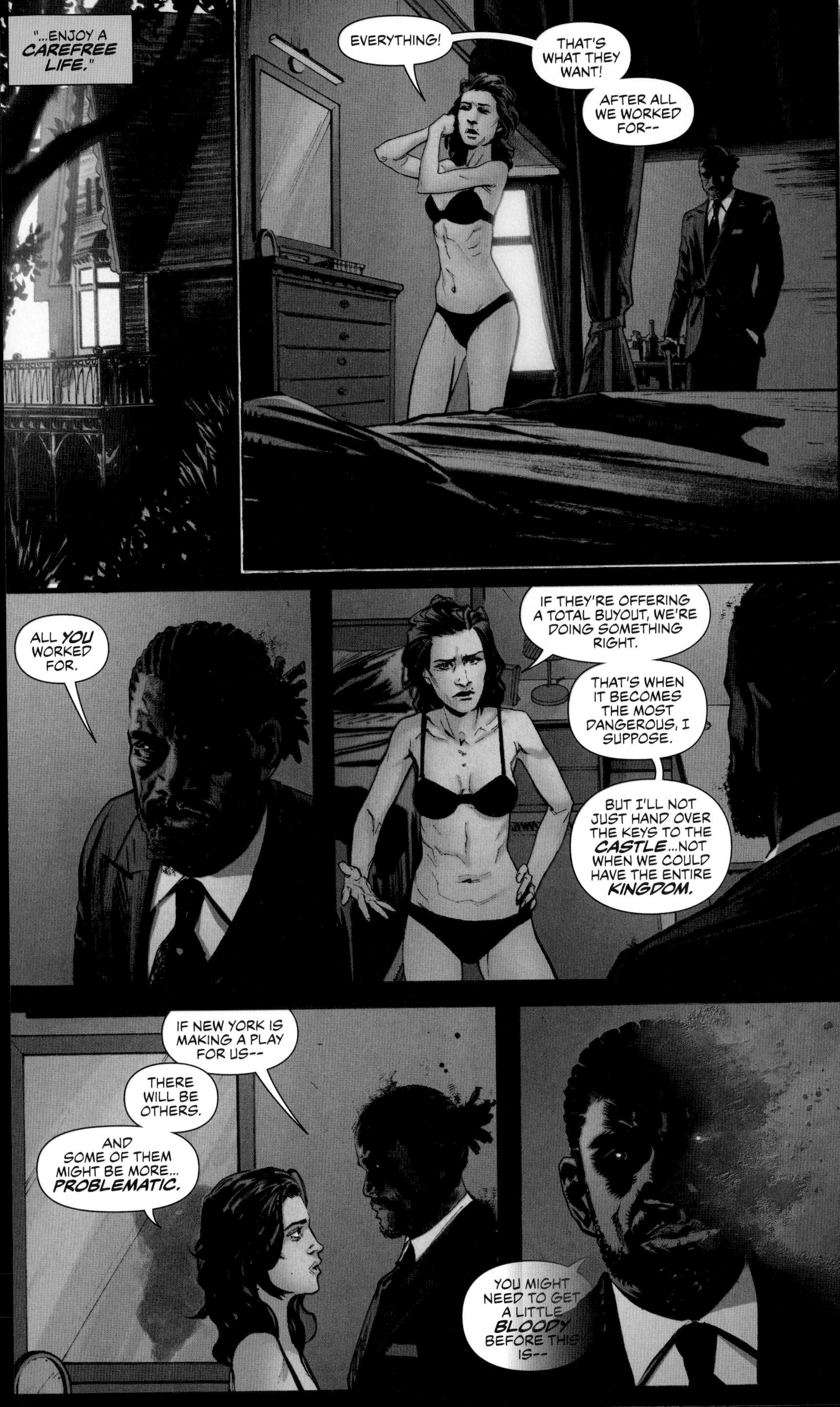
"...ENJOY A CAREFREE LIFE."
EVERYTHING!
THAT'S WHAT THEY WANT!
AFTER ALL WE WORKED FOR--
ALL YOU WORKED FOR.
IF THEY'RE OFFERING A TOTAL BUYOUT, WE'RE DOING SOMETHING RIGHT.
THAT'S WHEN IT BECOMES THE MOST DANGEROUS, I SUPPOSE.
BUT I'LL NOT JUST HAND OVER THE KEYS TO THE CASTLE...NOT WHEN WE COULD HAVE THE ENTIRE KINGDOM.
IF NEW YORK IS MAKING A PLAY FOR US--
THERE WILL BE OTHERS.
AND SOME OF THEM MIGHT BE MORE... PROBLEMATIC.
YOU MIGHT NEED TO GET A LITTLE BLOODY BEFORE THIS IS--

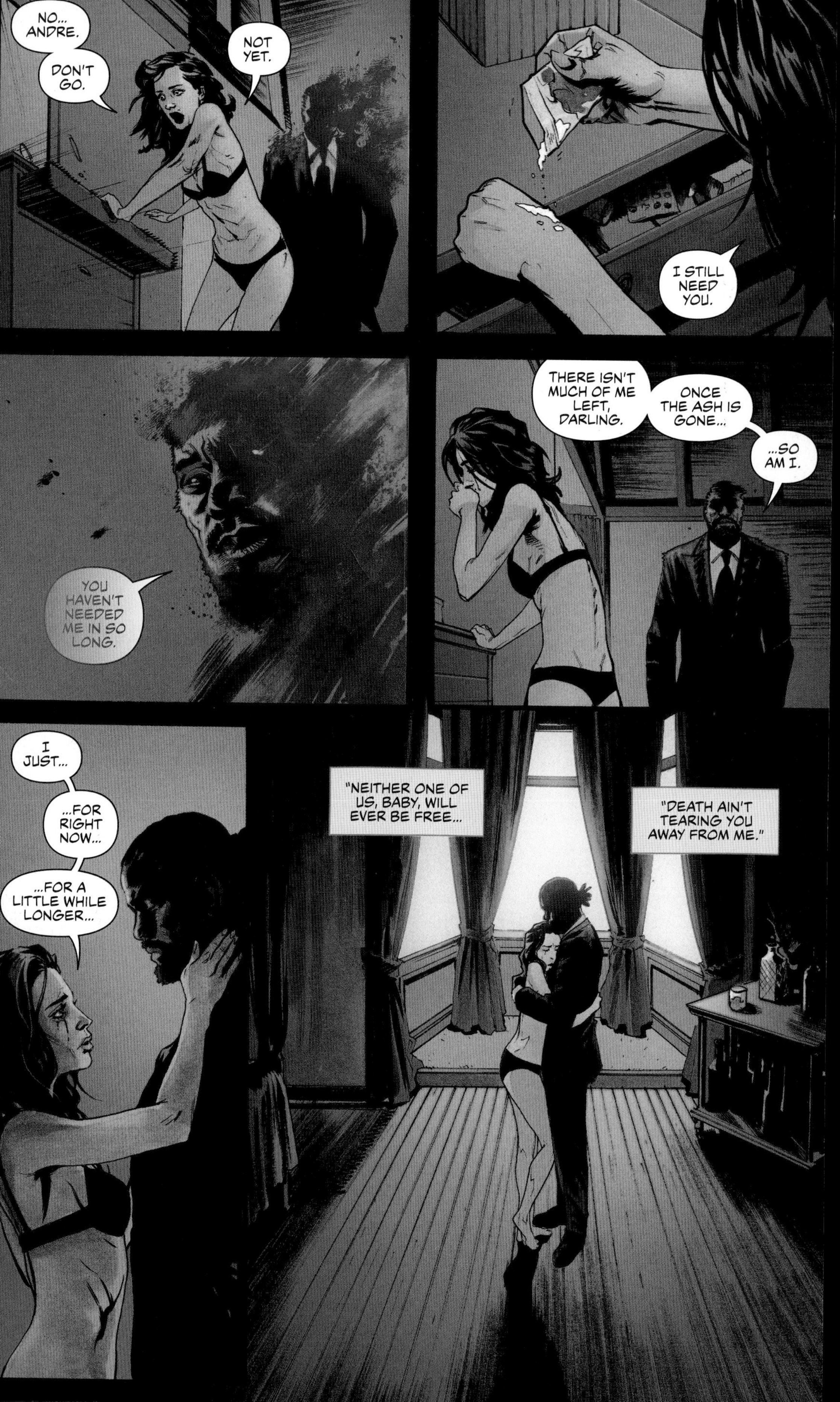
NO... ANDRE.
DON'T GO.
NOT YET.
I STILL NEED YOU.
YOU HAVEN'T NEEDED ME IN SO LONG.
THERE ISN'T MUCH OF ME LEFT, DARLING.
ONCE THE ASH IS GONE...
...SO AM I.
I JUST...
...FOR RIGHT NOW...
...FOR A LITTLE WHILE LONGER...
"NEITHER ONE OF US, BABY, WILL EVER BE FREE...
"DEATH AIN'T TEARING YOU AWAY FROM ME."

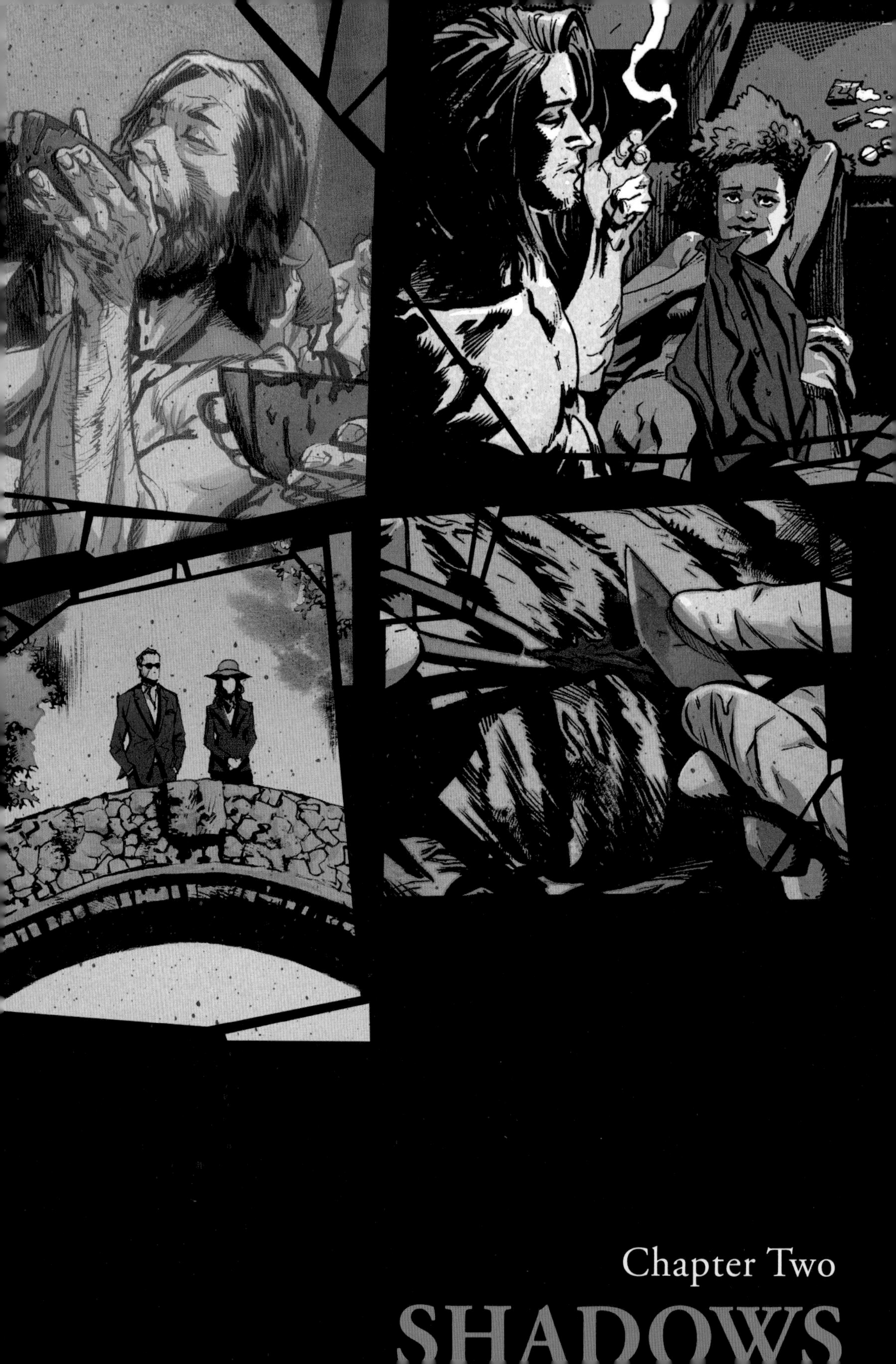

Chapter Two

SHADOWS

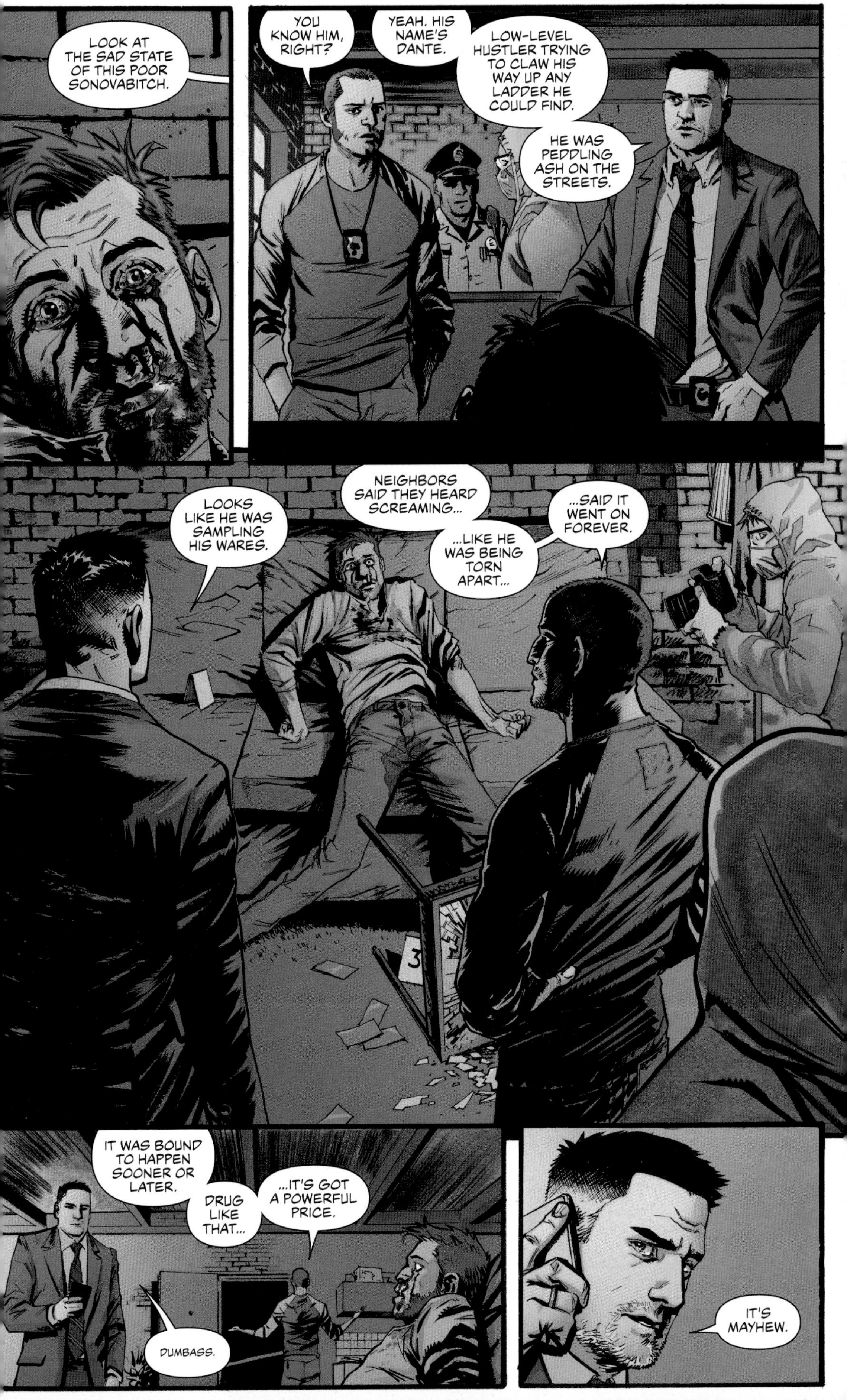
LOOK AT THE SAD STATE OF THIS POOR SONOVABITCH.
YOU KNOW HIM, RIGHT?
YEAH. HIS NAME'S DANTE.
LOW-LEVEL HUSTLER TRYING TO CLAW HIS WAY UP ANY LADDER HE COULD FIND.
HE WAS PEDDLING ASH ON THE STREETS.
LOOKS LIKE HE WAS SAMPLING HIS WARES.
NEIGHBORS SAID THEY HEARD SCREAMING...
...LIKE HE WAS BEING TORN APART...
...SAID IT WENT ON FOREVER.
3
IT WAS BOUND TO HAPPEN SOONER OR LATER.
DRUG LIKE THAT...
...IT'S GOT A POWERFUL PRICE.
DUMBASS.
IT'S MAYHEW.

"WE'VE GOT A PROBLEM."

HMM.

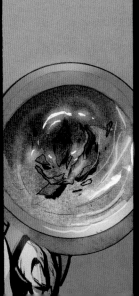

BRAE.
GOOD MORNING.

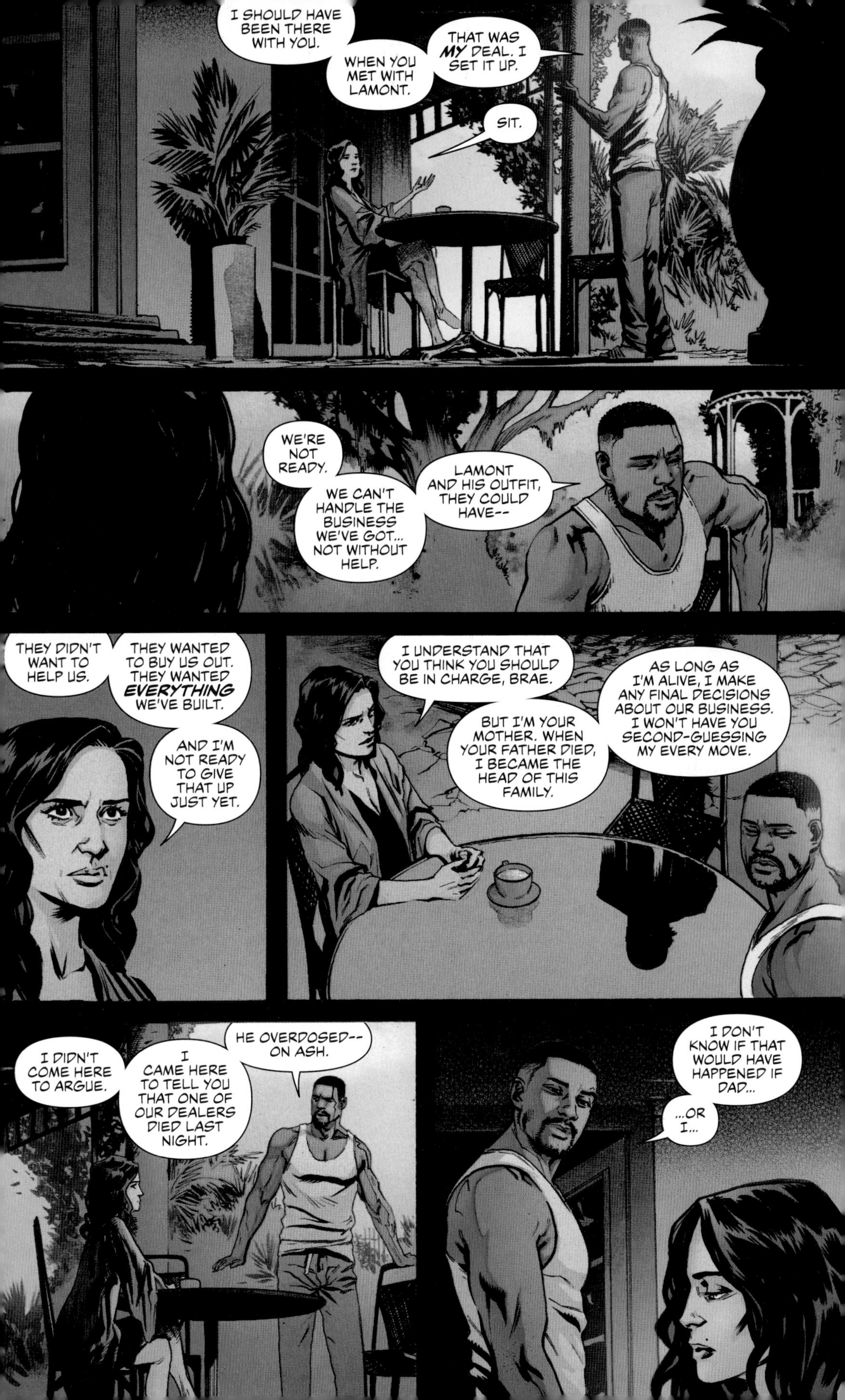
I SHOULD HAVE BEEN THERE WITH YOU.
WHEN YOU MET WITH LAMONT.
THAT WAS MY DEAL. I SET IT UP.
SIT.
WE'RE NOT READY.
WE CAN'T HANDLE THE BUSINESS WE'VE GOT... NOT WITHOUT HELP.
LAMONT AND HIS OUTFIT, THEY COULD HAVE--
THEY DIDN'T WANT TO HELP US.
THEY WANTED TO BUY US OUT. THEY WANTED EVERYTHING WE'VE BUILT.
AND I'M NOT READY TO GIVE THAT UP JUST YET.
I UNDERSTAND THAT YOU THINK YOU SHOULD BE IN CHARGE, BRAE.
BUT I'M YOUR MOTHER. WHEN YOUR FATHER DIED, I BECAME THE HEAD OF THIS FAMILY.
AS LONG AS I'M ALIVE, I MAKE ANY FINAL DECISIONS ABOUT OUR BUSINESS. I WON'T HAVE YOU SECOND-GUESSING MY EVERY MOVE.
I DIDN'T COME HERE TO ARGUE.
I CAME HERE TO TELL YOU THAT ONE OF OUR DEALERS DIED LAST NIGHT.
HE OVERDOSED-- ON ASH.
I DON'T KNOW IF THAT WOULD HAVE HAPPENED IF DAD...
...OR I...

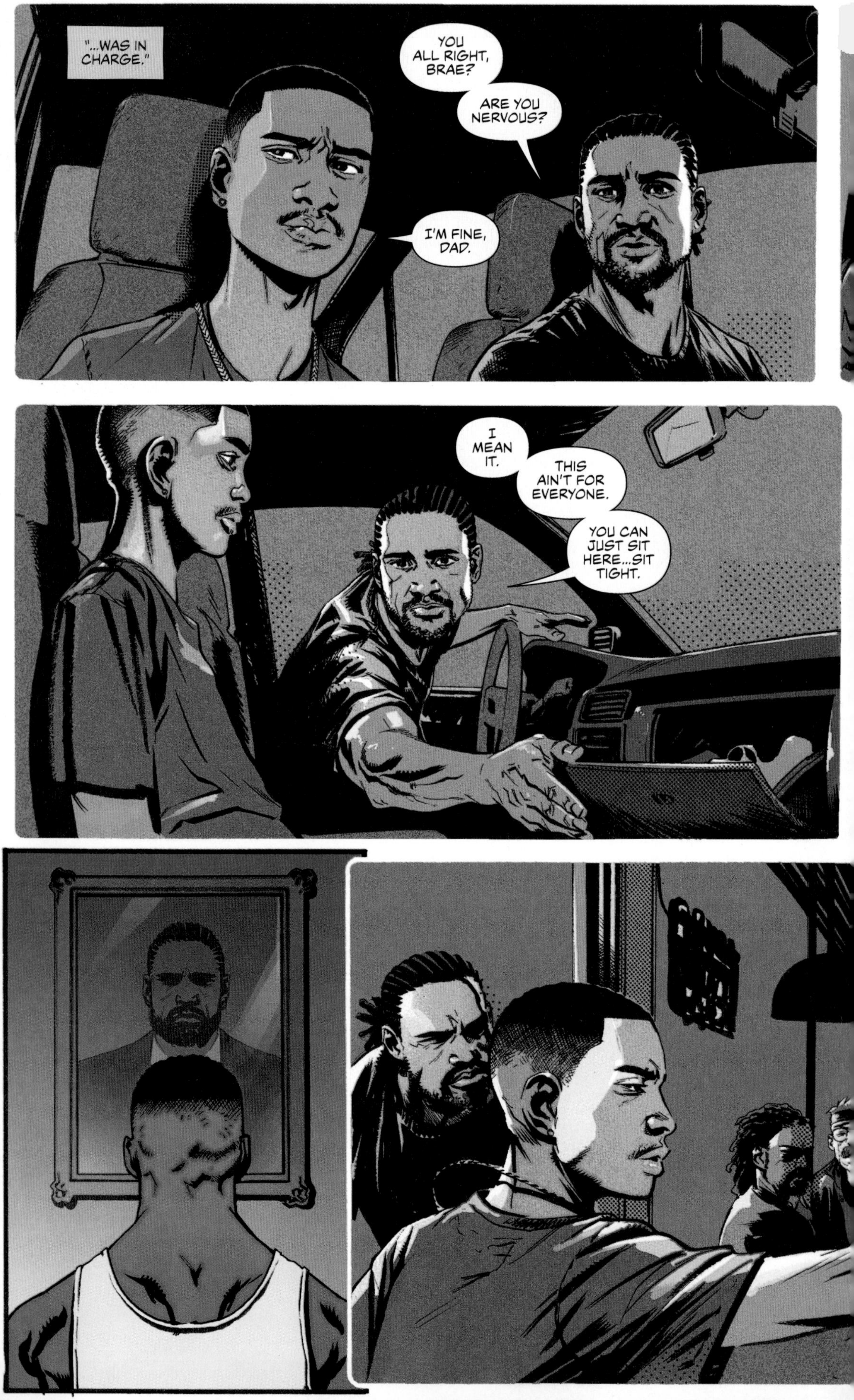
"...WAS IN CHARGE."
YOU ALL RIGHT, BRAE?
ARE YOU NERVOUS?
I'M FINE, DAD.
I MEAN IT.
THIS AIN'T FOR EVERYONE.
YOU CAN JUST SIT HERE...SIT TIGHT.

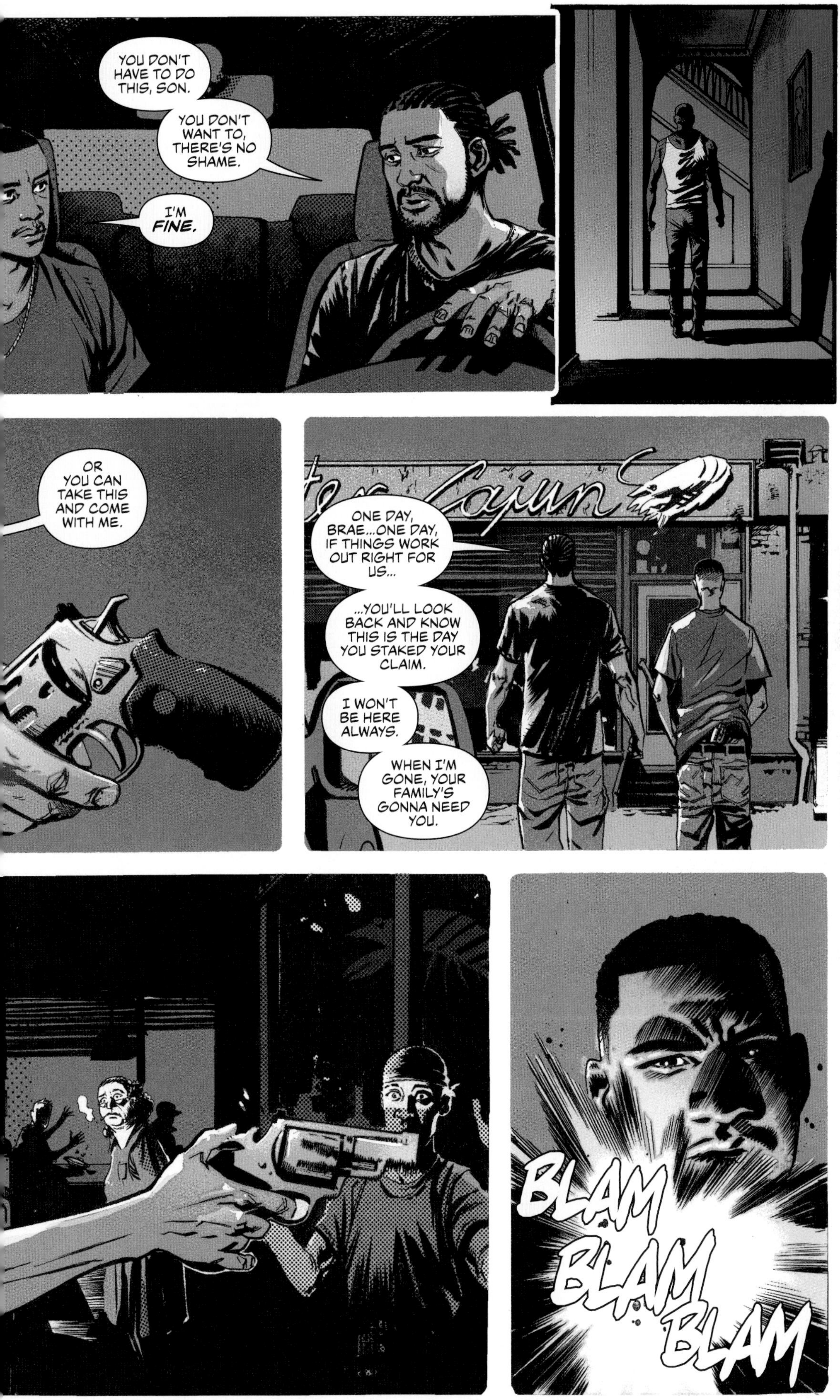
YOU DON'T HAVE TO DO THIS, SON.
YOU DON'T WANT TO, THERE'S NO SHAME.
I'M *FINE.*
OR YOU CAN TAKE THIS AND COME WITH ME.
ONE DAY, BRAE...ONE DAY, IF THINGS WORK OUT RIGHT FOR US...
...YOU'LL LOOK BACK AND KNOW THIS IS THE DAY YOU STAKED YOUR CLAIM.
I WON'T BE HERE ALWAYS.
WHEN I'M GONE, YOUR FAMILY'S GONNA NEED YOU.
BLAM
BLAM
BLAM

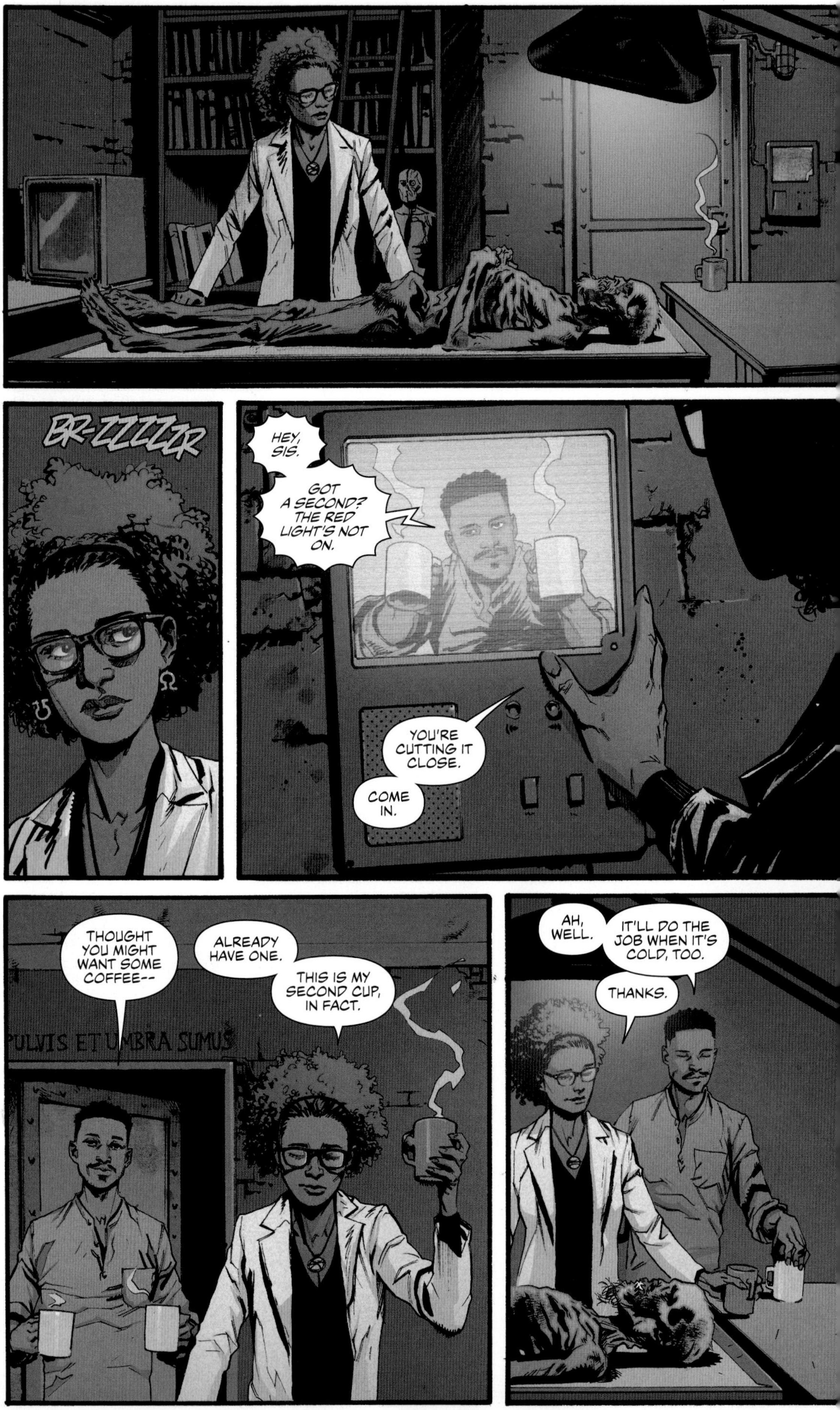
BR-ZZZZZR
HEY, SIS.
GOT A SECOND? THE RED LIGHT'S NOT ON.
YOU'RE CUTTING IT CLOSE.
COME IN.
THOUGHT YOU MIGHT WANT SOME COFFEE--
ALREADY HAVE ONE.
THIS IS MY SECOND CUP, IN FACT.
PULVIS ET UMBRA SUMUS
AH, WELL.
IT'LL DO THE JOB WHEN IT'S COLD, TOO.
THANKS.

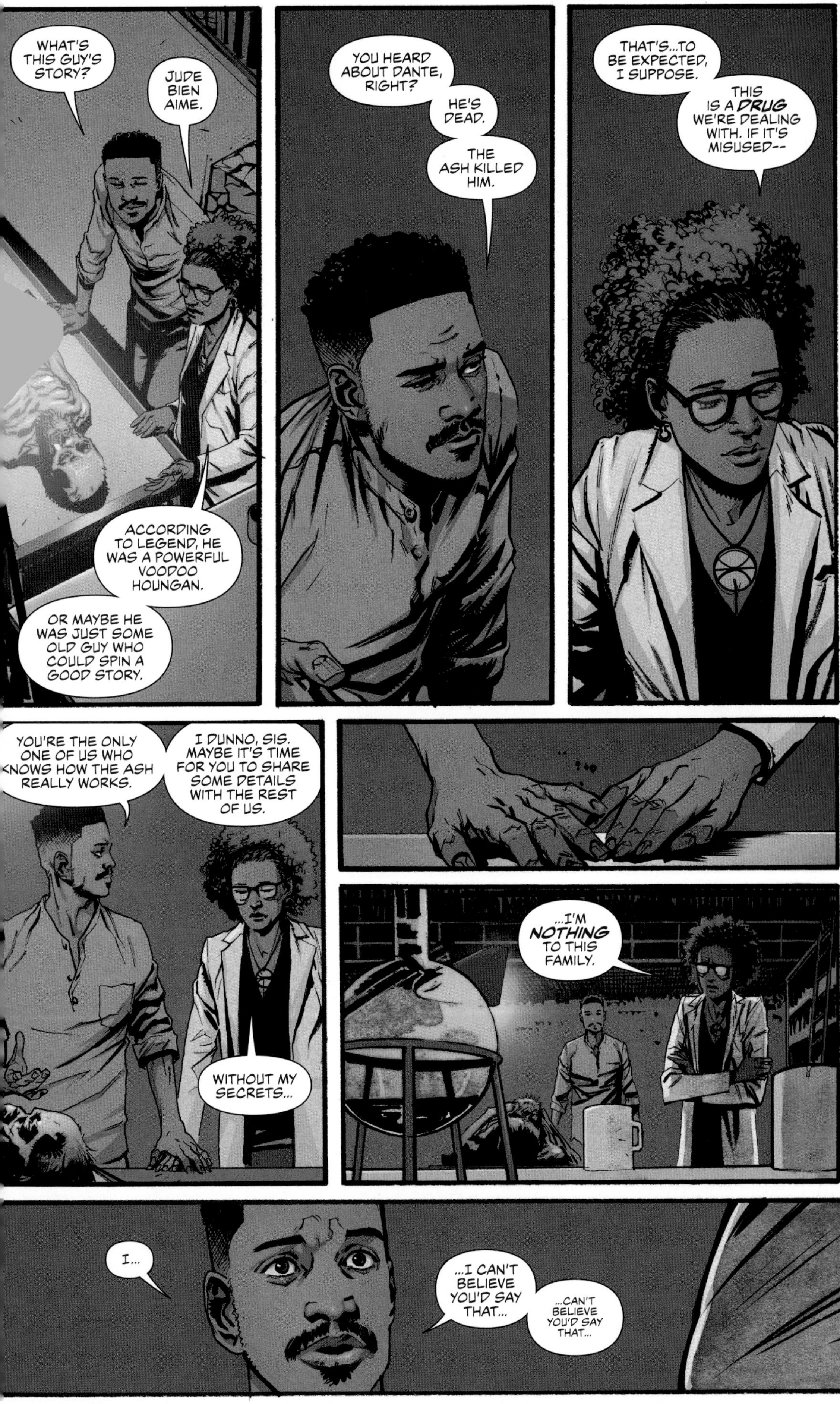
WHAT'S THIS GUY'S STORY?
JUDE BIEN AIME.
ACCORDING TO LEGEND, HE WAS A POWERFUL VOODOO HOUNGAN.
OR MAYBE HE WAS JUST SOME OLD GUY WHO COULD SPIN A GOOD STORY.
YOU HEARD ABOUT DANTE, RIGHT?
HE'S DEAD.
THE ASH KILLED HIM.
THAT'S...TO BE EXPECTED, I SUPPOSE.
THIS IS A DRUG WE'RE DEALING WITH. IF IT'S MISUSED--
YOU'RE THE ONLY ONE OF US WHO KNOWS HOW THE ASH REALLY WORKS.
I DUNNO, SIS. MAYBE IT'S TIME FOR YOU TO SHARE SOME DETAILS WITH THE REST OF US.
WITHOUT MY SECRETS...
...I'M NOTHING TO THIS FAMILY.
I...
...I CAN'T BELIEVE YOU'D SAY THAT...
...CAN'T BELIEVE YOU'D SAY THAT...

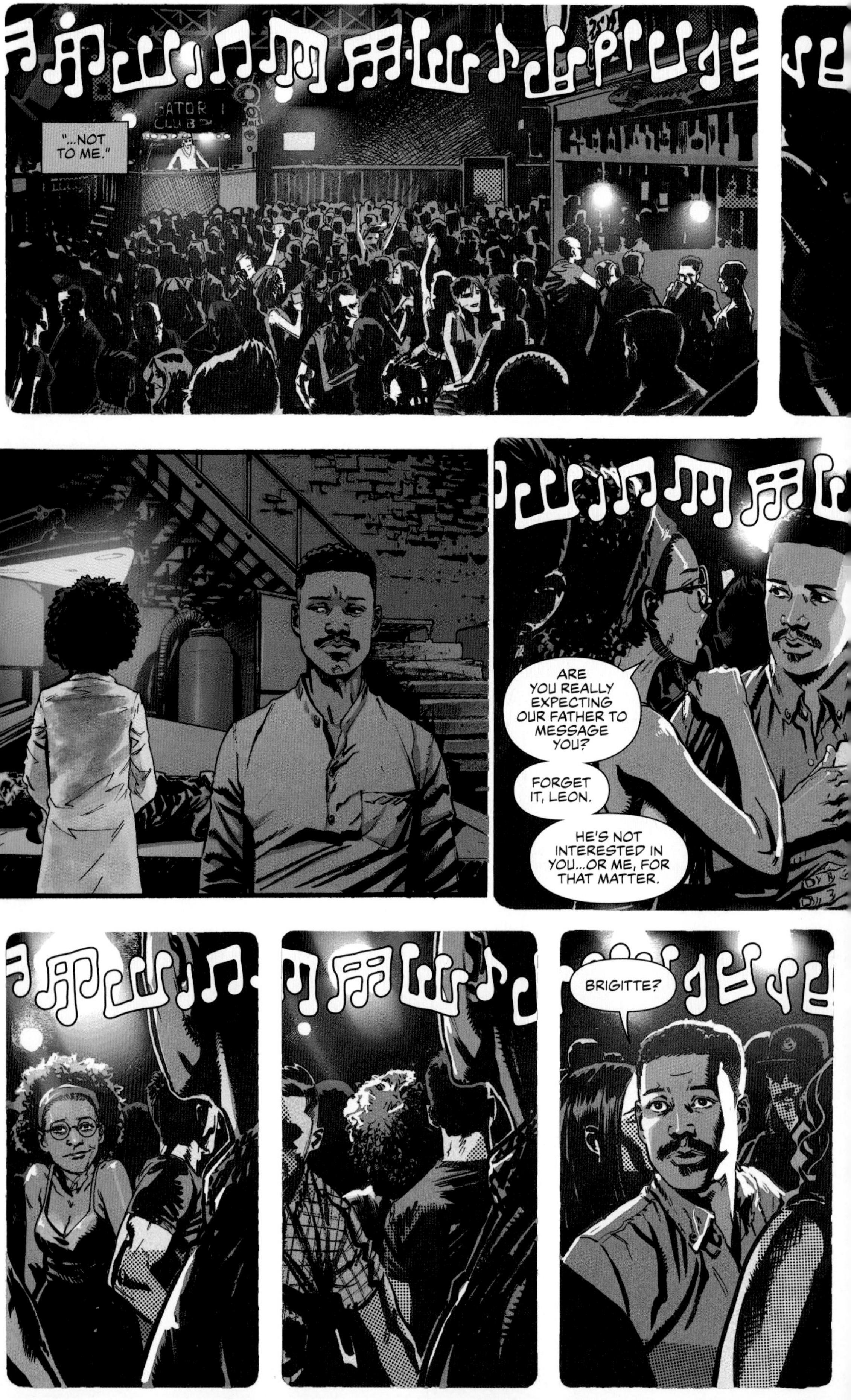
"...NOT TO ME."
GATOR CLUB
ARE YOU REALLY EXPECTING OUR FATHER TO MESSAGE YOU?
FORGET IT, LEON.
HE'S NOT INTERESTED IN YOU...OR ME, FOR THAT MATTER.
BRIGITTE?

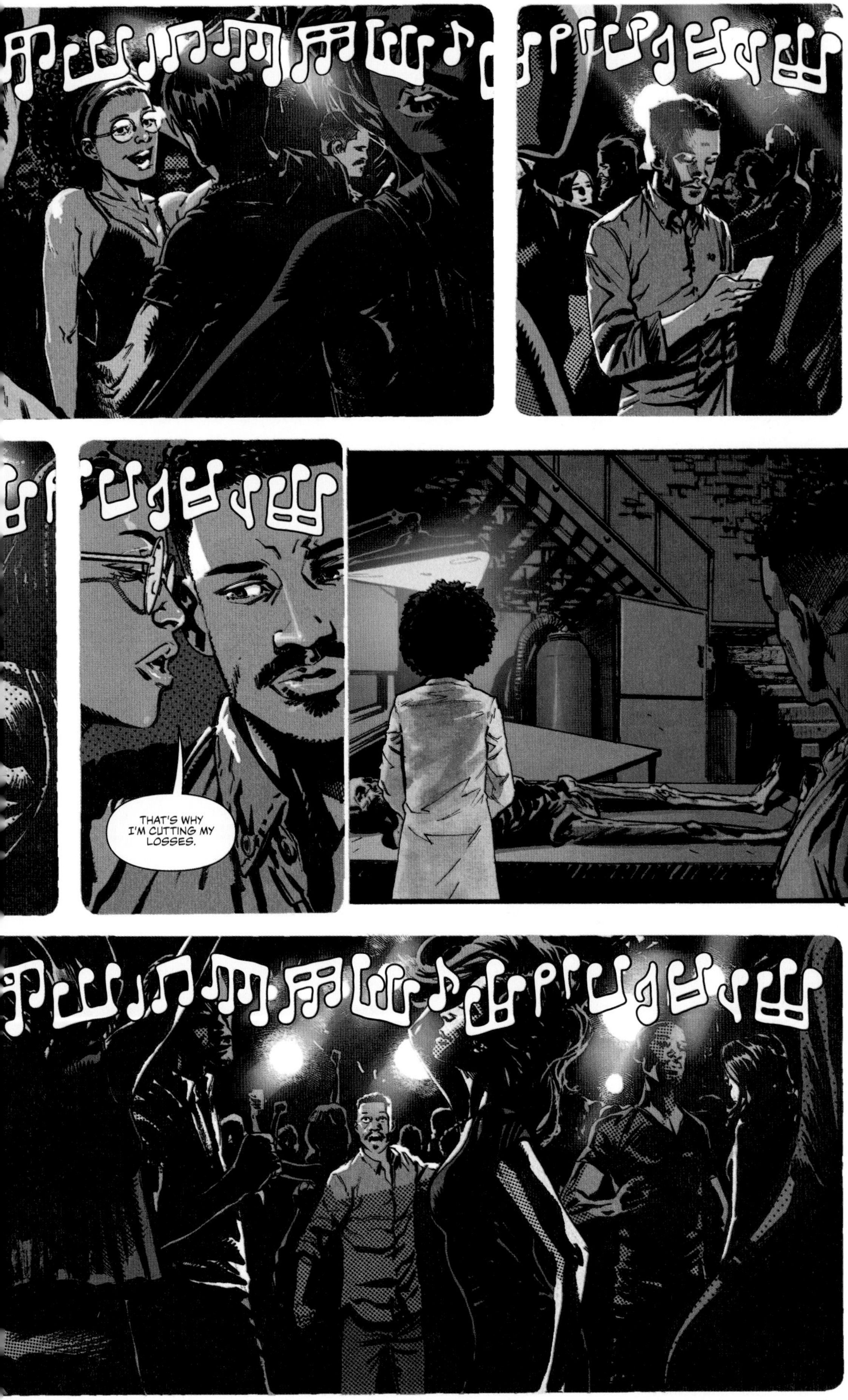
THAT'S WHY I'M CUTTING MY LOSSES.

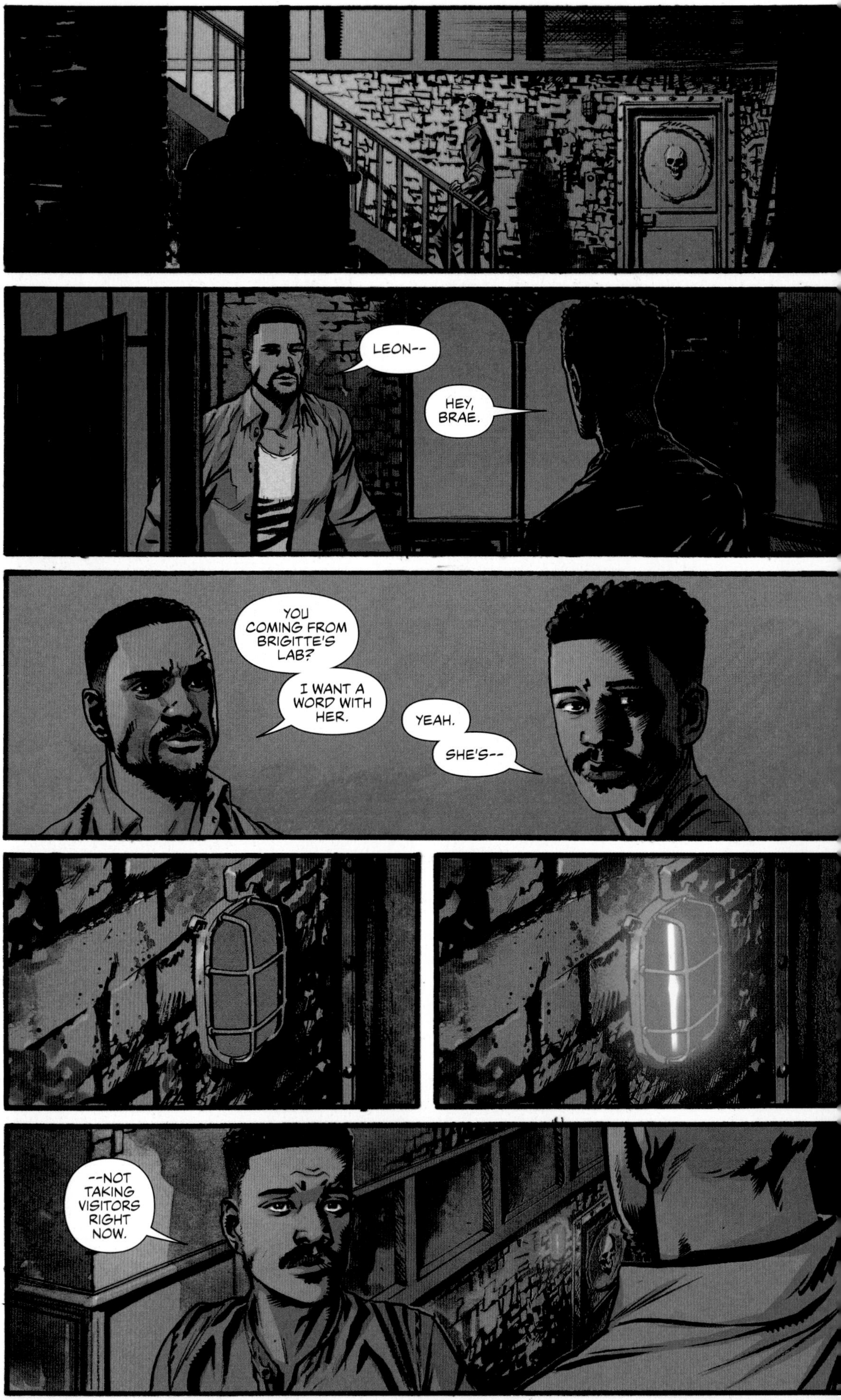
LEON--
HEY, BRAE.
YOU COMING FROM BRIGITTE'S LAB?
I WANT A WORD WITH HER.
YEAH.
SHE'S--
--NOT TAKING VISITORS RIGHT NOW.

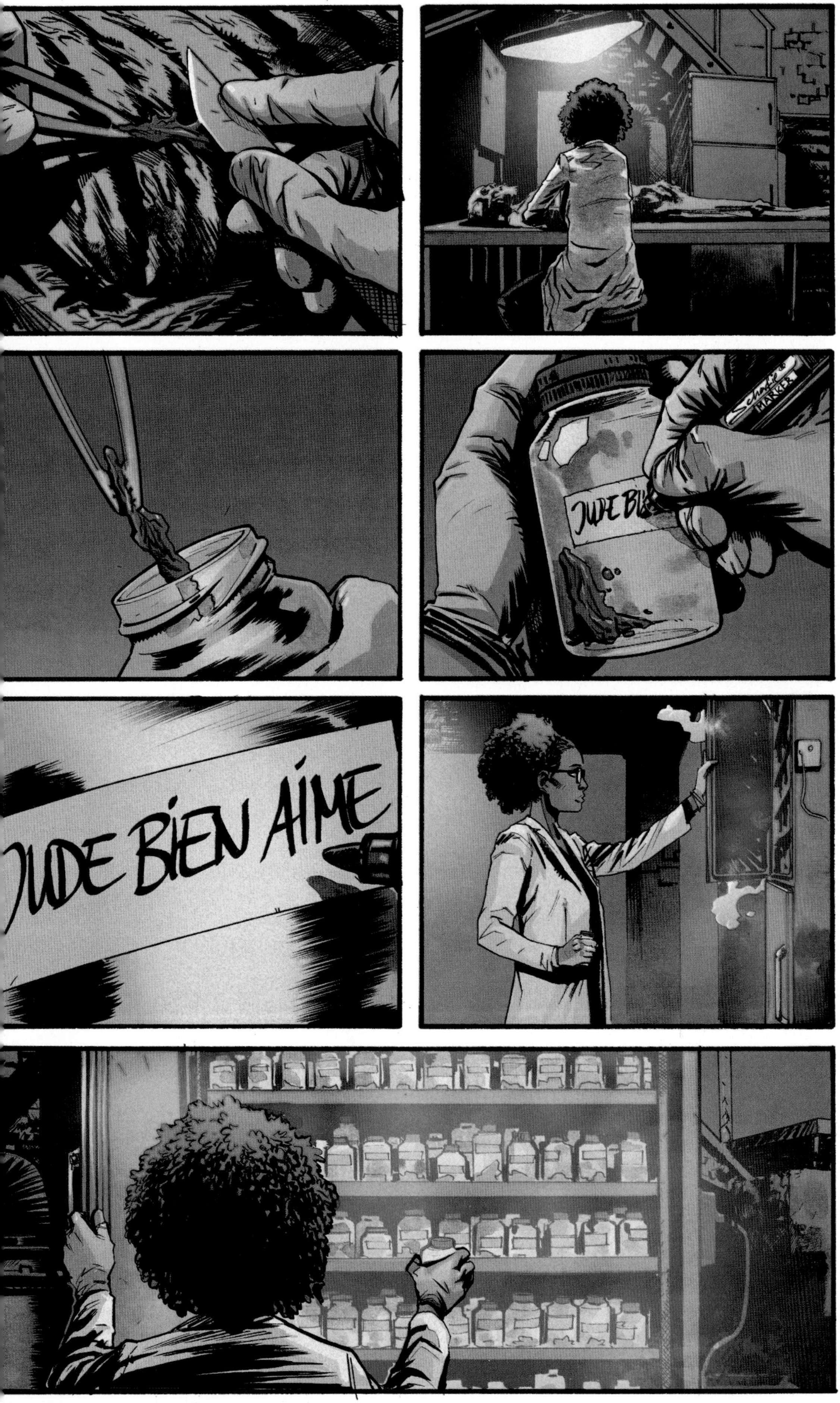
MARKER
JUDE BIEN AIME

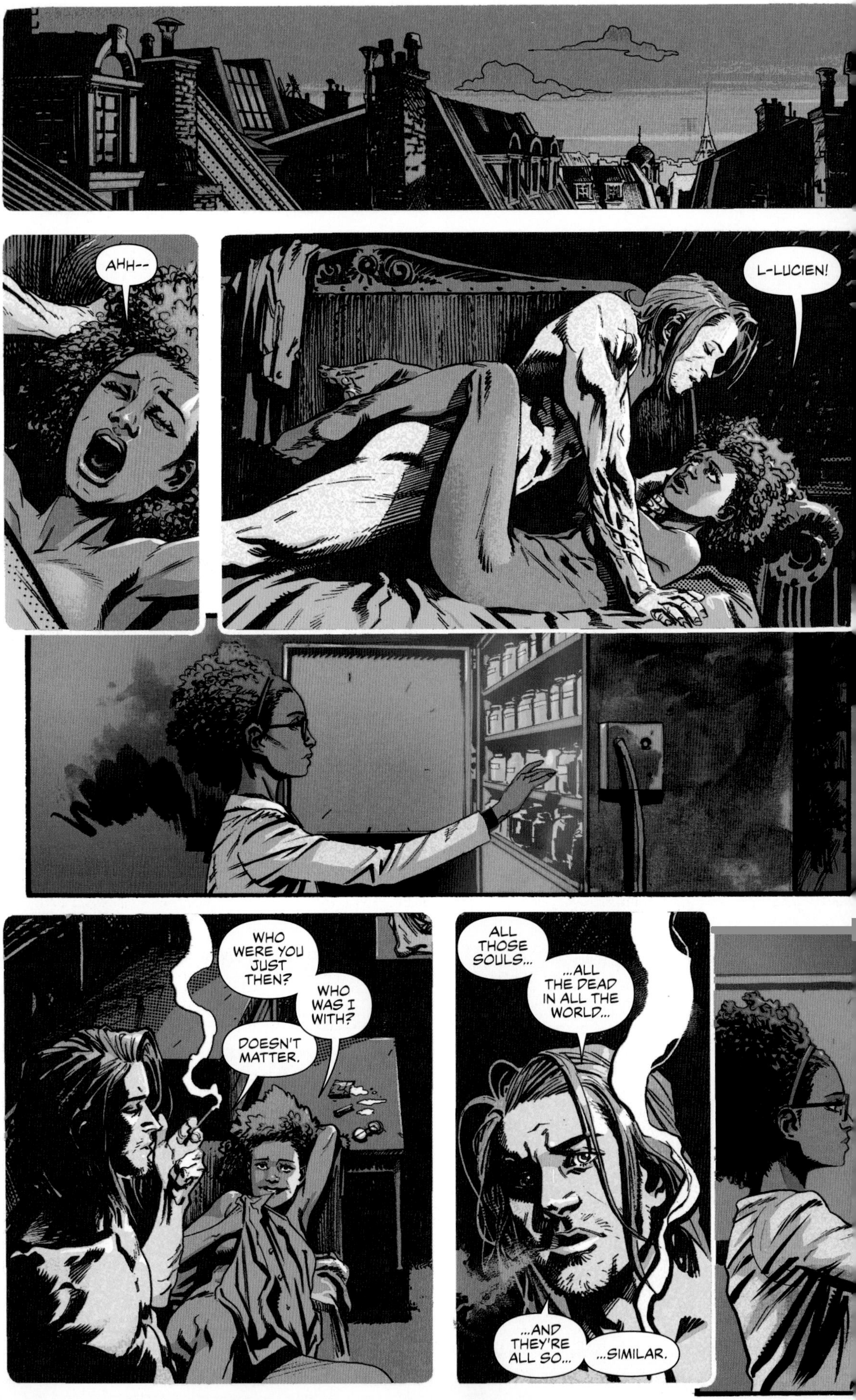
AHH--
L-LUCIEN!
WHO WERE YOU JUST THEN?
WHO WAS I WITH?
DOESN'T MATTER.
ALL THOSE SOULS...
...ALL THE DEAD IN ALL THE WORLD...
...AND THEY'RE ALL SO...
...SIMILAR.

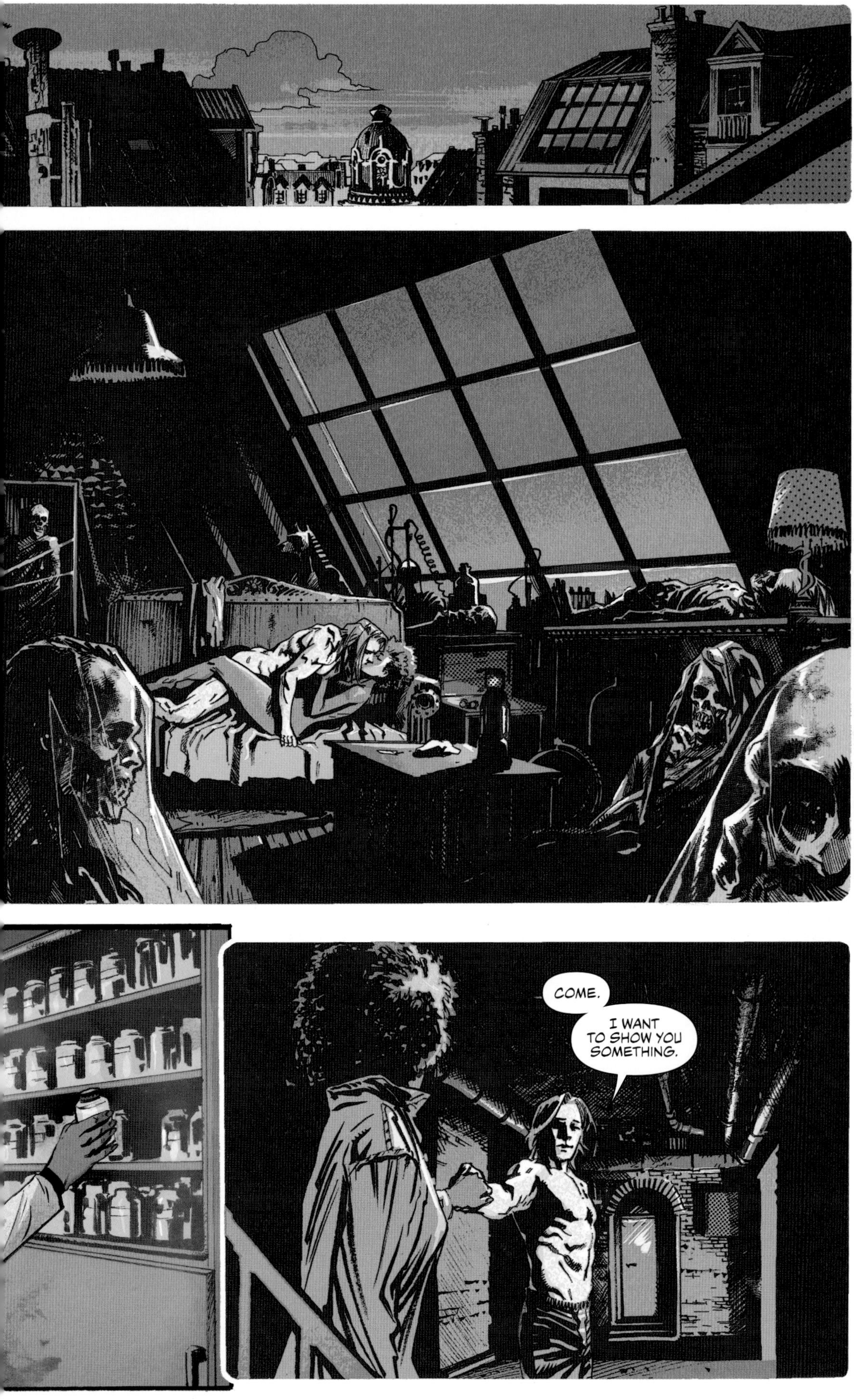
COME.
I WANT TO SHOW YOU SOMETHING.

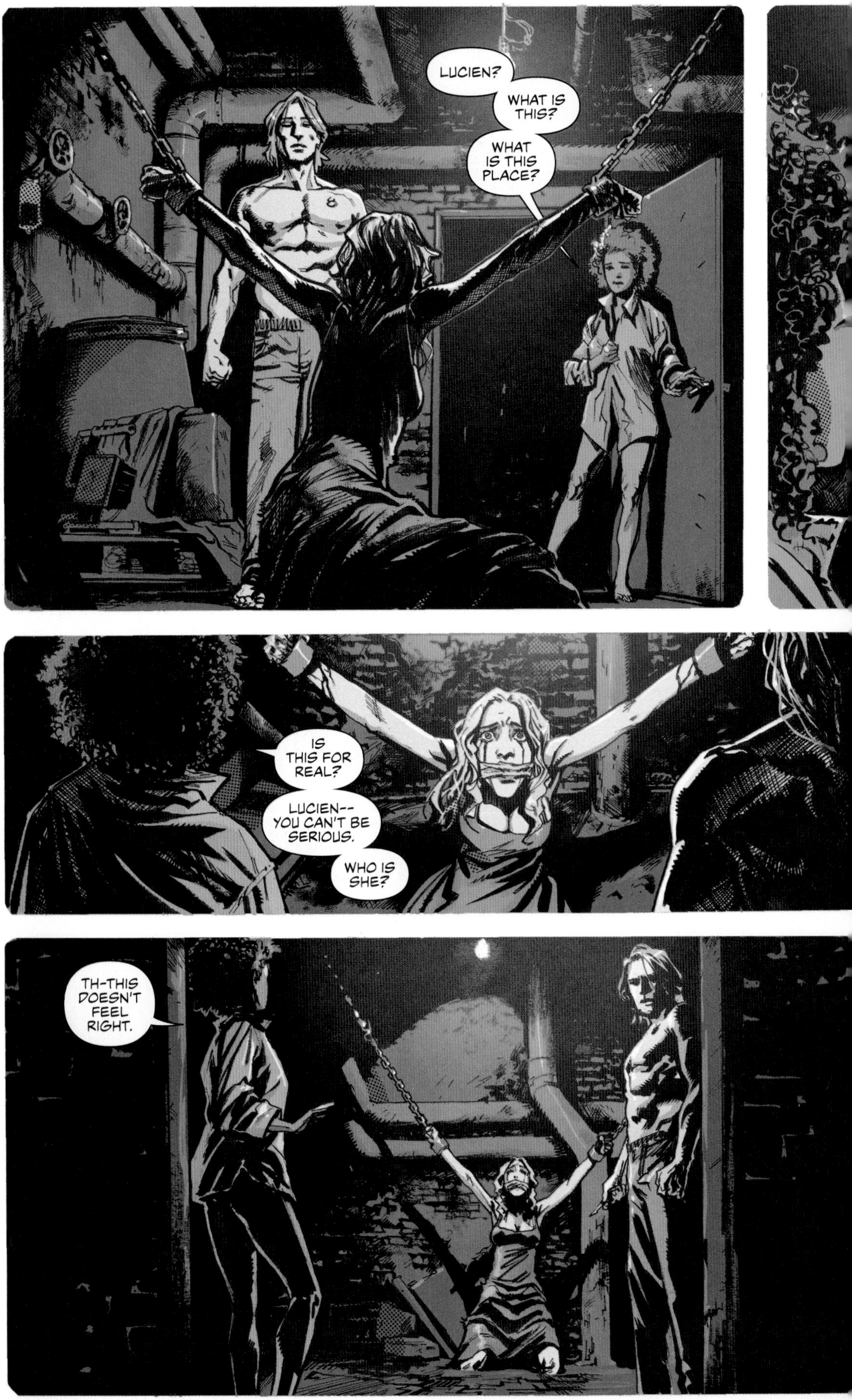
LUCIEN?
WHAT IS THIS?
WHAT IS THIS PLACE?
IS THIS FOR REAL?
LUCIEN-- YOU CAN'T BE SERIOUS.
WHO IS SHE?
TH-THIS DOESN'T FEEL RIGHT.

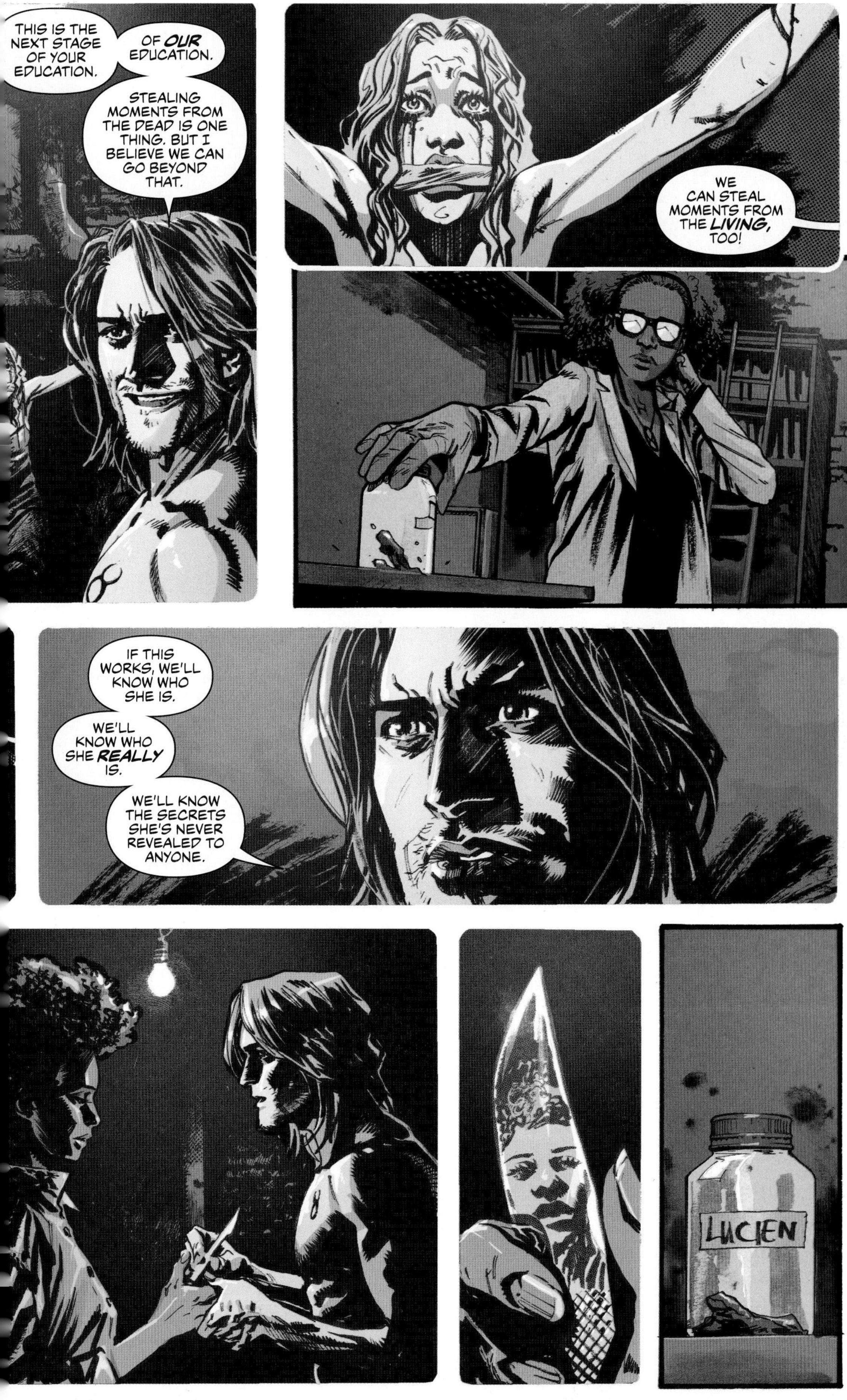

THIS IS THE NEXT STAGE OF YOUR EDUCATION.
OF OUR EDUCATION.
STEALING MOMENTS FROM THE DEAD IS ONE THING. BUT I BELIEVE WE CAN GO BEYOND THAT.
WE CAN STEAL MOMENTS FROM THE LIVING, TOO!
IF THIS WORKS, WE'LL KNOW WHO SHE IS.
WE'LL KNOW WHO SHE REALLY IS.
WE'LL KNOW THE SECRETS SHE'S NEVER REVEALED TO ANYONE.
LUCIEN

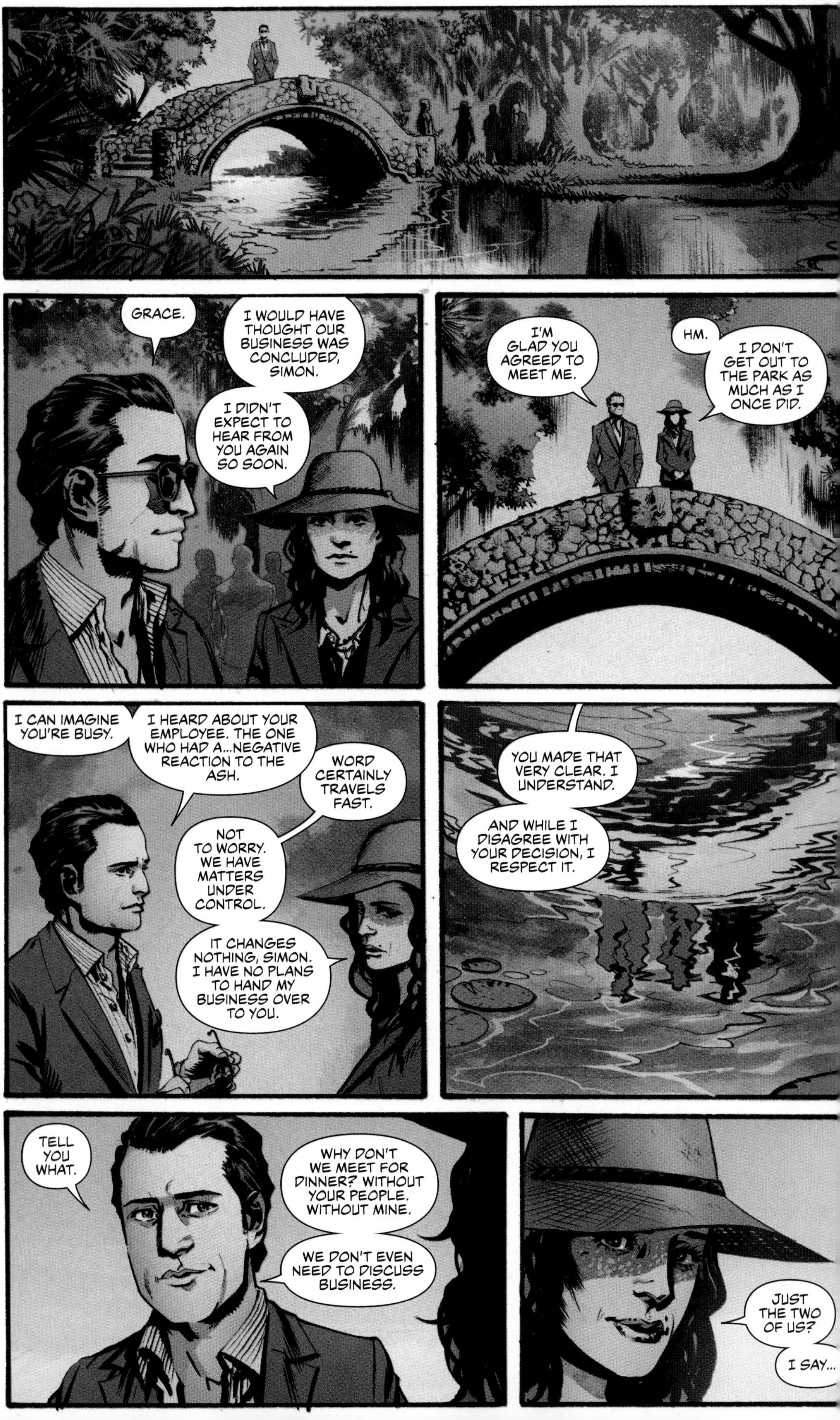
GRACE.
I WOULD HAVE THOUGHT OUR BUSINESS WAS CONCLUDED, SIMON.
I DIDN'T EXPECT TO HEAR FROM YOU AGAIN SO SOON.
I'M GLAD YOU AGREED TO MEET ME.
HM.
I DON'T GET OUT TO THE PARK AS MUCH AS I ONCE DID.
I CAN IMAGINE YOU'RE BUSY.
I HEARD ABOUT YOUR EMPLOYEE. THE ONE WHO HAD A...NEGATIVE REACTION TO THE ASH.
WORD CERTAINLY TRAVELS FAST.
NOT TO WORRY. WE HAVE MATTERS UNDER CONTROL.
IT CHANGES NOTHING, SIMON. I HAVE NO PLANS TO HAND MY BUSINESS OVER TO YOU.
YOU MADE THAT VERY CLEAR. I UNDERSTAND.
AND WHILE I DISAGREE WITH YOUR DECISION, I RESPECT IT.
TELL YOU WHAT.
WHY DON'T WE MEET FOR DINNER? WITHOUT YOUR PEOPLE. WITHOUT MINE.
WE DON'T EVEN NEED TO DISCUSS BUSINESS.
JUST THE TWO OF US?
I SAY...

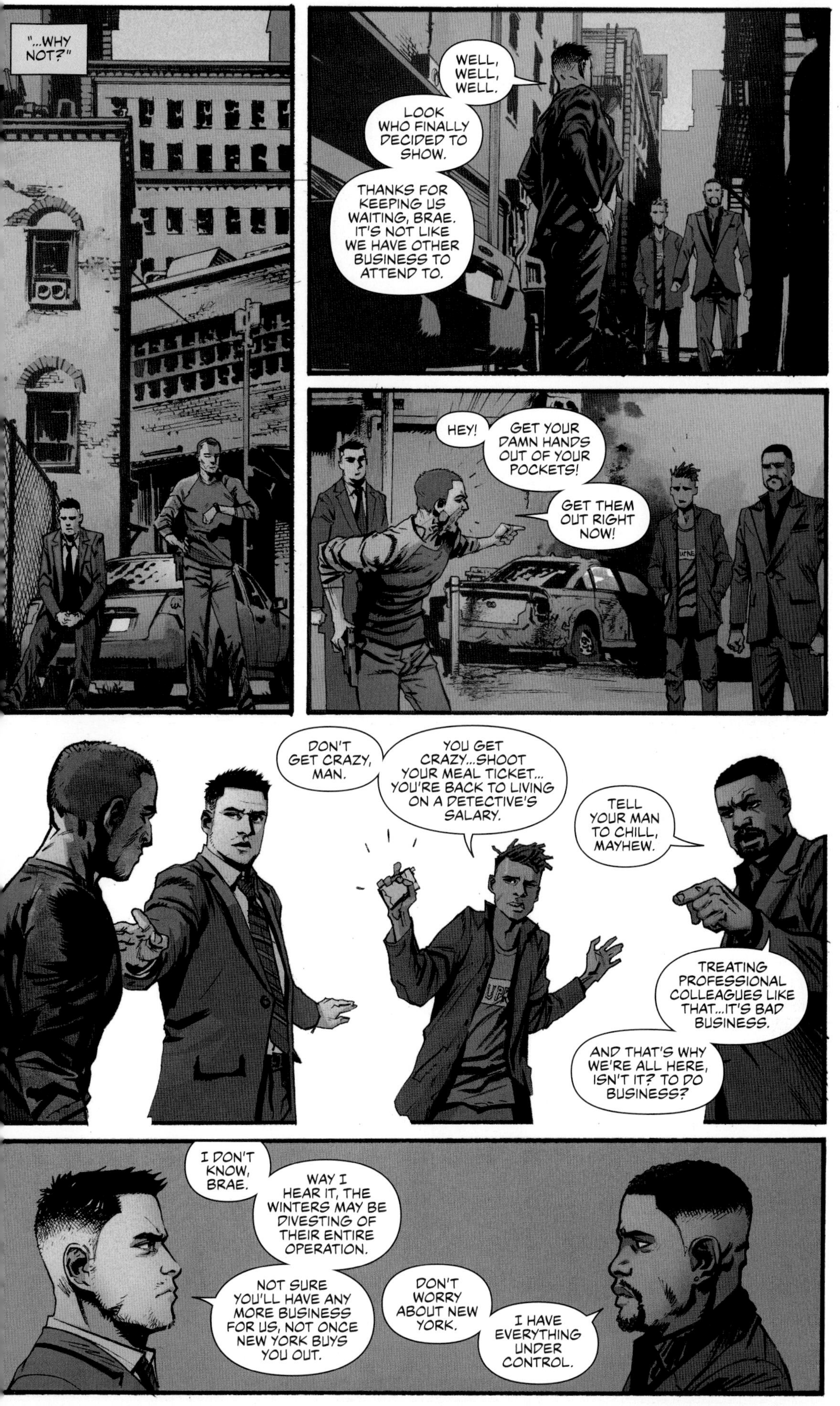
"...WHY NOT?"
WELL, WELL, WELL.
LOOK WHO FINALLY DECIDED TO SHOW.
THANKS FOR KEEPING US WAITING, BRAE. IT'S NOT LIKE WE HAVE OTHER BUSINESS TO ATTEND TO.
HEY!
GET YOUR DAMN HANDS OUT OF YOUR POCKETS!
GET THEM OUT RIGHT NOW!
DON'T GET CRAZY, MAN.
YOU GET CRAZY...SHOOT YOUR MEAL TICKET... YOU'RE BACK TO LIVING ON A DETECTIVE'S SALARY.
TELL YOUR MAN TO CHILL, MAYHEW.
TREATING PROFESSIONAL COLLEAGUES LIKE THAT...IT'S BAD BUSINESS.
AND THAT'S WHY WE'RE ALL HERE, ISN'T IT? TO DO BUSINESS?
I DON'T KNOW, BRAE.
WAY I HEAR IT, THE WINTERS MAY BE DIVESTING OF THEIR ENTIRE OPERATION.
NOT SURE YOU'LL HAVE ANY MORE BUSINESS FOR US, NOT ONCE NEW YORK BUYS YOU OUT.
DON'T WORRY ABOUT NEW YORK.
I HAVE EVERYTHING UNDER CONTROL.

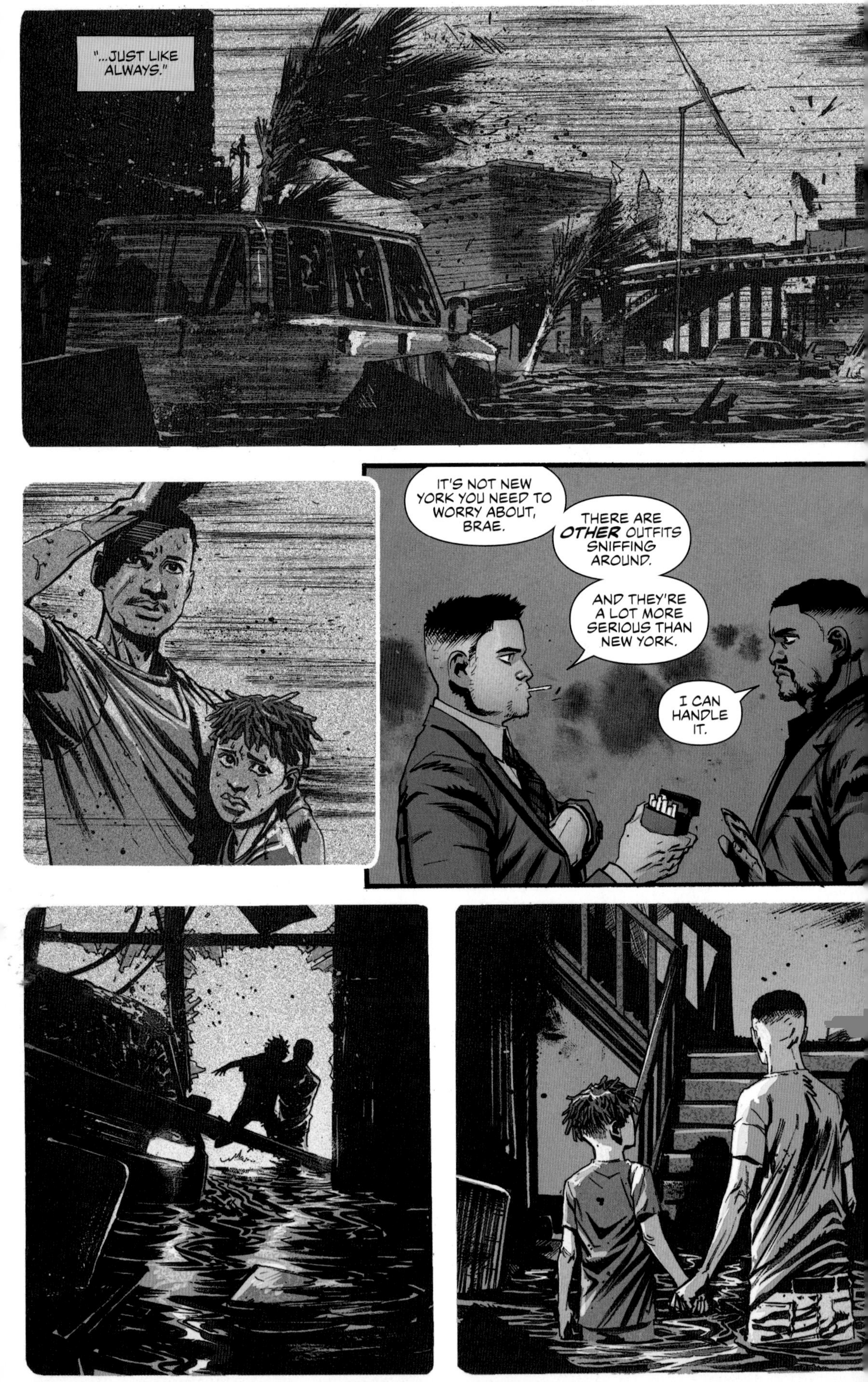
"...JUST LIKE ALWAYS."
IT'S NOT NEW YORK YOU NEED TO WORRY ABOUT, BRAE.
THERE ARE *OTHER* OUTFITS SNIFFING AROUND.
AND THEY'RE A LOT MORE SERIOUS THAN NEW YORK.
I CAN HANDLE IT.

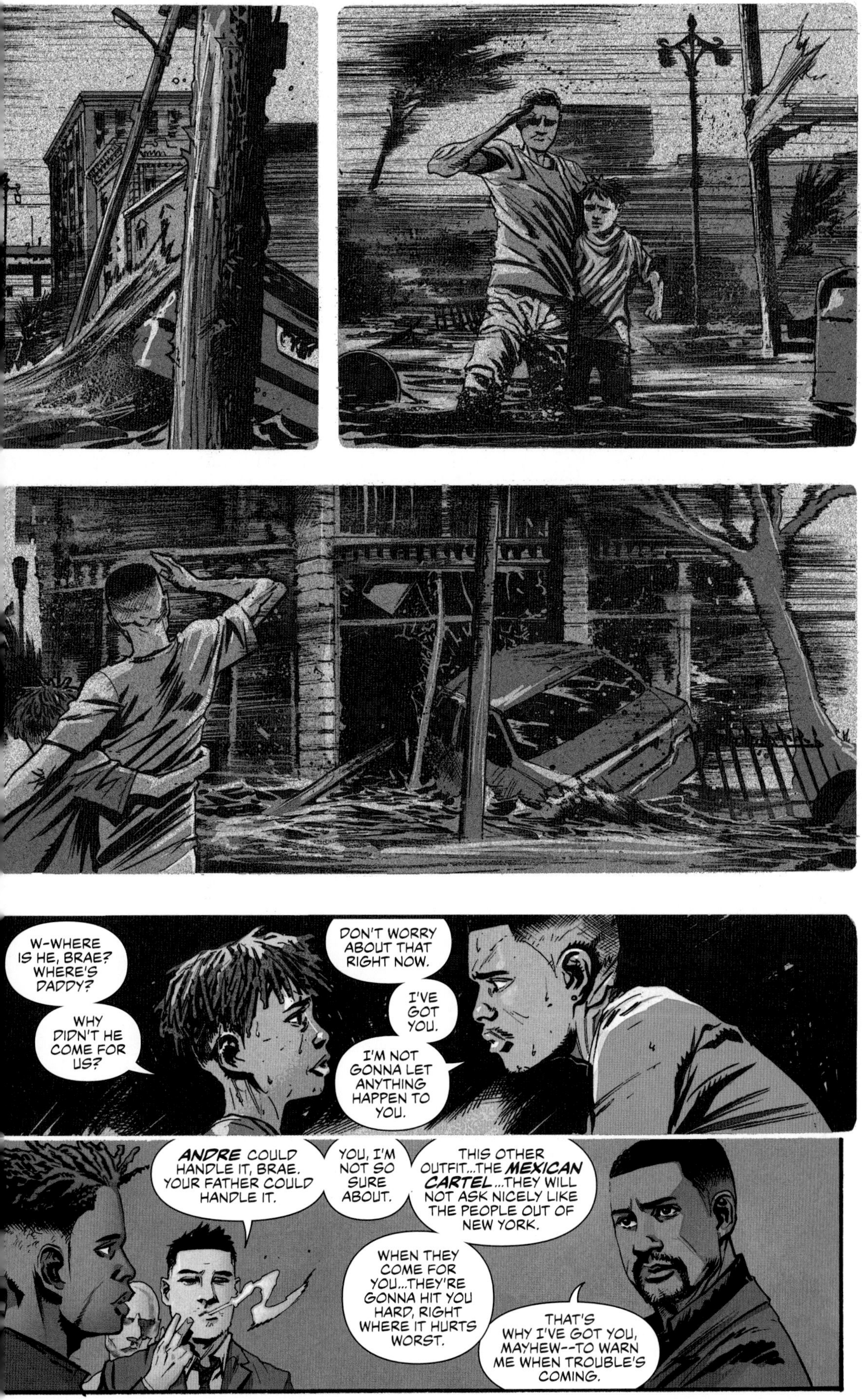
W-WHERE IS HE, BRAE? WHERE'S DADDY?
WHY DIDN'T HE COME FOR US?
DON'T WORRY ABOUT THAT RIGHT NOW.
I'VE GOT YOU.
I'M NOT GONNA LET ANYTHING HAPPEN TO YOU.
ANDRE COULD HANDLE IT, BRAE. YOUR FATHER COULD HANDLE IT.
YOU, I'M NOT SO SURE ABOUT.
THIS OTHER OUTFIT...THE MEXICAN CARTEL...THEY WILL NOT ASK NICELY LIKE THE PEOPLE OUT OF NEW YORK.
WHEN THEY COME FOR YOU...THEY'RE GONNA HIT YOU HARD, RIGHT WHERE IT HURTS WORST.
THAT'S WHY I'VE GOT YOU, MAYHEW--TO WARN ME WHEN TROUBLE'S COMING.

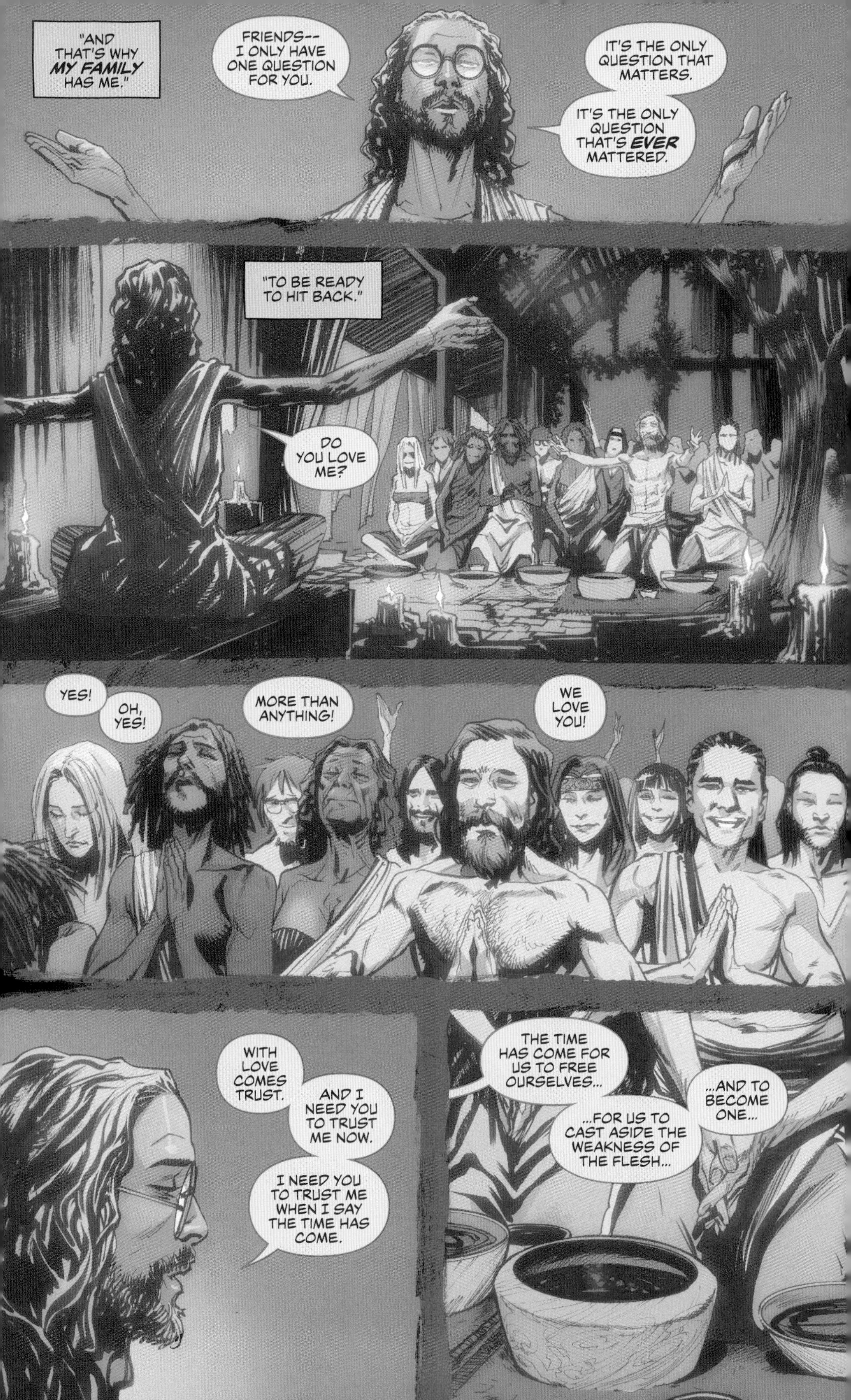
"AND THAT'S WHY *MY FAMILY* HAS ME."
FRIENDS-- I ONLY HAVE ONE QUESTION FOR YOU.
IT'S THE ONLY QUESTION THAT MATTERS.
IT'S THE ONLY QUESTION THAT'S *EVER* MATTERED.
"TO BE READY TO HIT BACK."
DO YOU LOVE ME?
YES!
OH, YES!
MORE THAN ANYTHING!
WE LOVE YOU!
WITH LOVE COMES TRUST.
AND I NEED YOU TO TRUST ME NOW.
I NEED YOU TO TRUST ME WHEN I SAY THE TIME HAS COME.
THE TIME HAS COME FOR US TO FREE OURSELVES...
...FOR US TO CAST ASIDE THE WEAKNESS OF THE FLESH...
...AND TO BECOME ONE...

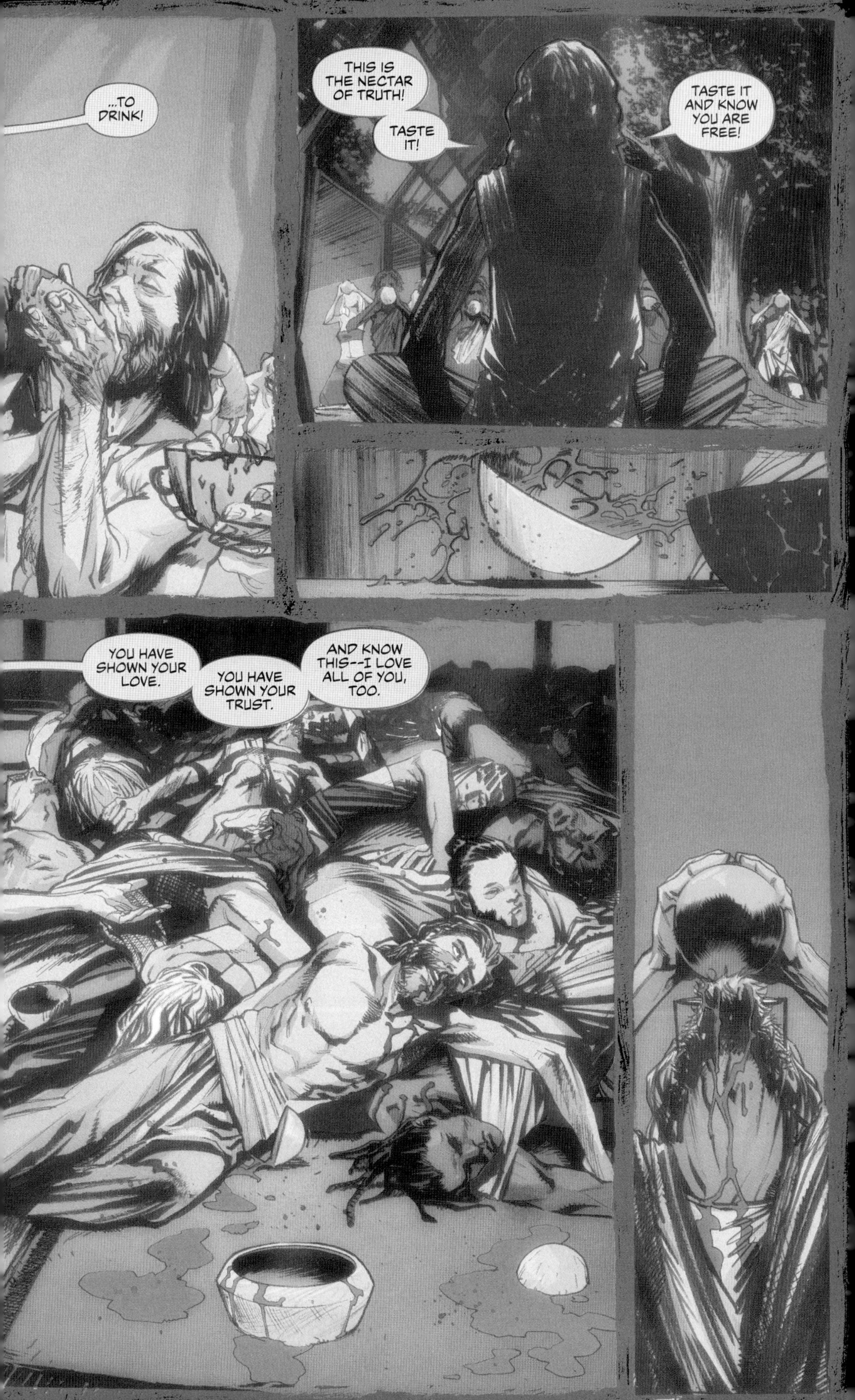
...TO DRINK!
THIS IS THE NECTAR OF TRUTH!
TASTE IT!
TASTE IT AND KNOW YOU ARE FREE!
YOU HAVE SHOWN YOUR LOVE.
YOU HAVE SHOWN YOUR TRUST.
AND KNOW THIS--I LOVE ALL OF YOU, TOO.

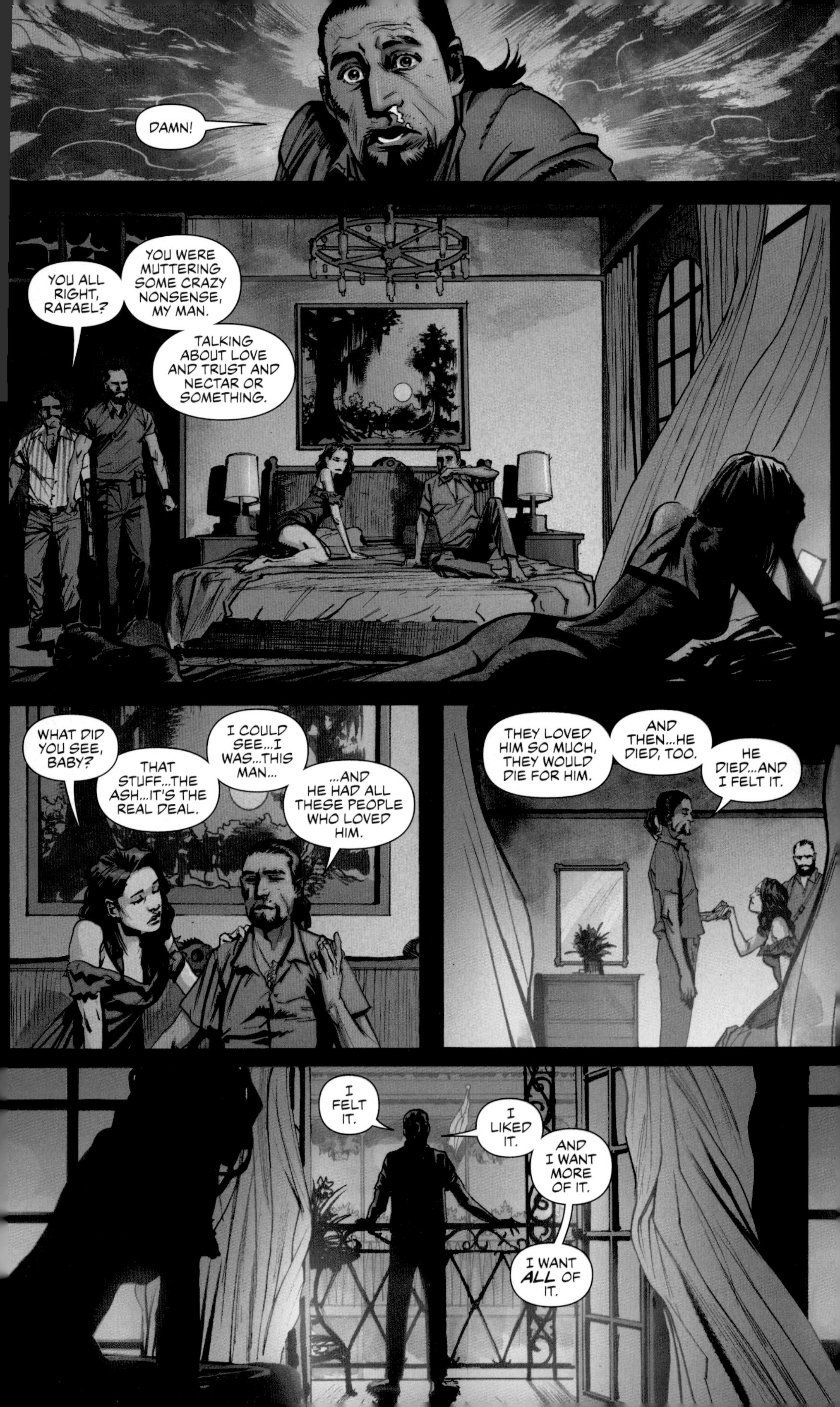
DAMN!
YOU ALL RIGHT, RAFAEL?
YOU WERE MUTTERING SOME CRAZY NONSENSE, MY MAN.
TALKING ABOUT LOVE AND TRUST AND NECTAR OR SOMETHING.
WHAT DID YOU SEE, BABY?
THAT STUFF...THE ASH...IT'S THE REAL DEAL.
I COULD SEE...I WAS...THIS MAN...
...AND HE HAD ALL THESE PEOPLE WHO LOVED HIM.
THEY LOVED HIM SO MUCH, THEY WOULD DIE FOR HIM.
AND THEN...HE DIED, TOO.
HE DIED...AND I FELT IT.
I FELT IT.
I LIKED IT.
AND I WANT MORE OF IT.
I WANT ALL OF IT.

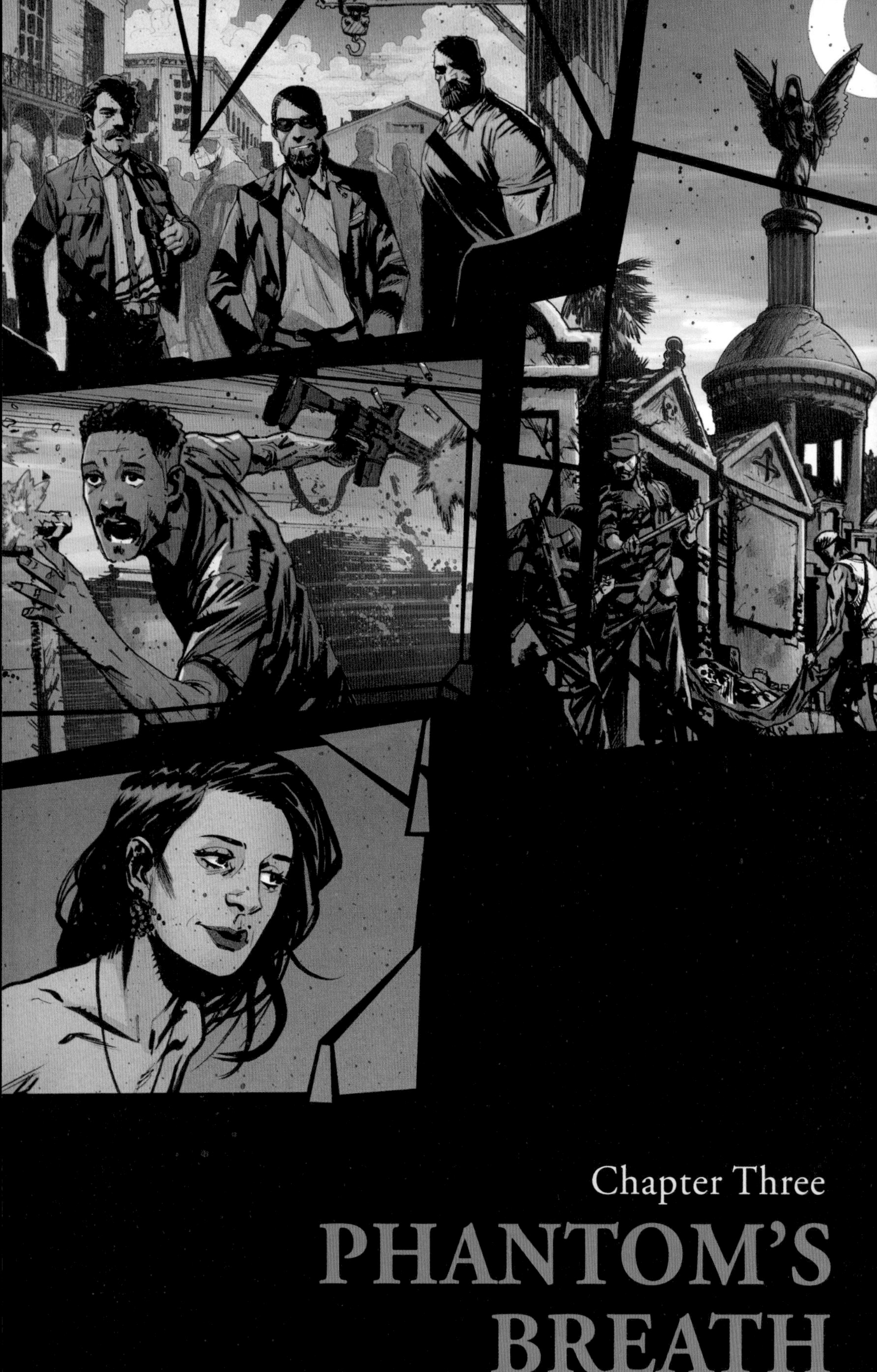

Chapter Three

PHANTOM'S BREATH

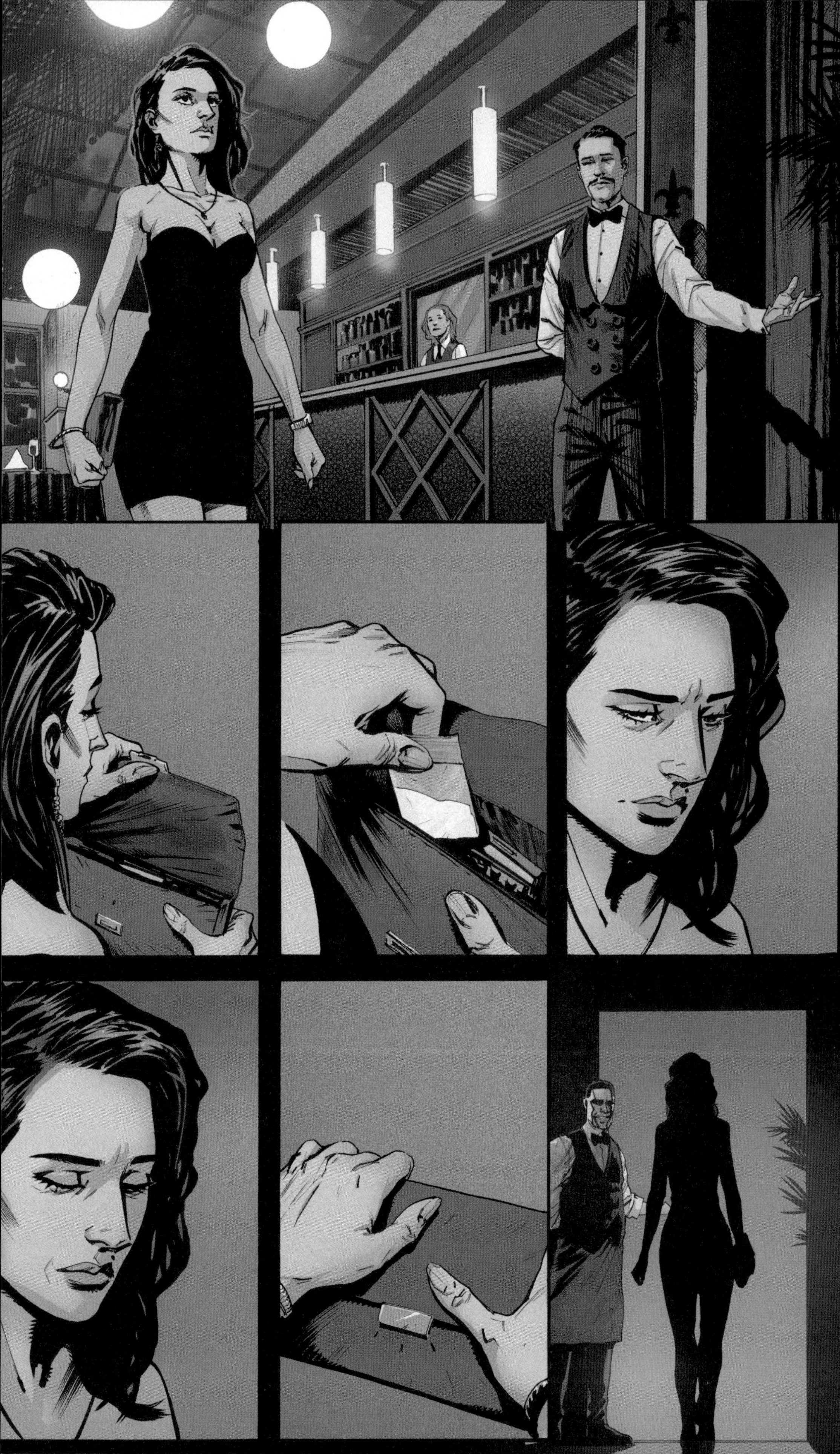

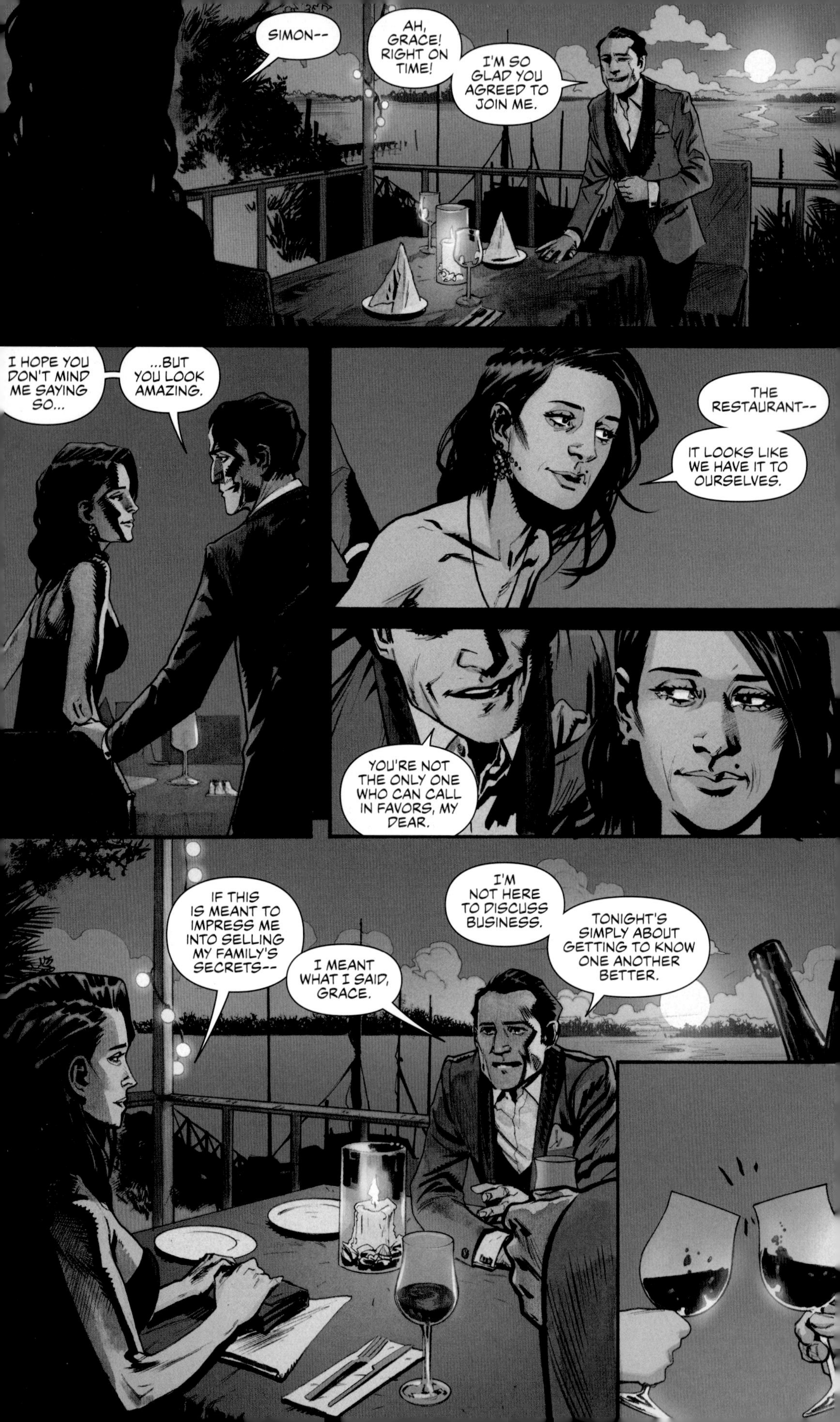
SIMON--
AH, GRACE! RIGHT ON TIME!
I'M SO GLAD YOU AGREED TO JOIN ME.
I HOPE YOU DON'T MIND ME SAYING SO...
...BUT YOU LOOK AMAZING.
THE RESTAURANT--
IT LOOKS LIKE WE HAVE IT TO OURSELVES.
YOU'RE NOT THE ONLY ONE WHO CAN CALL IN FAVORS, MY DEAR.
IF THIS IS MEANT TO IMPRESS ME INTO SELLING MY FAMILY'S SECRETS--
I MEANT WHAT I SAID, GRACE.
I'M NOT HERE TO DISCUSS BUSINESS.
TONIGHT'S SIMPLY ABOUT GETTING TO KNOW ONE ANOTHER BETTER.

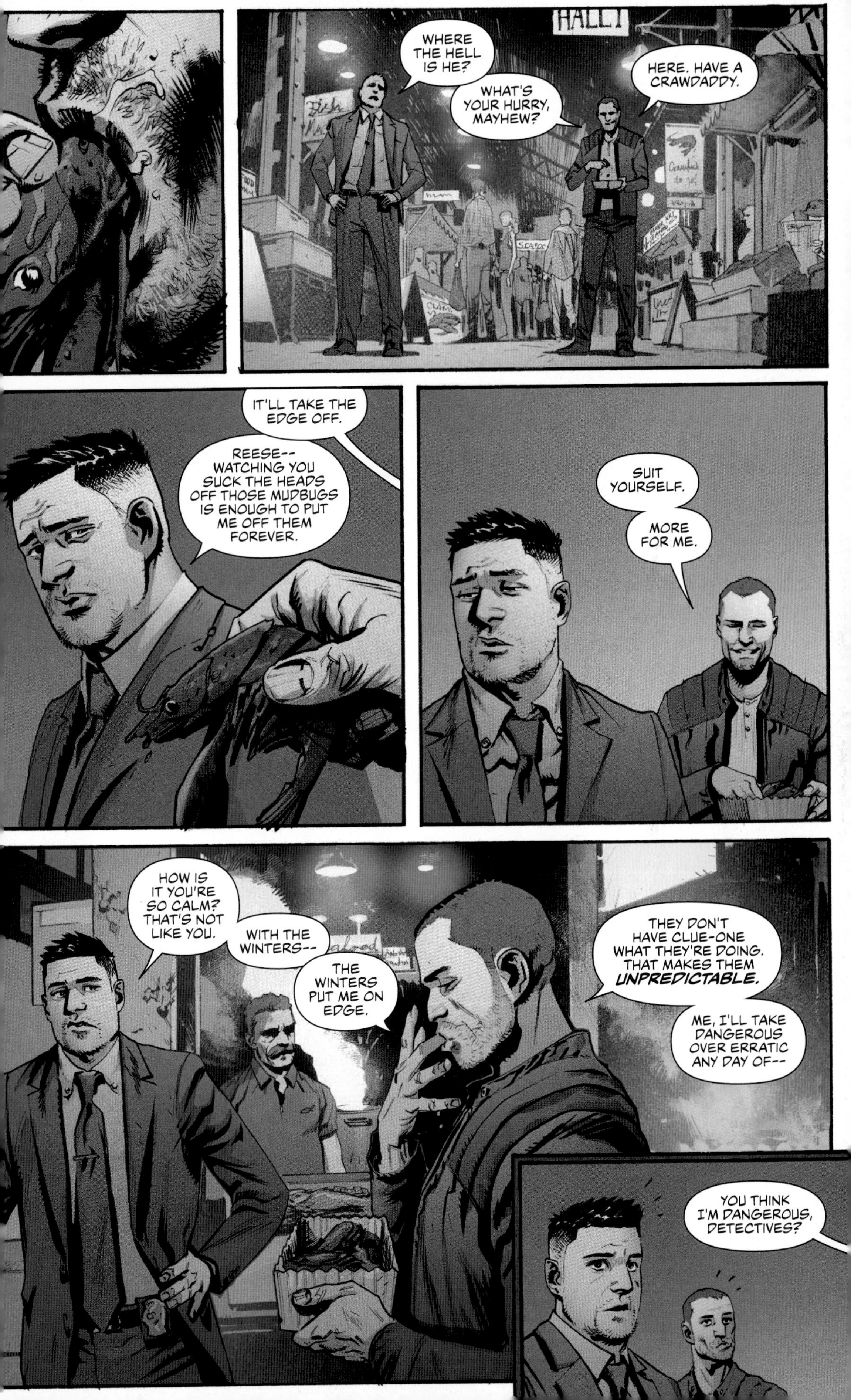
HALLT
WHERE THE HELL IS HE?
WHAT'S YOUR HURRY, MAYHEW?
HERE. HAVE A CRAWDADDY.
IT'LL TAKE THE EDGE OFF.
REESE-- WATCHING YOU SUCK THE HEADS OFF THOSE MUDBUGS IS ENOUGH TO PUT ME OFF THEM FOREVER.
SUIT YOURSELF.
MORE FOR ME.
HOW IS IT YOU'RE SO CALM? THAT'S NOT LIKE YOU.
WITH THE WINTERS--
THE WINTERS PUT ME ON EDGE.
THEY DON'T HAVE CLUE-ONE WHAT THEY'RE DOING. THAT MAKES THEM *UNPREDICTABLE.*
ME, I'LL TAKE DANGEROUS OVER ERRATIC ANY DAY OF--
YOU THINK I'M DANGEROUS, DETECTIVES?

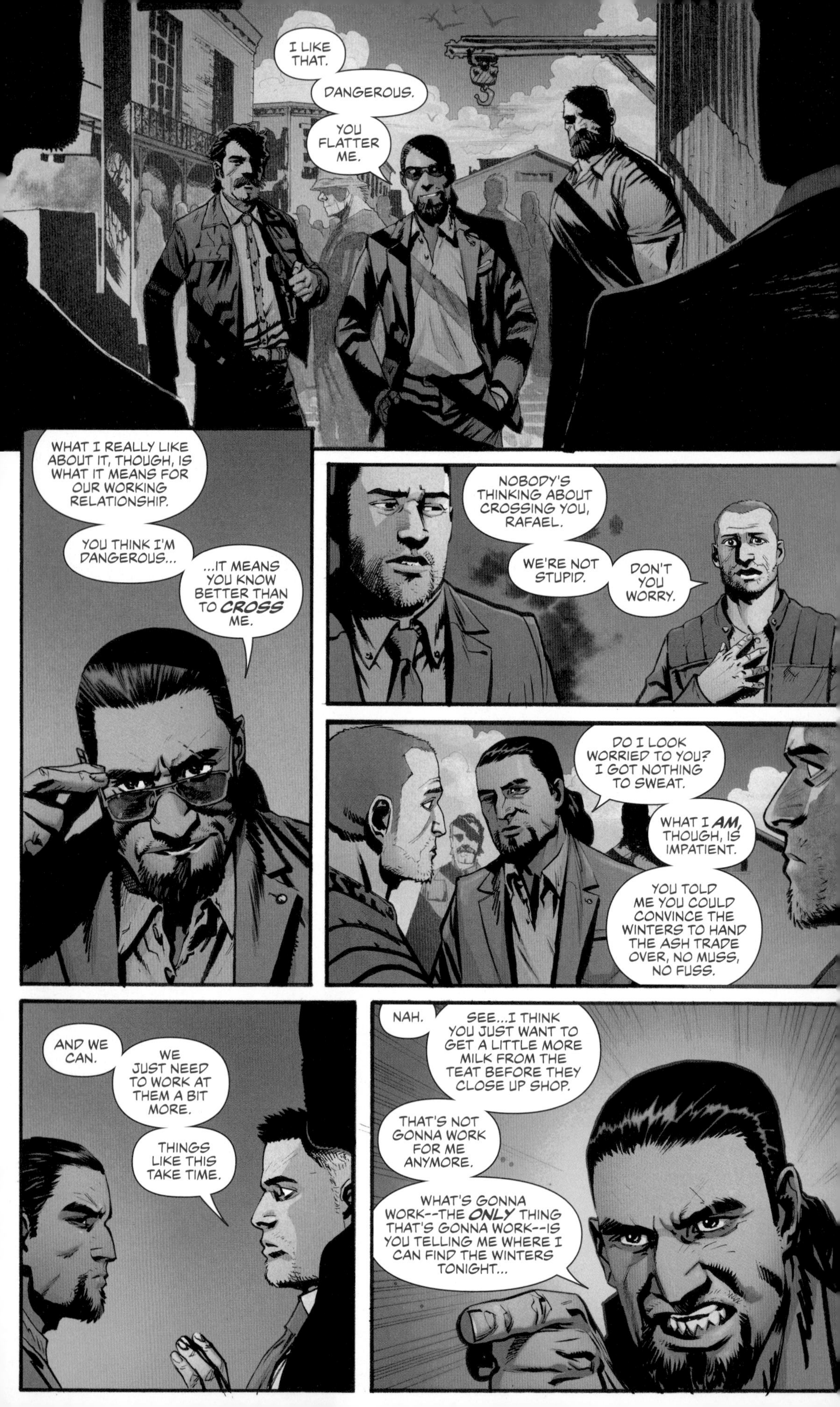
I LIKE THAT.
DANGEROUS.
YOU FLATTER ME.
WHAT I REALLY LIKE ABOUT IT, THOUGH, IS WHAT IT MEANS FOR OUR WORKING RELATIONSHIP.
YOU THINK I'M DANGEROUS...
...IT MEANS YOU KNOW BETTER THAN TO *CROSS* ME.
NOBODY'S THINKING ABOUT CROSSING YOU, RAFAEL.
WE'RE NOT STUPID.
DON'T YOU WORRY.
DO I LOOK WORRIED TO YOU? I GOT NOTHING TO SWEAT.
WHAT I *AM,* THOUGH, IS IMPATIENT.
YOU TOLD ME YOU COULD CONVINCE THE WINTERS TO HAND THE ASH TRADE OVER, NO MUSS, NO FUSS.
AND WE CAN.
WE JUST NEED TO WORK AT THEM A BIT MORE.
THINGS LIKE THIS TAKE TIME.
NAH.
SEE...I THINK YOU JUST WANT TO GET A LITTLE MORE MILK FROM THE TEAT BEFORE THEY CLOSE UP SHOP.
THAT'S NOT GONNA WORK FOR ME ANYMORE.
WHAT'S GONNA WORK--THE *ONLY* THING THAT'S GONNA WORK--IS YOU TELLING ME WHERE I CAN FIND THE WINTERS TONIGHT...

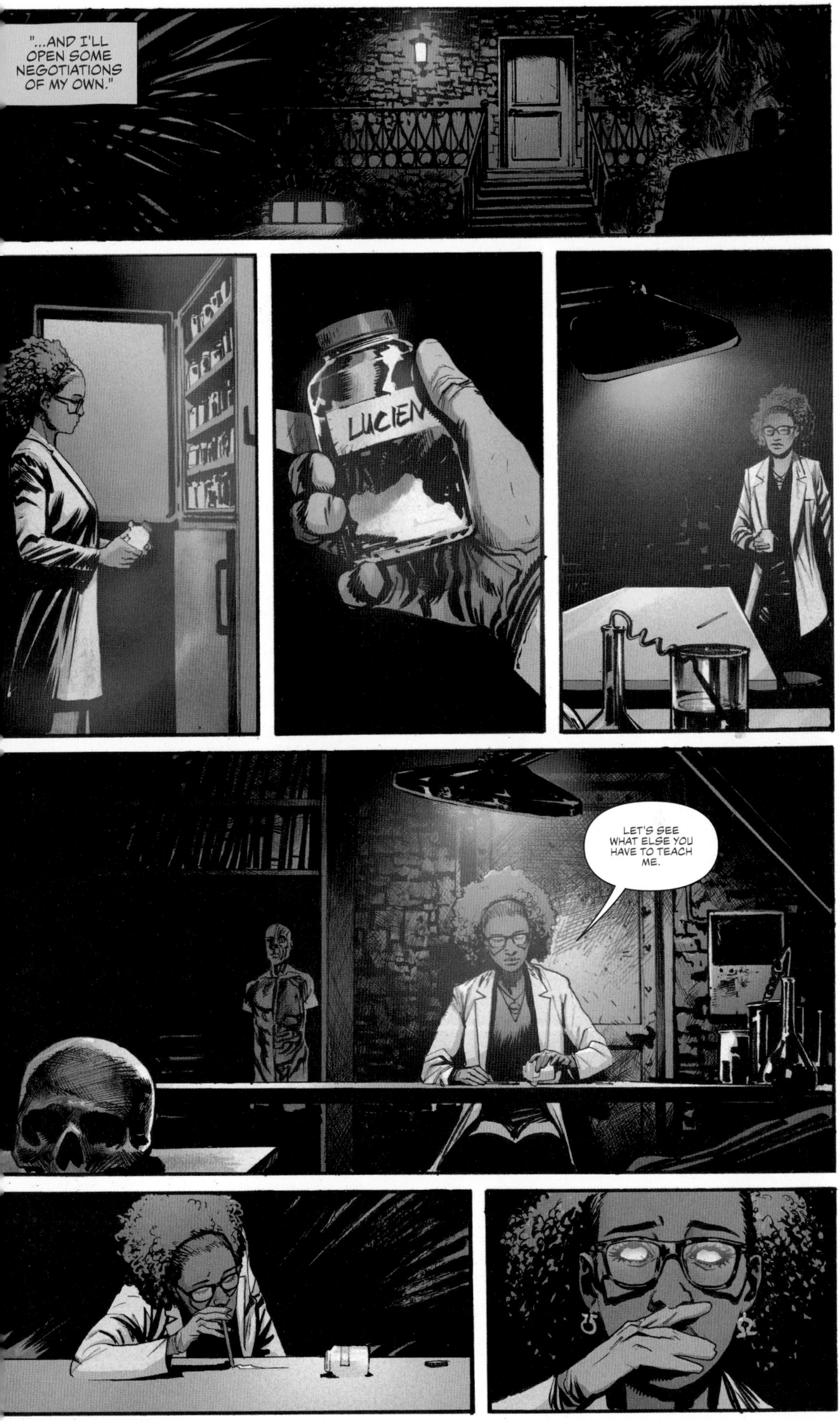
"...AND I'LL OPEN SOME NEGOTIATIONS OF MY OWN."
LUCIEN
LET'S SEE WHAT ELSE YOU HAVE TO TEACH ME.

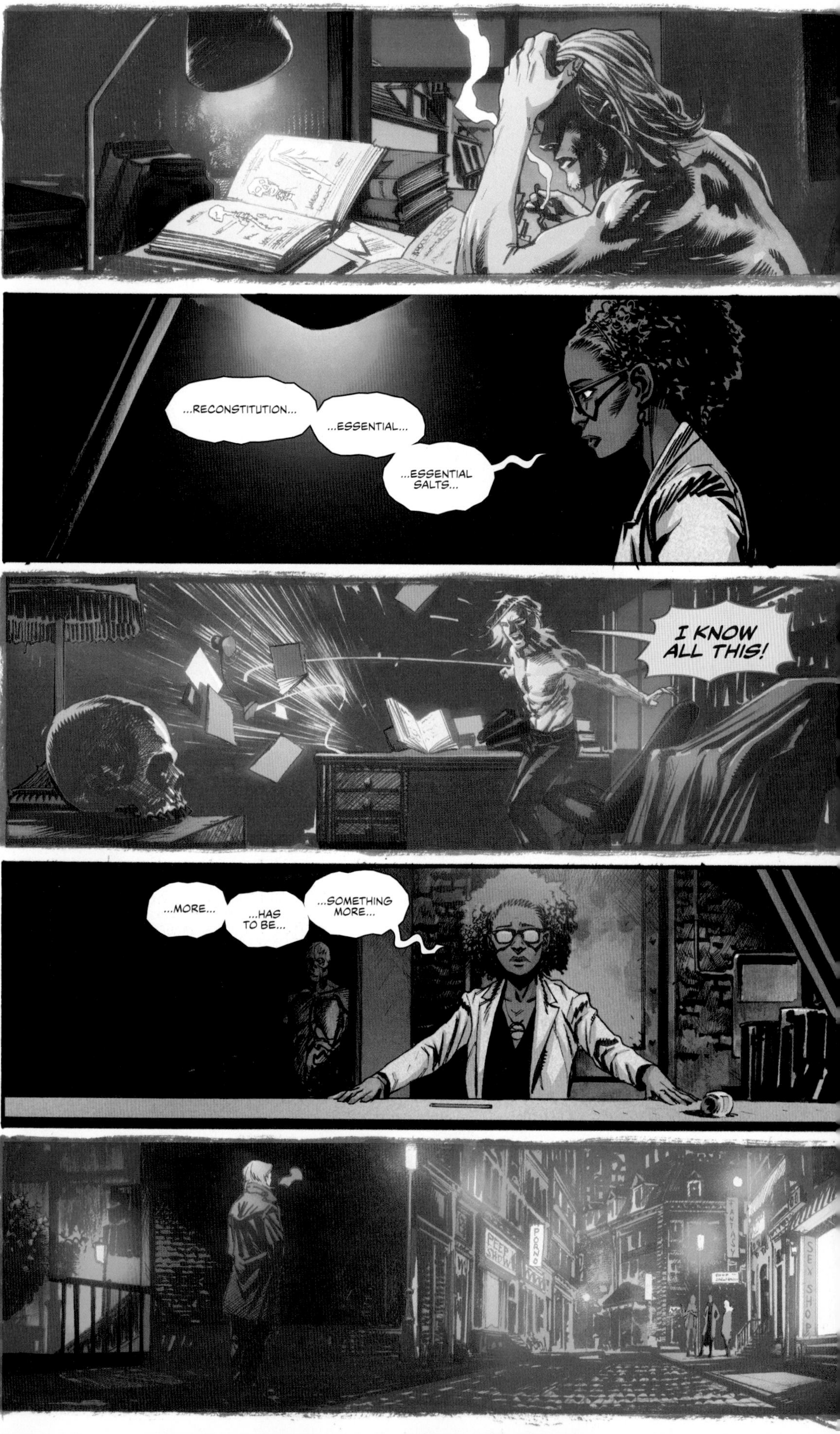
...RECONSTITUTION...
...ESSENTIAL...
...ESSENTIAL SALTS...
I KNOW ALL THIS!
...MORE...
...HAS TO BE...
...SOMETHING MORE...
PEEP SHOW
PORNO
FANTASY
SEX SHOP

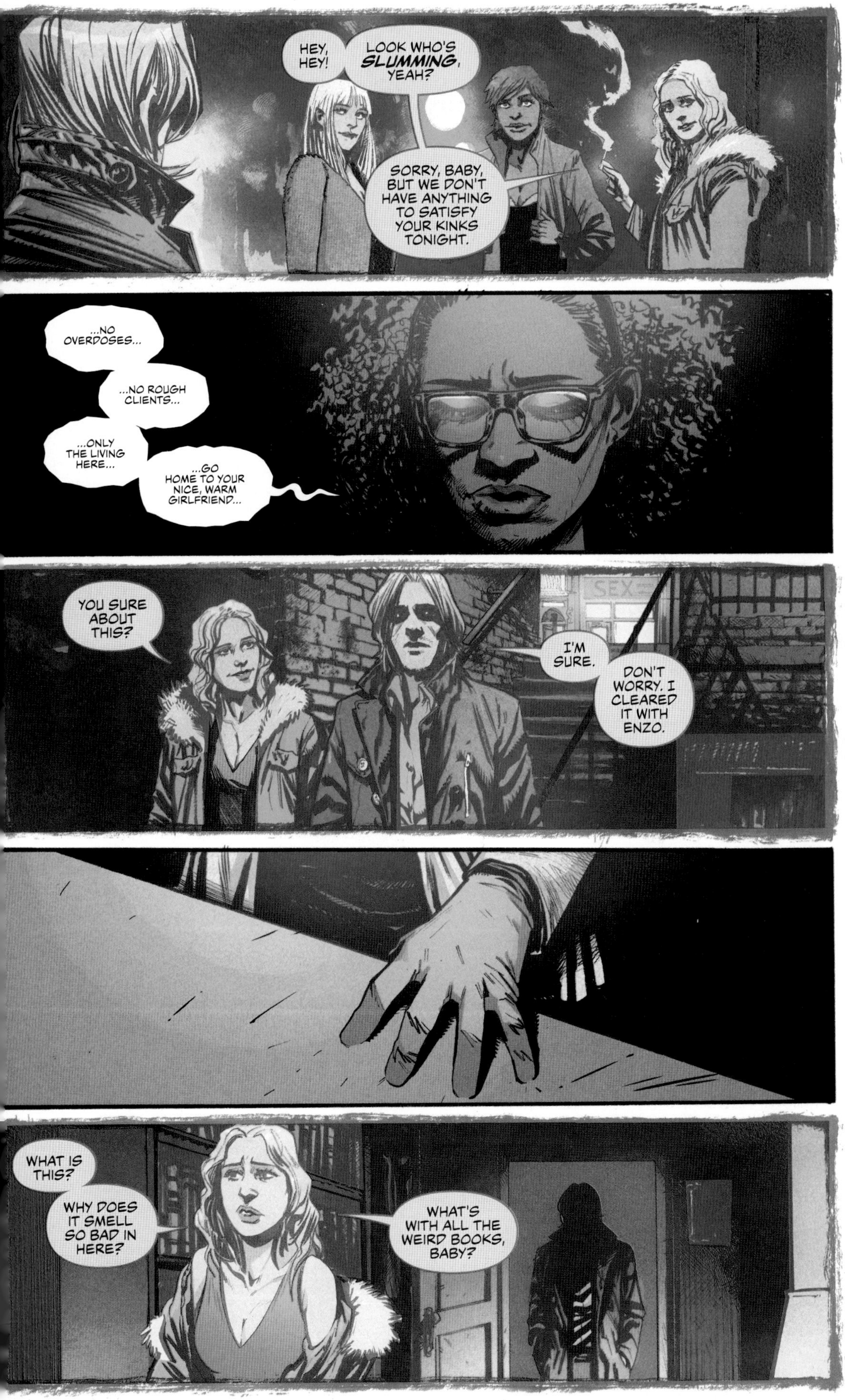
HEY, HEY!
LOOK WHO'S SLUMMING, YEAH?
SORRY, BABY, BUT WE DON'T HAVE ANYTHING TO SATISFY YOUR KINKS TONIGHT.
...NO OVERDOSES...
...NO ROUGH CLIENTS...
...ONLY THE LIVING HERE...
...GO HOME TO YOUR NICE, WARM GIRLFRIEND...
SEX
YOU SURE ABOUT THIS?
I'M SURE.
DON'T WORRY. I CLEARED IT WITH ENZO.
WHAT IS THIS?
WHY DOES IT SMELL SO BAD IN HERE?
WHAT'S WITH ALL THE WEIRD BOOKS, BABY?

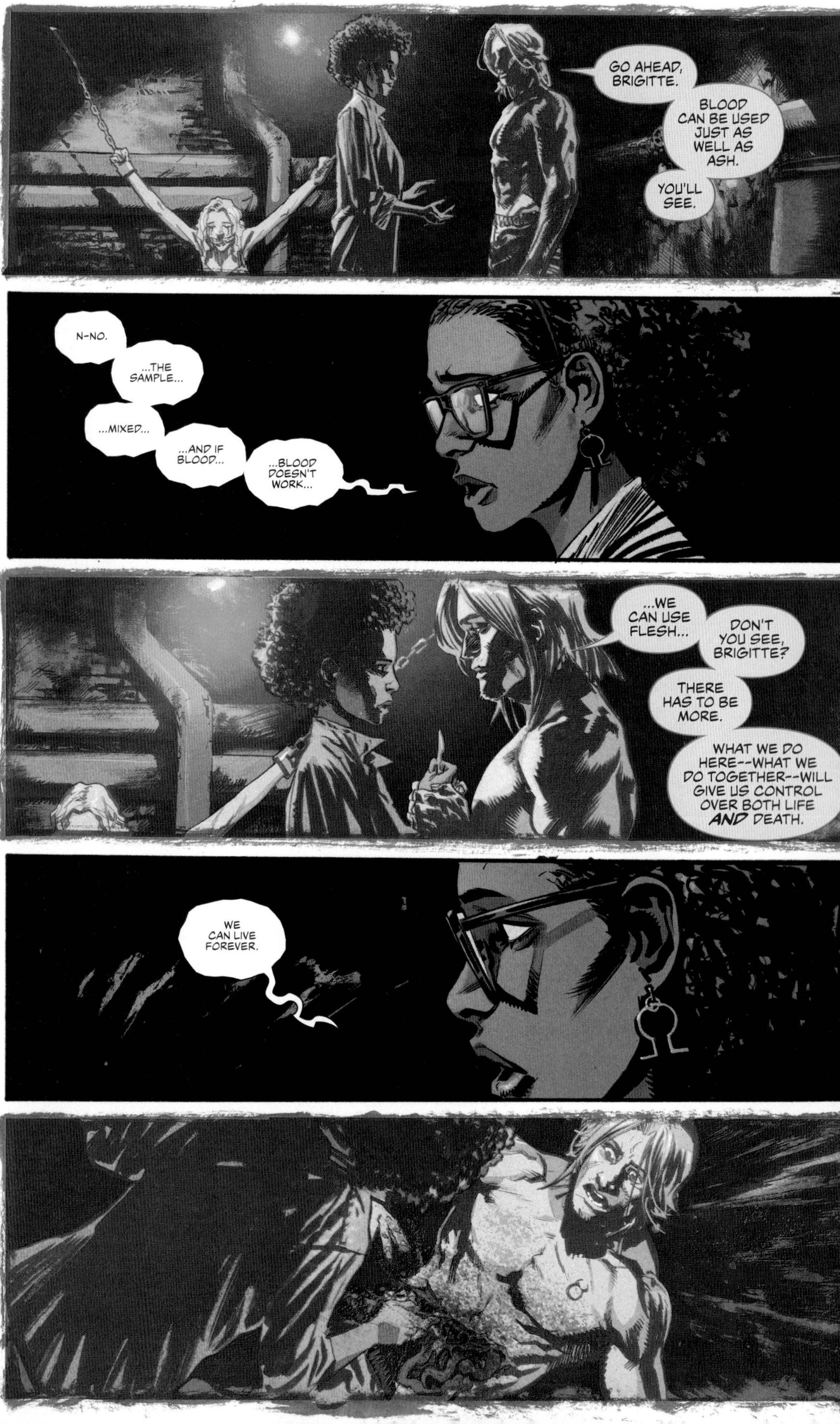
GO AHEAD, BRIGITTE.
BLOOD CAN BE USED JUST AS WELL AS ASH.
YOU'LL SEE.
N-NO.
...THE SAMPLE...
...MIXED...
...AND IF BLOOD...
...BLOOD DOESN'T WORK...
...WE CAN USE FLESH...
DON'T YOU SEE, BRIGITTE?
THERE HAS TO BE MORE.
WHAT WE DO HERE--WHAT WE DO TOGETHER--WILL GIVE US CONTROL OVER BOTH LIFE AND DEATH.
WE CAN LIVE FOREVER.

‹GASP›

OH...OH, LORD.

HIS DEATH.

I WASN'T SUPPOSED TO SEE.

FELT LIKE I WAS KILLING MY--

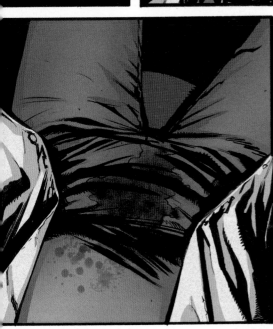

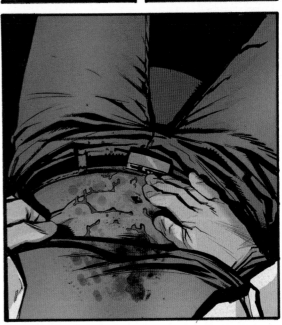

FELT LIKE...

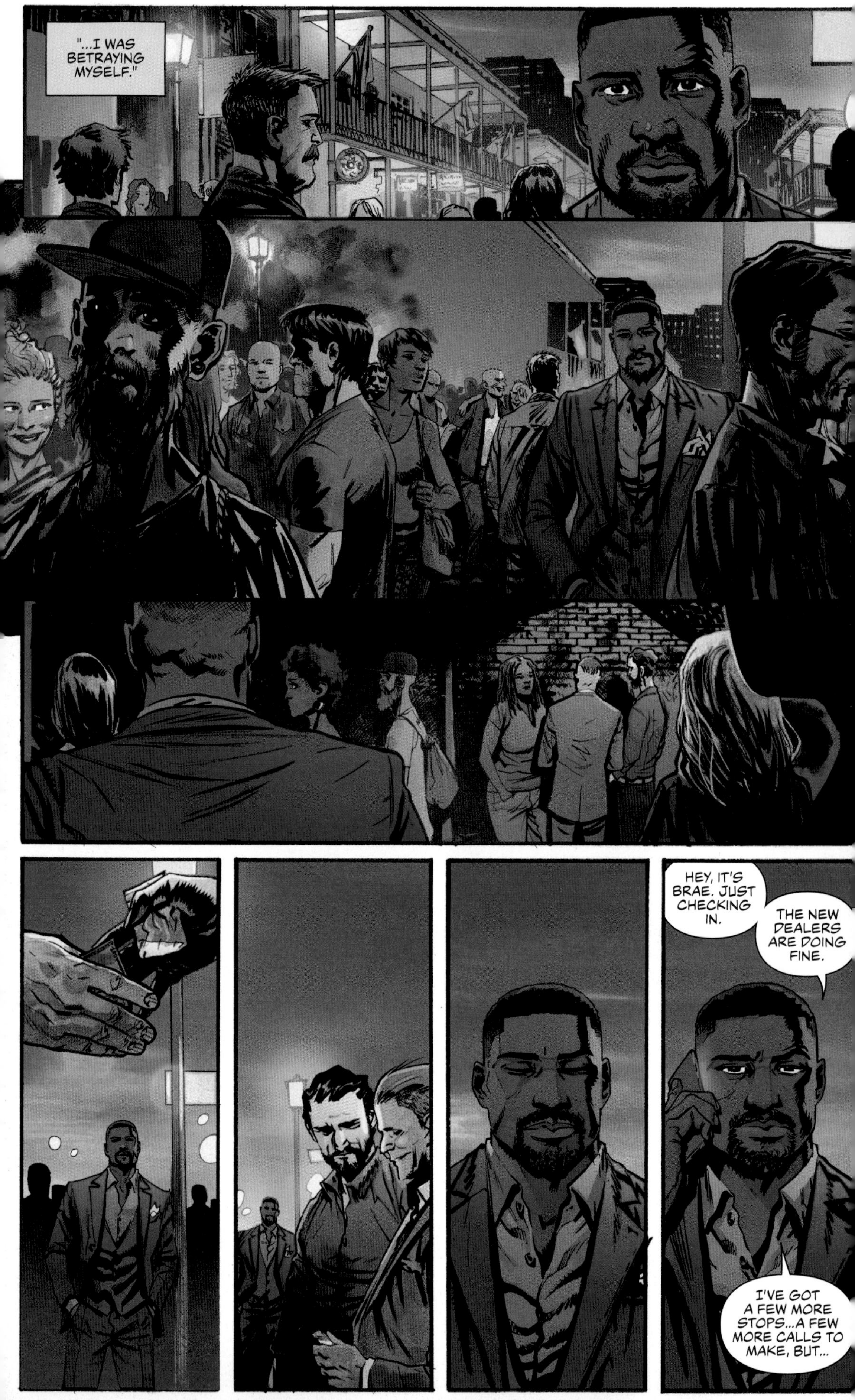
"...I WAS BETRAYING MYSELF."
HEY, IT'S BRAE. JUST CHECKING IN.
THE NEW DEALERS ARE DOING FINE.
I'VE GOT A FEW MORE STOPS...A FEW MORE CALLS TO MAKE, BUT...

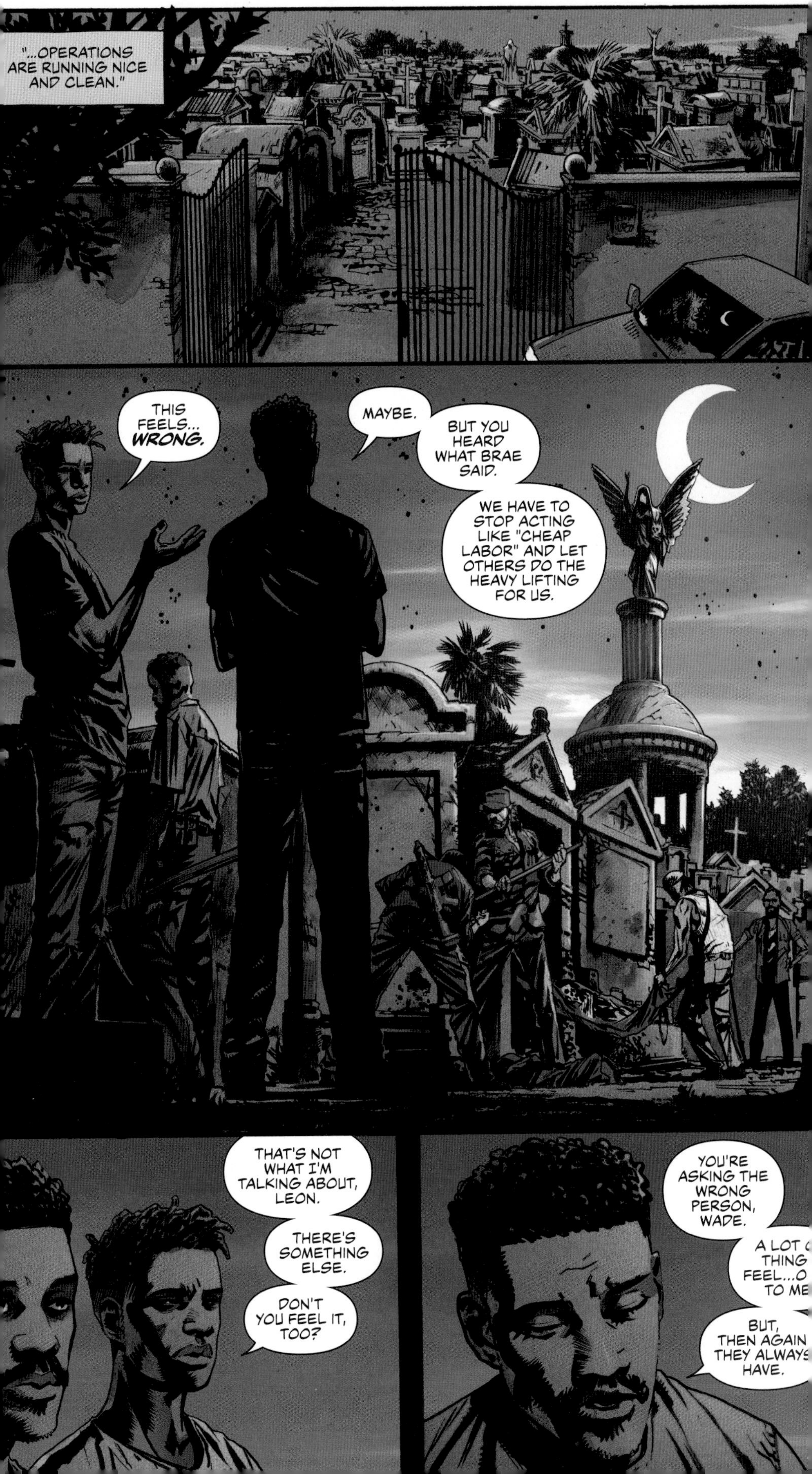
"...OPERATIONS ARE RUNNING NICE AND CLEAN."
THIS FEELS... WRONG.
MAYBE.
BUT YOU HEARD WHAT BRAE SAID.
WE HAVE TO STOP ACTING LIKE "CHEAP LABOR" AND LET OTHERS DO THE HEAVY LIFTING FOR US.
THAT'S NOT WHAT I'M TALKING ABOUT, LEON.
THERE'S SOMETHING ELSE.
DON'T YOU FEEL IT, TOO?
YOU'RE ASKING THE WRONG PERSON, WADE.
A LOT THING FEEL...O TO ME
BUT, THEN AGAIN THEY ALWAYS HAVE.

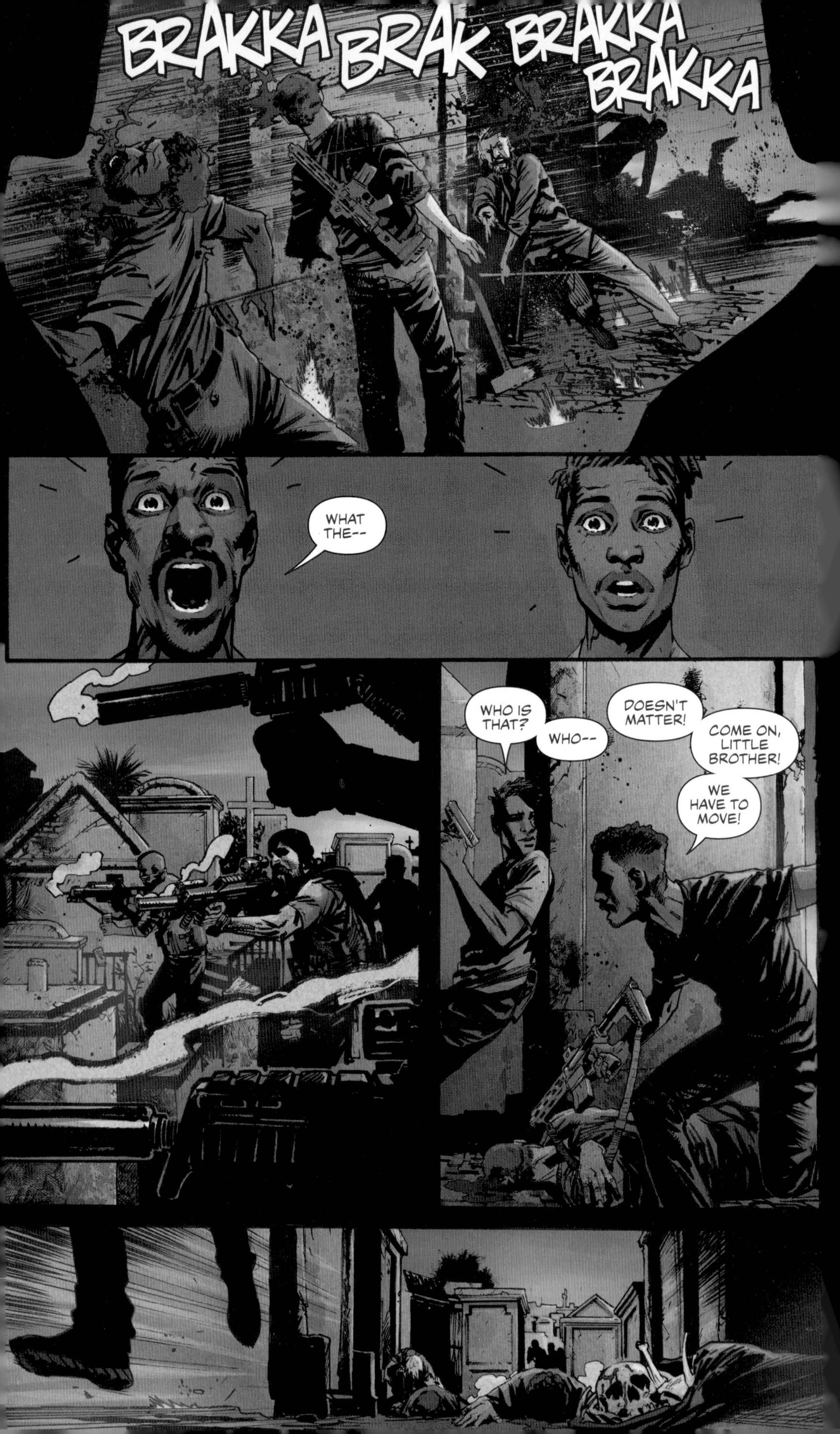
BRAKKA BRAK BRAKKA BRAKKA
WHAT THE--
WHO IS THAT?
WHO--
DOESN'T MATTER!
COME ON, LITTLE BROTHER!
WE HAVE TO MOVE!

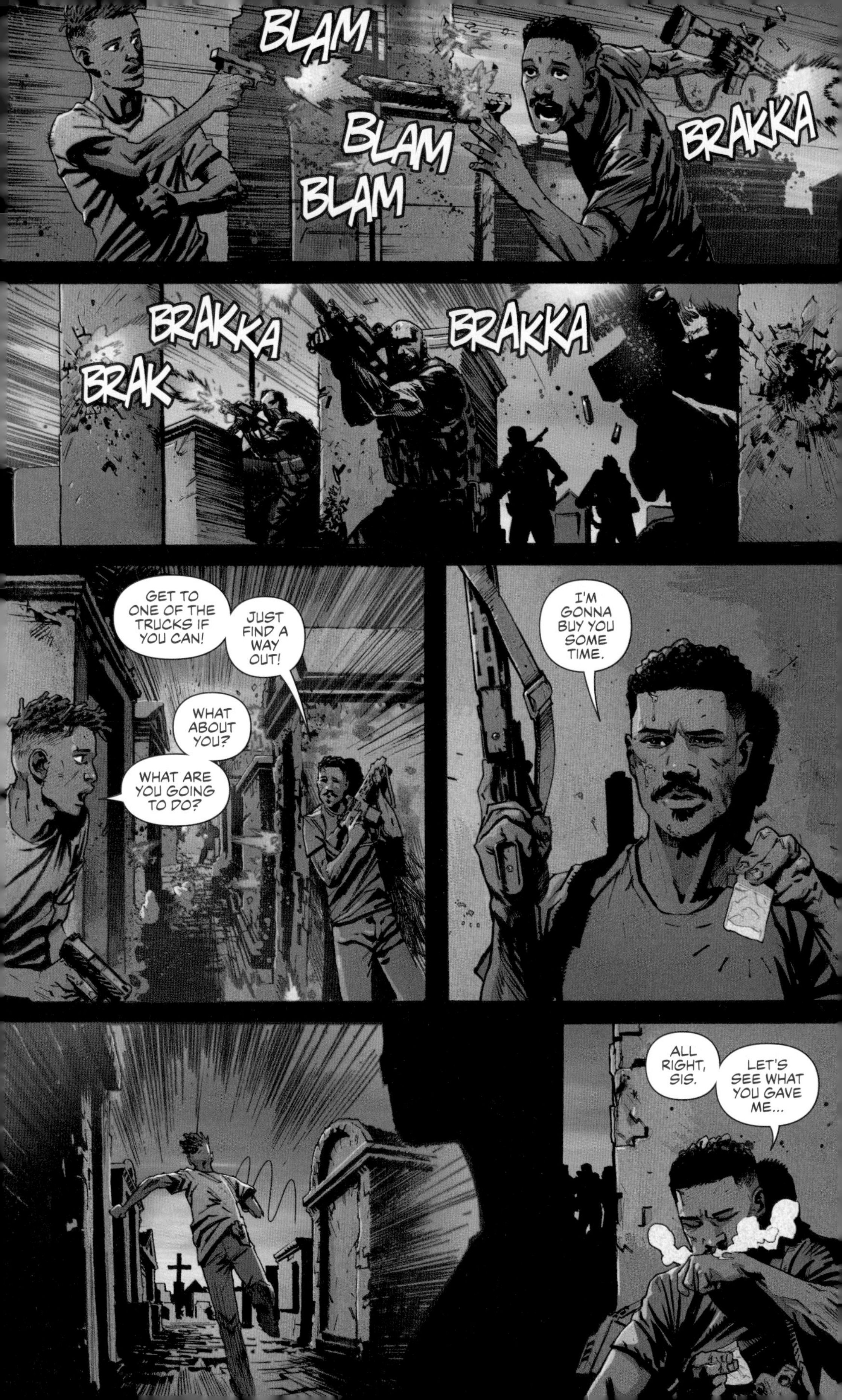
BLAM
BLAM
BLAM
BRAKKA
BRAK
BRAKKA
BRAKKA
GET TO ONE OF THE TRUCKS IF YOU CAN!
JUST FIND A WAY OUT!
WHAT ABOUT YOU?
WHAT ARE YOU GOING TO DO?
I'M GONNA BUY YOU SOME TIME.
ALL RIGHT, SIS.
LET'S SEE WHAT YOU GAVE ME...

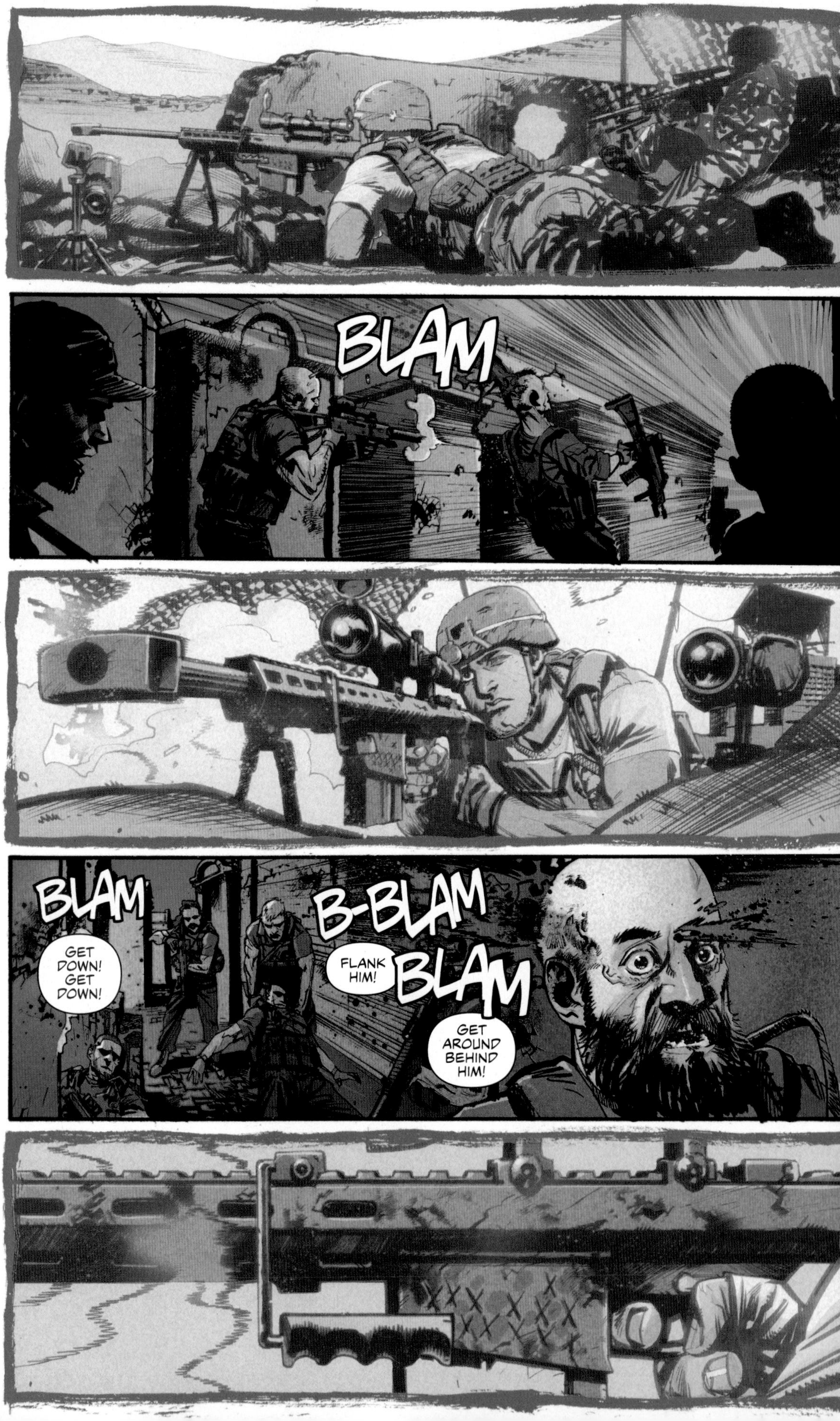
BLAM
BLAM
GET DOWN! GET DOWN!
B-BLAM
FLANK HIM!
BLAM
GET AROUND BEHIND HIM!

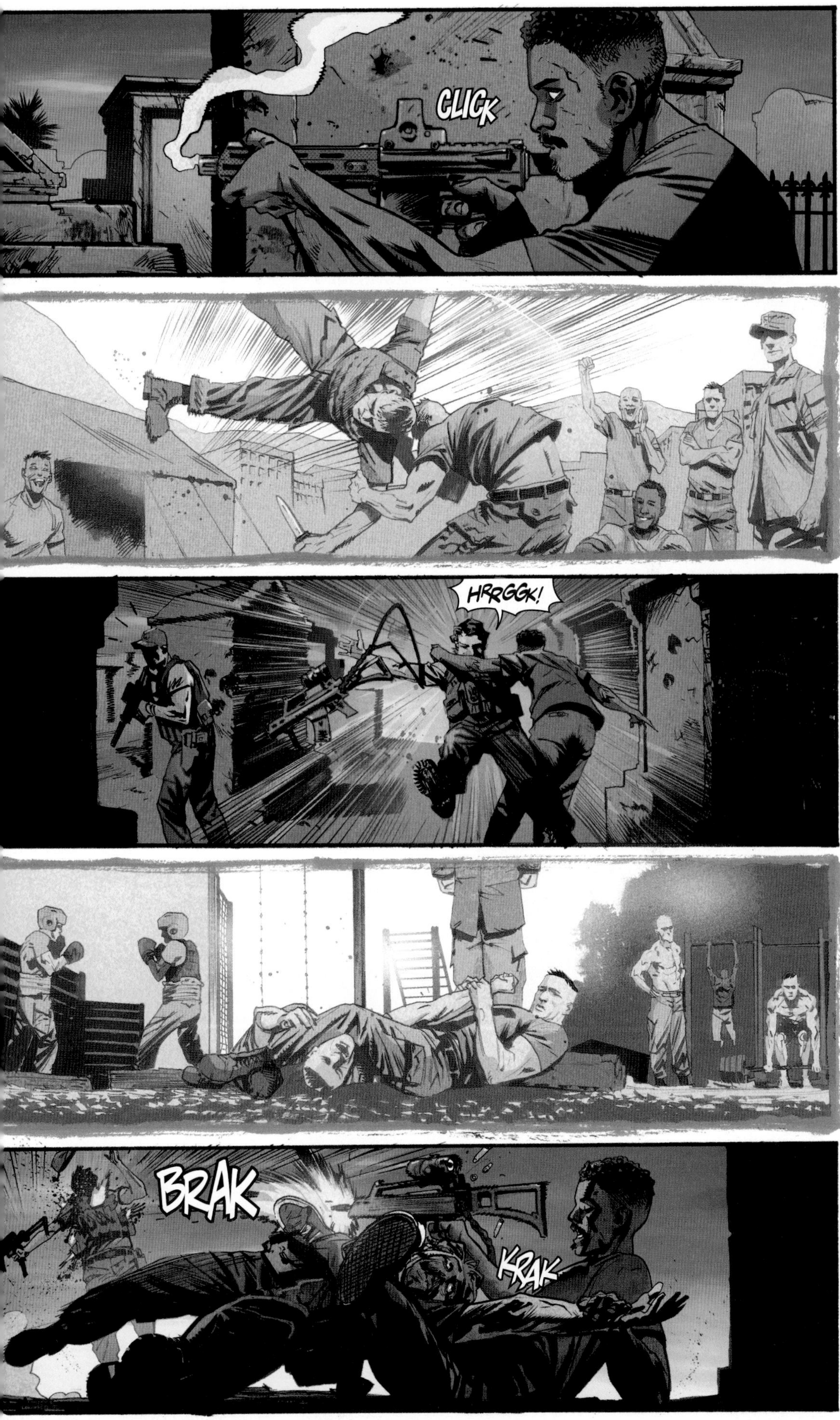
CLICK
HRRGGK!
BRAK
KRAK

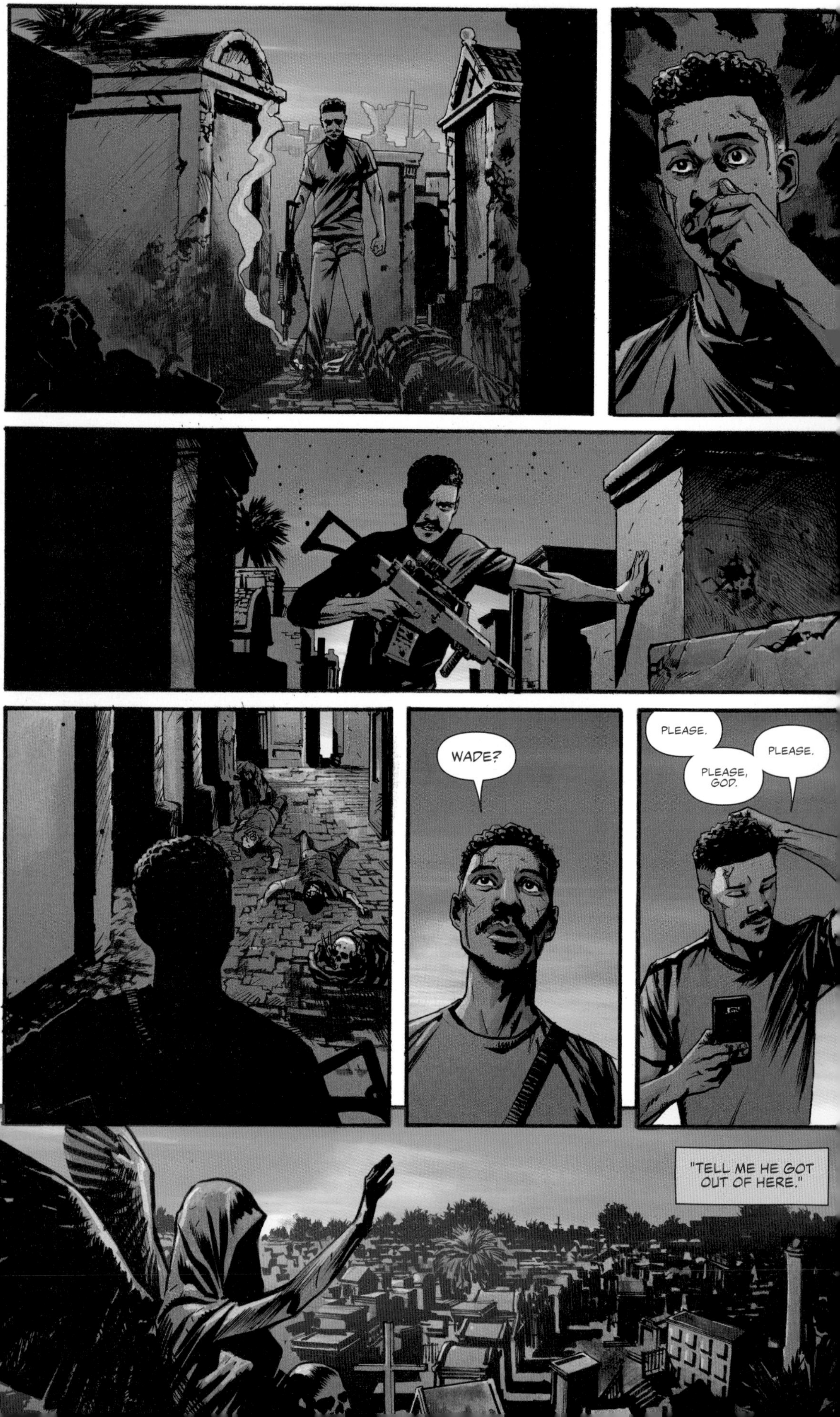
WADE?
PLEASE.
PLEASE, GOD.
PLEASE.
"TELL ME HE GOT OUT OF HERE."

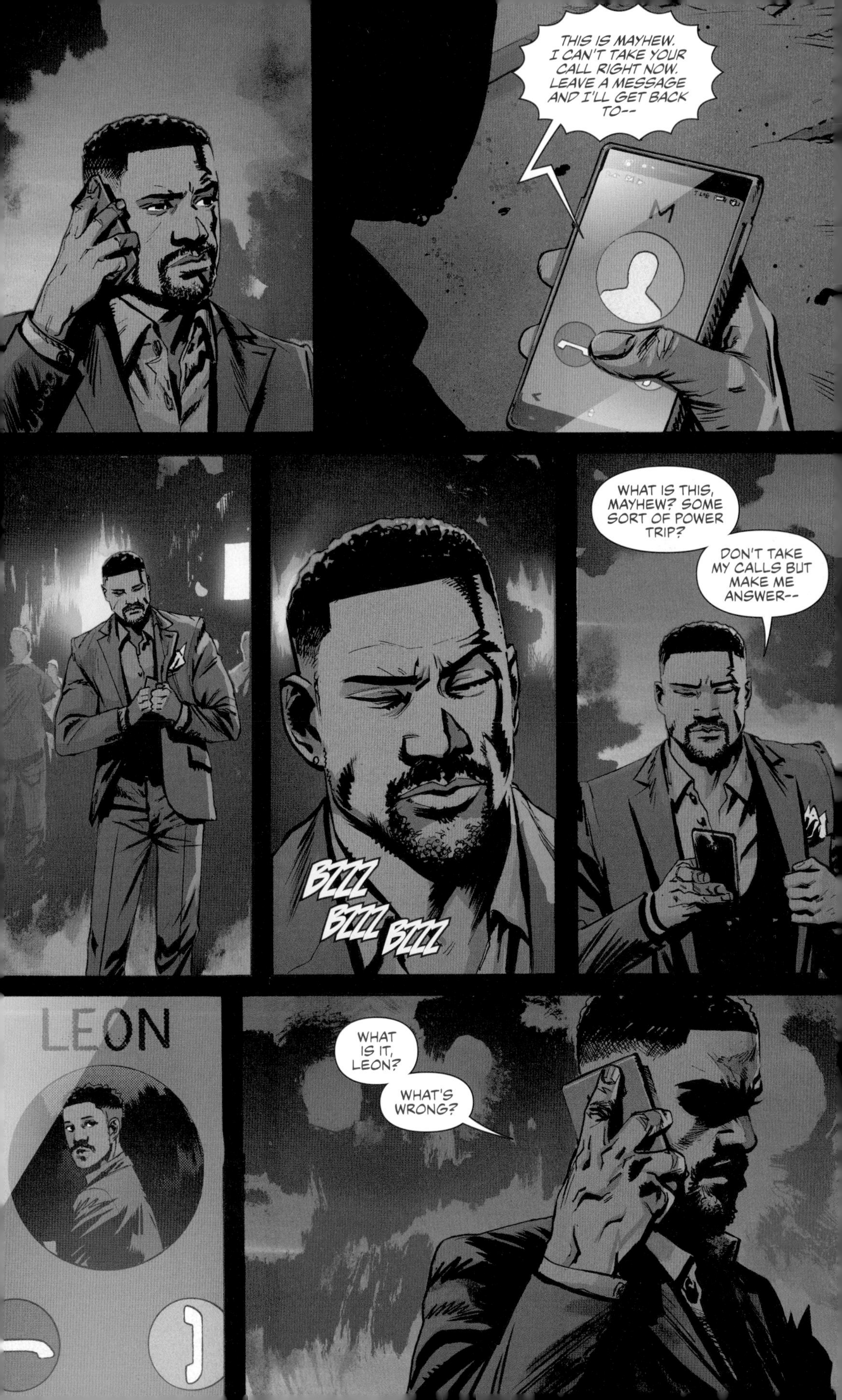

THIS IS MAYHEW. I CAN'T TAKE YOUR CALL RIGHT NOW. LEAVE A MESSAGE AND I'LL GET BACK TO--
M
BZZZ BZZZ BZZZ
WHAT IS THIS, MAYHEW? SOME SORT OF POWER TRIP?
DON'T TAKE MY CALLS BUT MAKE ME ANSWER--
LEON
WHAT IS IT, LEON?
WHAT'S WRONG?

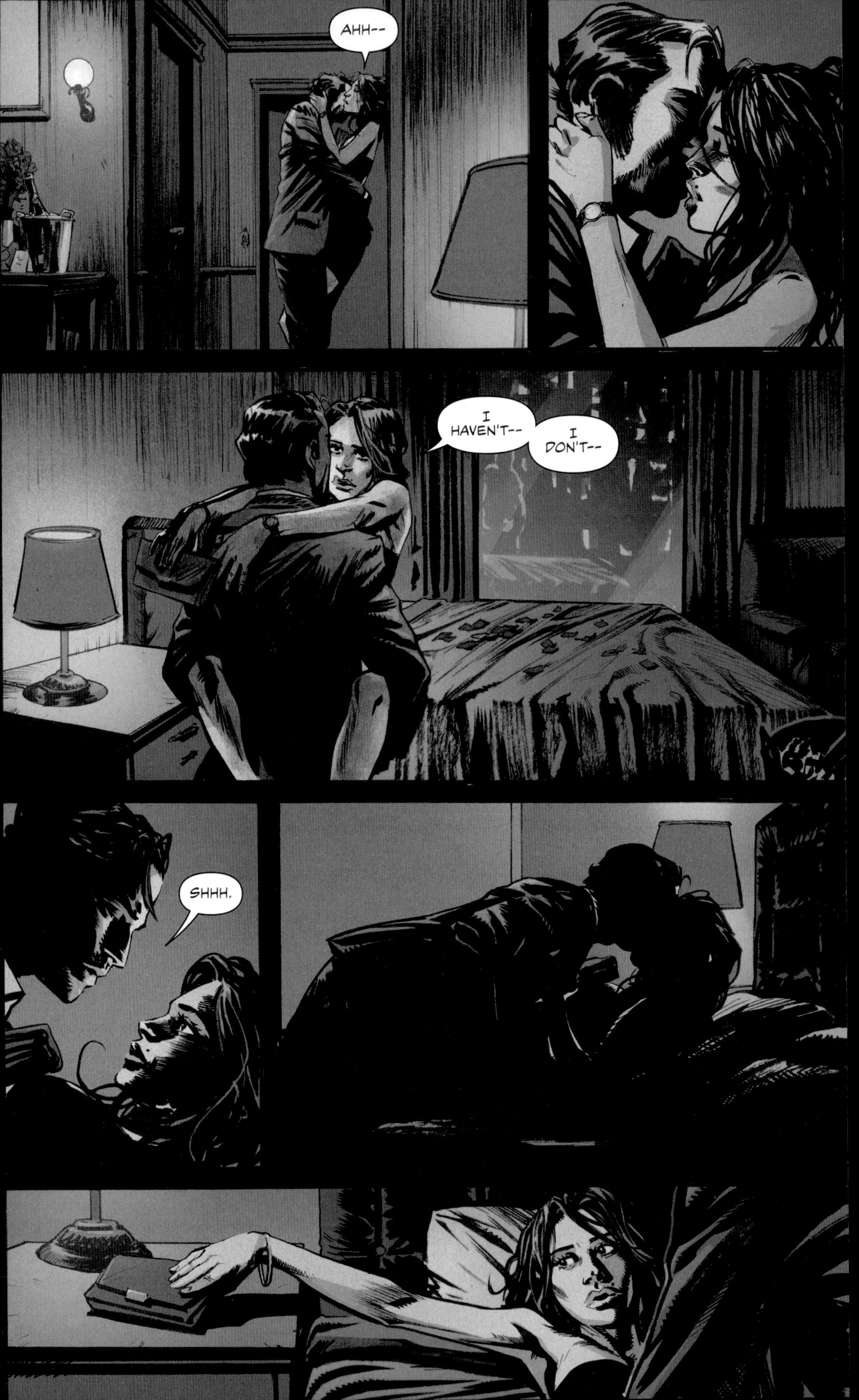
AHH--
I HAVEN'T--
I DON'T--
SHHH.

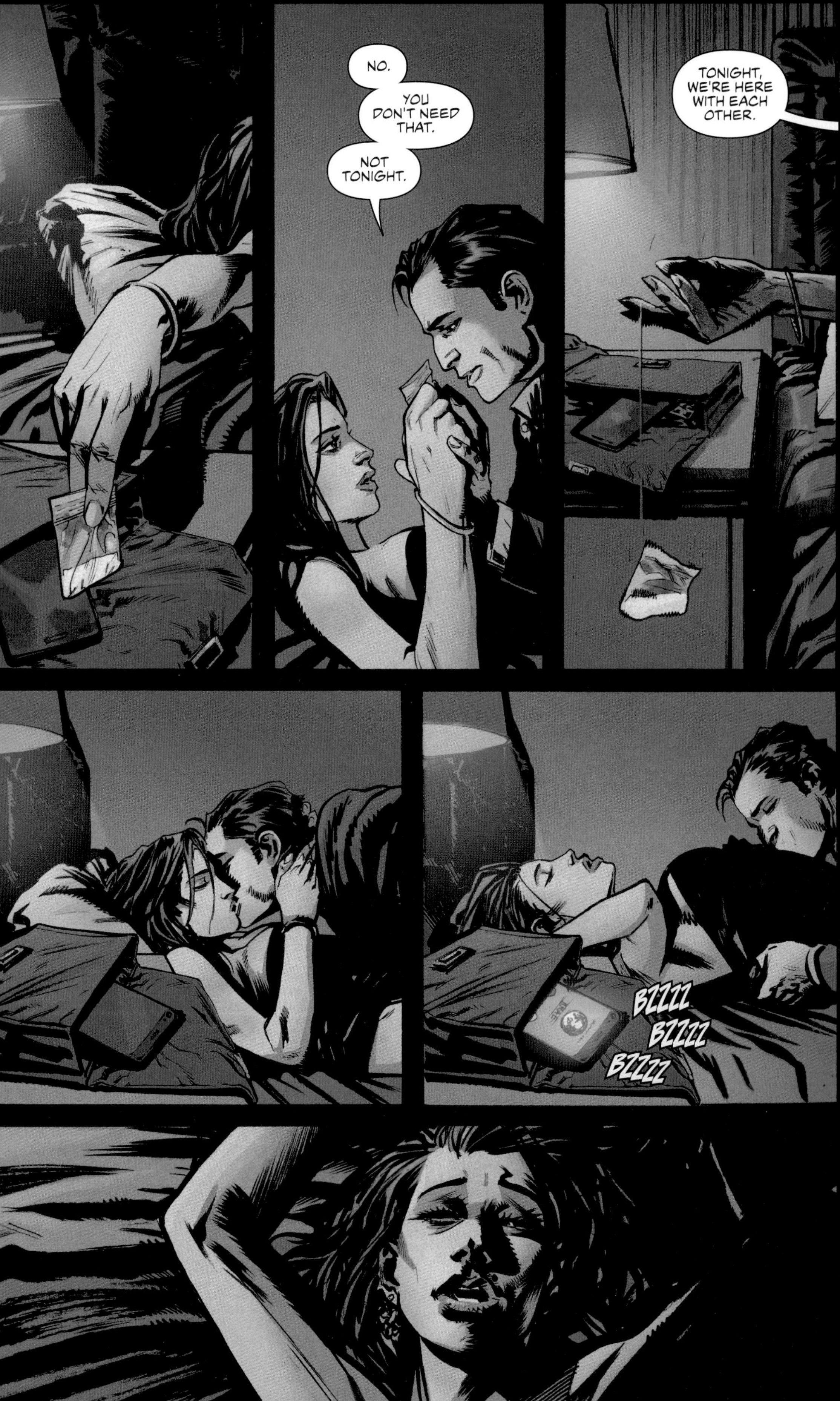
NO.
YOU DON'T NEED THAT.
NOT TONIGHT.
TONIGHT, WE'RE HERE WITH EACH OTHER.
BZZZZ
BZZZZ
BZZZZ

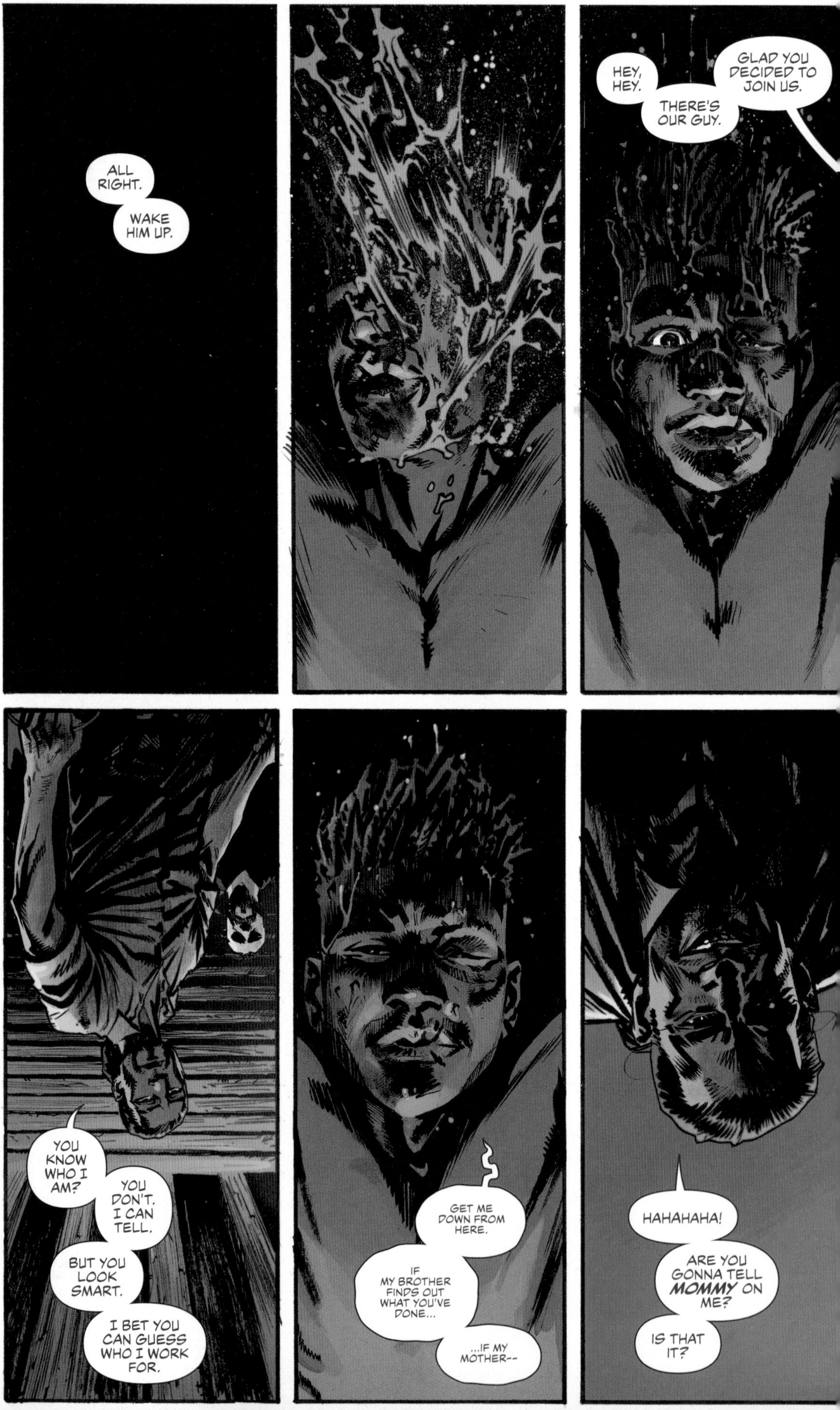
ALL RIGHT.
WAKE HIM UP.
HEY, HEY.
THERE'S OUR GUY.
GLAD YOU DECIDED TO JOIN US.
YOU KNOW WHO I AM?
YOU DON'T. I CAN TELL.
BUT YOU LOOK SMART.
I BET YOU CAN GUESS WHO I WORK FOR.
GET ME DOWN FROM HERE.
IF MY BROTHER FINDS OUT WHAT YOU'VE DONE...
...IF MY MOTHER--
HAHAHAHA!
ARE YOU GONNA TELL *MOMMY* ON ME?
IS THAT IT?

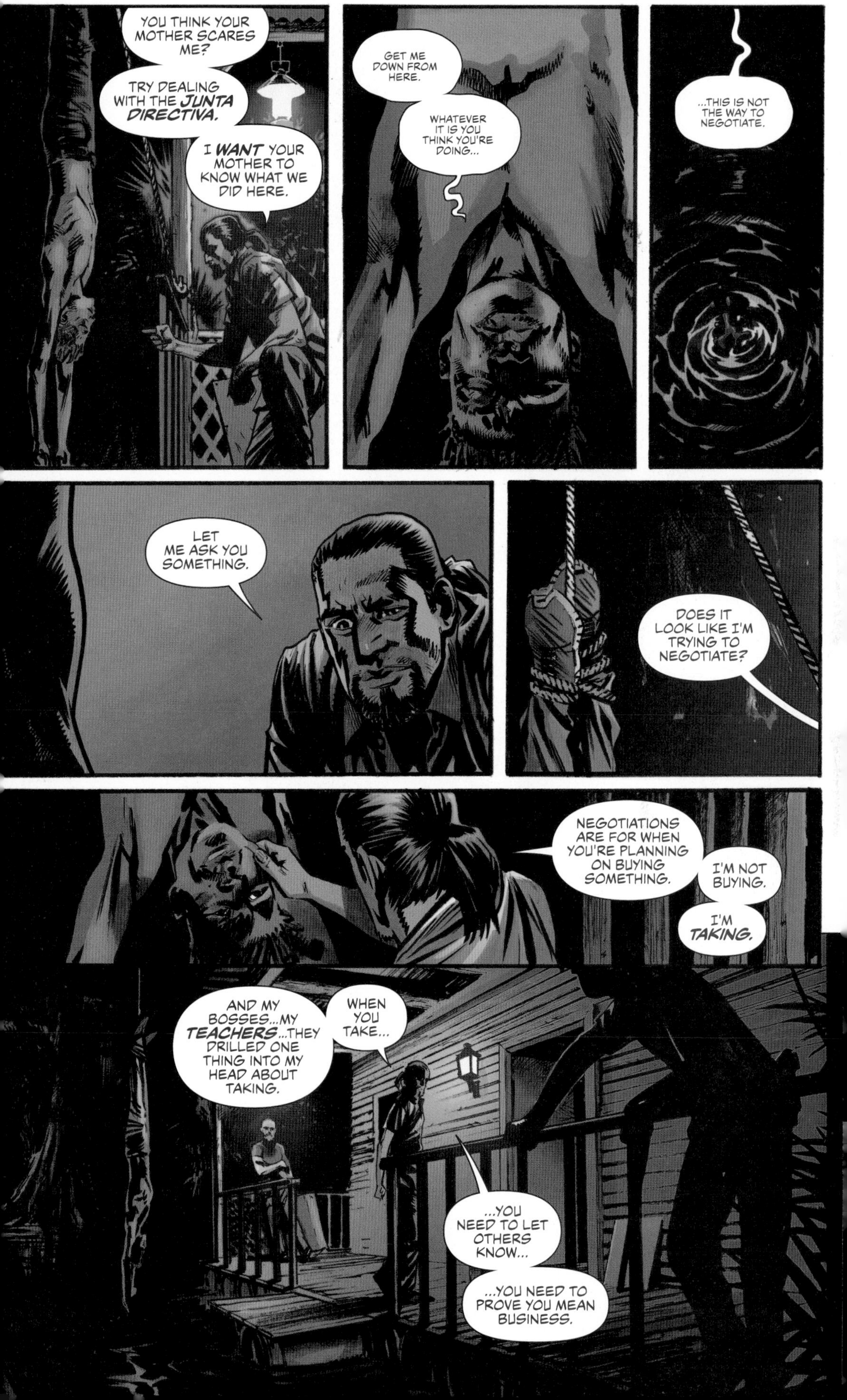
YOU THINK YOUR MOTHER SCARES ME?
TRY DEALING WITH THE JUNTA DIRECTIVA.
I WANT YOUR MOTHER TO KNOW WHAT WE DID HERE.
GET ME DOWN FROM HERE.
WHATEVER IT IS YOU THINK YOU'RE DOING...
...THIS IS NOT THE WAY TO NEGOTIATE.
LET ME ASK YOU SOMETHING.
DOES IT LOOK LIKE I'M TRYING TO NEGOTIATE?
NEGOTIATIONS ARE FOR WHEN YOU'RE PLANNING ON BUYING SOMETHING.
I'M NOT BUYING.
I'M TAKING.
WHEN YOU TAKE...
AND MY BOSSES...MY TEACHERS...THEY DRILLED ONE THING INTO MY HEAD ABOUT TAKING.
...YOU NEED TO LET OTHERS KNOW...
...YOU NEED TO PROVE YOU MEAN BUSINESS.

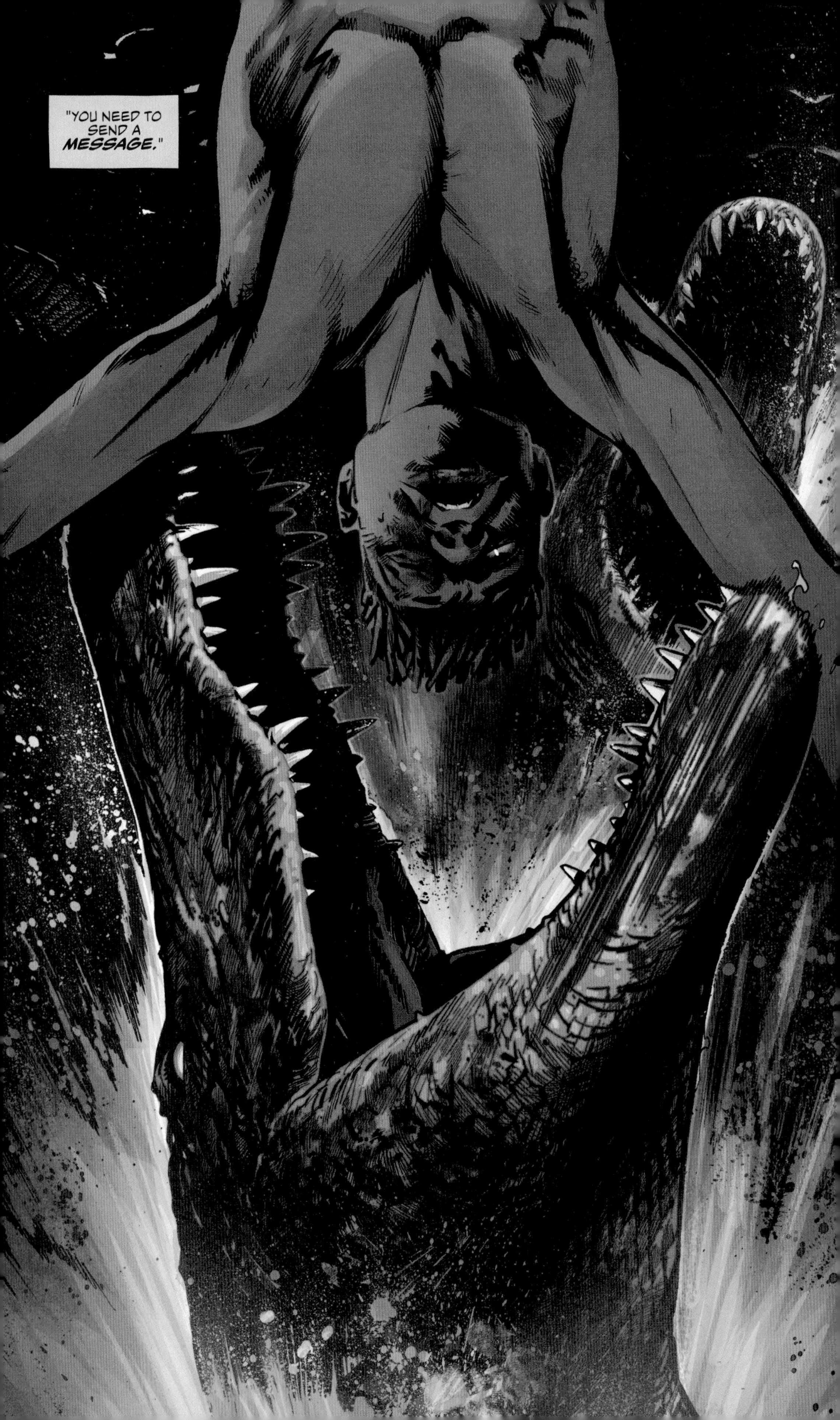
"YOU NEED TO SEND A MESSAGE."

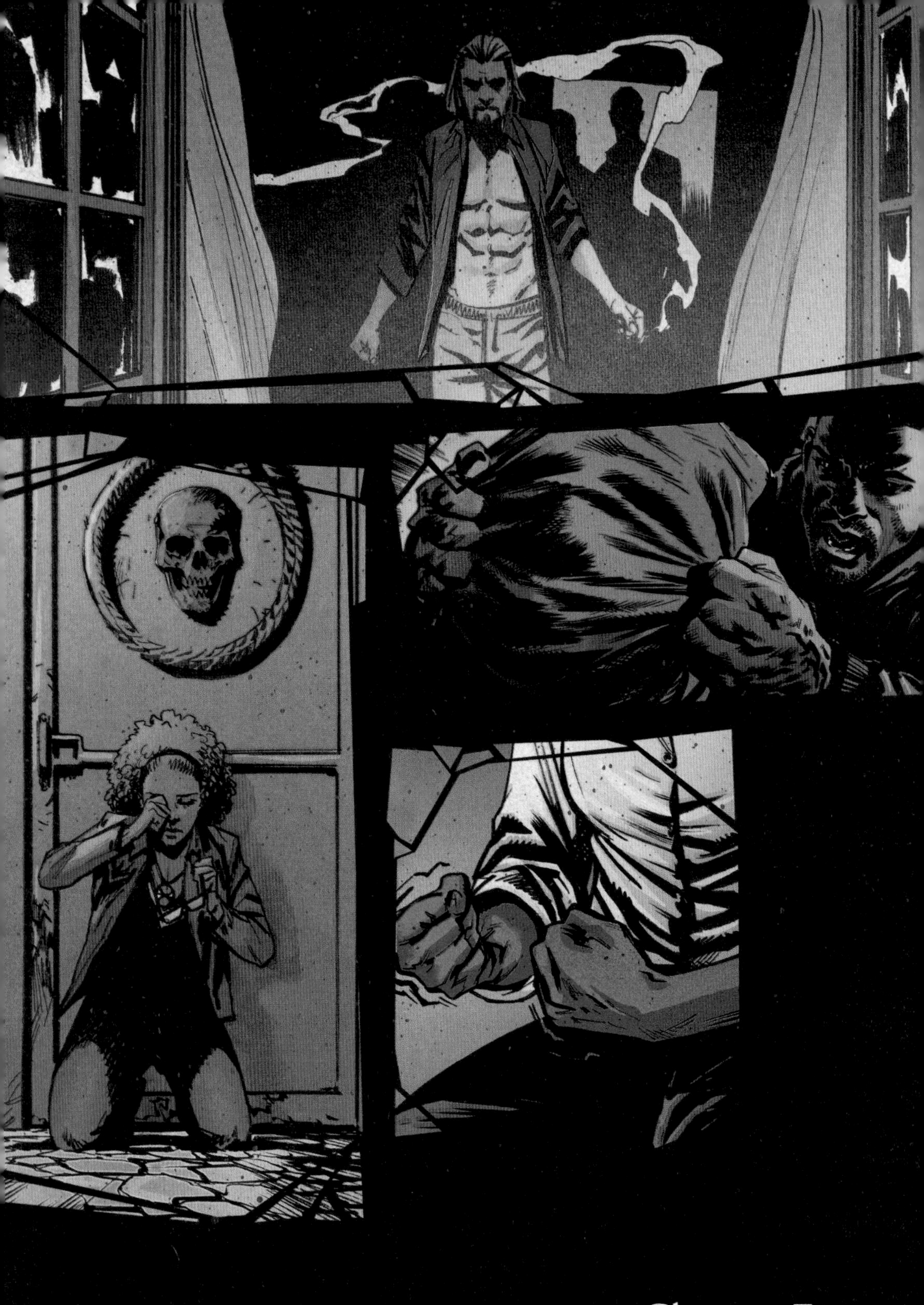

Chapter Four

THE FADE

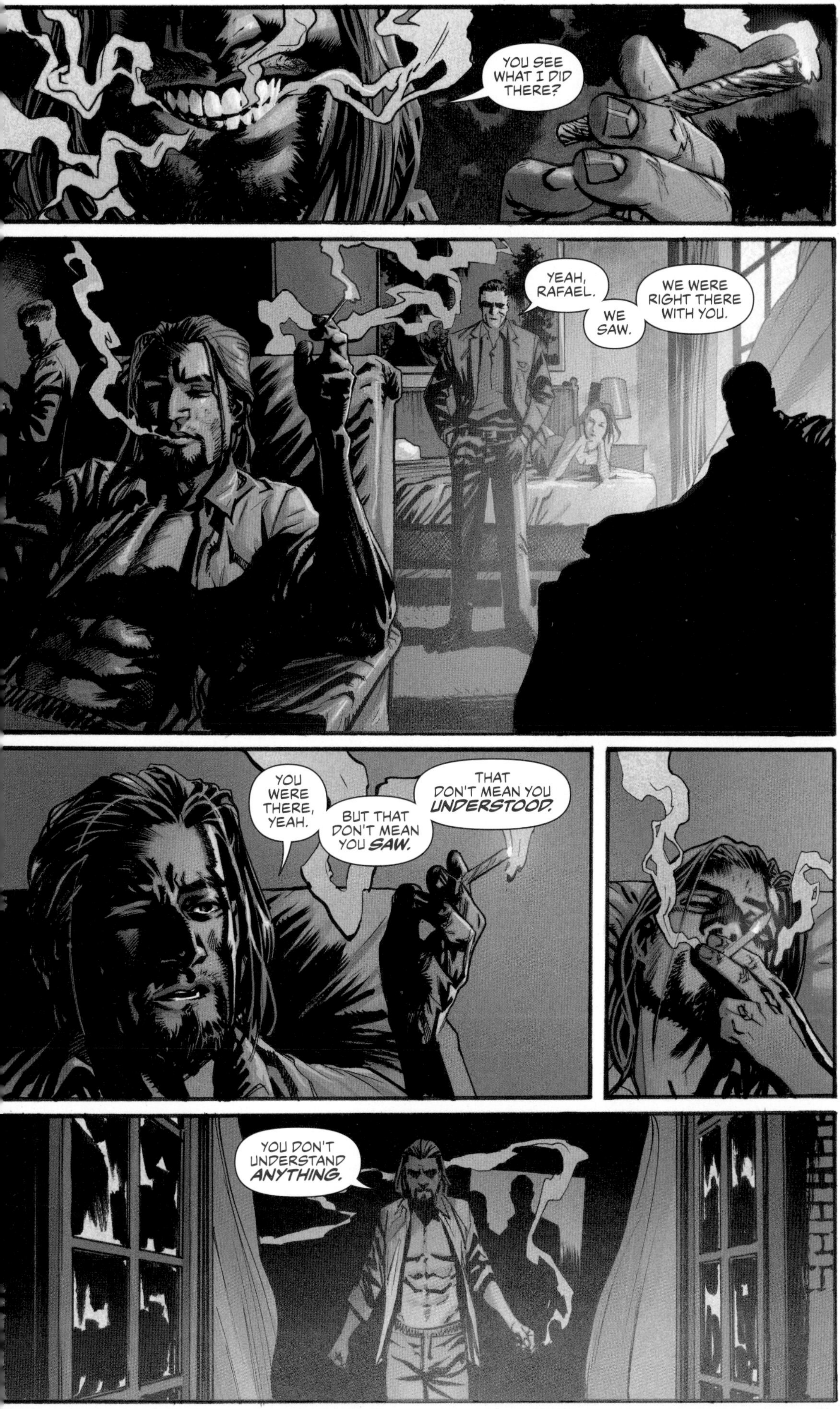
YOU SEE WHAT I DID THERE?
YEAH, RAFAEL.
WE SAW.
WE WERE RIGHT THERE WITH YOU.
YOU WERE THERE, YEAH.
BUT THAT DON'T MEAN YOU SAW.
THAT DON'T MEAN YOU UNDERSTOOD.
YOU DON'T UNDERSTAND ANYTHING.

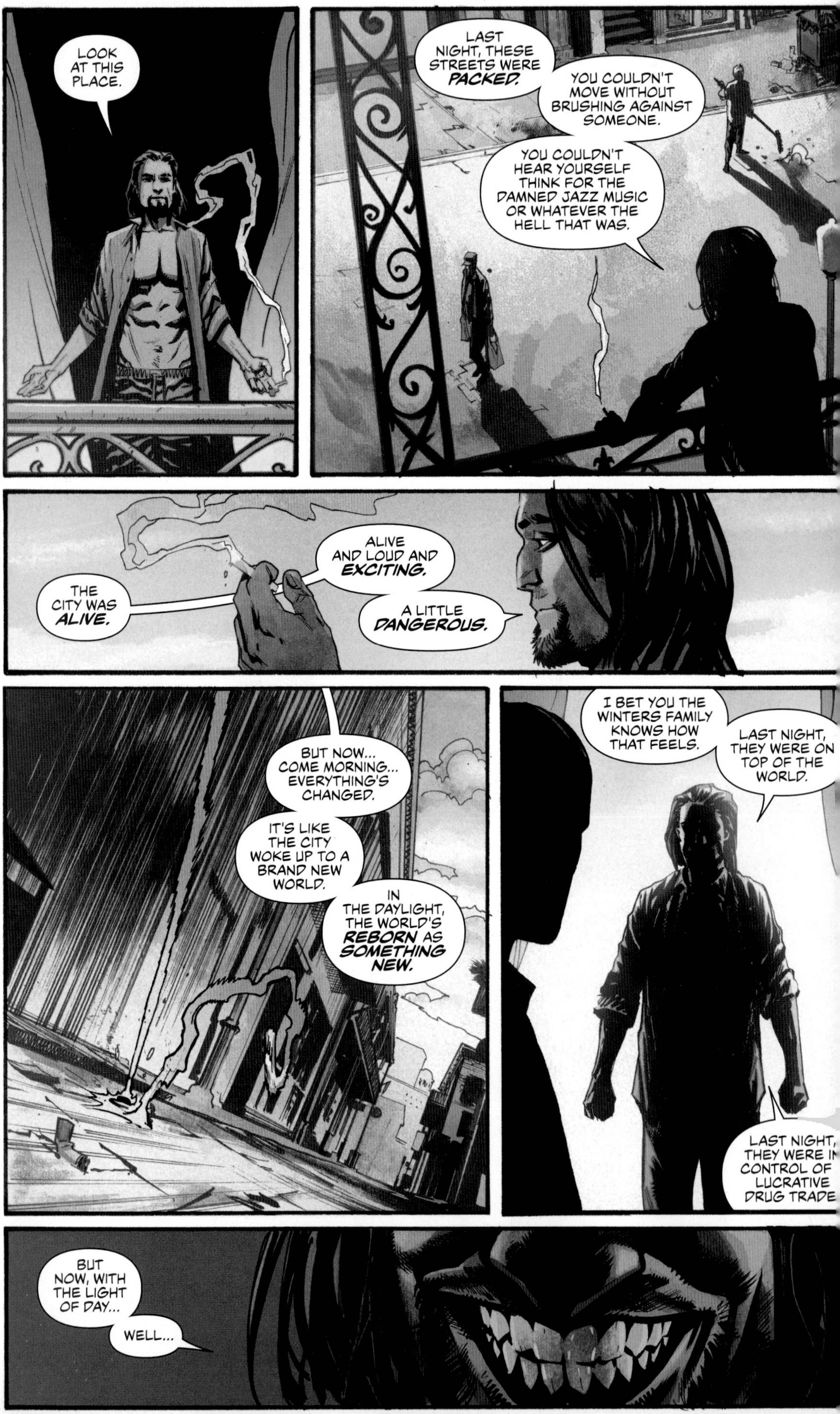
LOOK AT THIS PLACE.
LAST NIGHT, THESE STREETS WERE PACKED.
YOU COULDN'T MOVE WITHOUT BRUSHING AGAINST SOMEONE.
YOU COULDN'T HEAR YOURSELF THINK FOR THE DAMNED JAZZ MUSIC OR WHATEVER THE HELL THAT WAS.
THE CITY WAS ALIVE.
ALIVE AND LOUD AND EXCITING.
A LITTLE DANGEROUS.
BUT NOW... COME MORNING... EVERYTHING'S CHANGED.
IT'S LIKE THE CITY WOKE UP TO A BRAND NEW WORLD.
IN THE DAYLIGHT, THE WORLD'S REBORN AS SOMETHING NEW.
I BET YOU THE WINTERS FAMILY KNOWS HOW THAT FEELS.
LAST NIGHT, THEY WERE ON TOP OF THE WORLD.
LAST NIGHT, THEY WERE IN CONTROL OF LUCRATIVE DRUG TRADE
BUT NOW, WITH THE LIGHT OF DAY...
WELL...

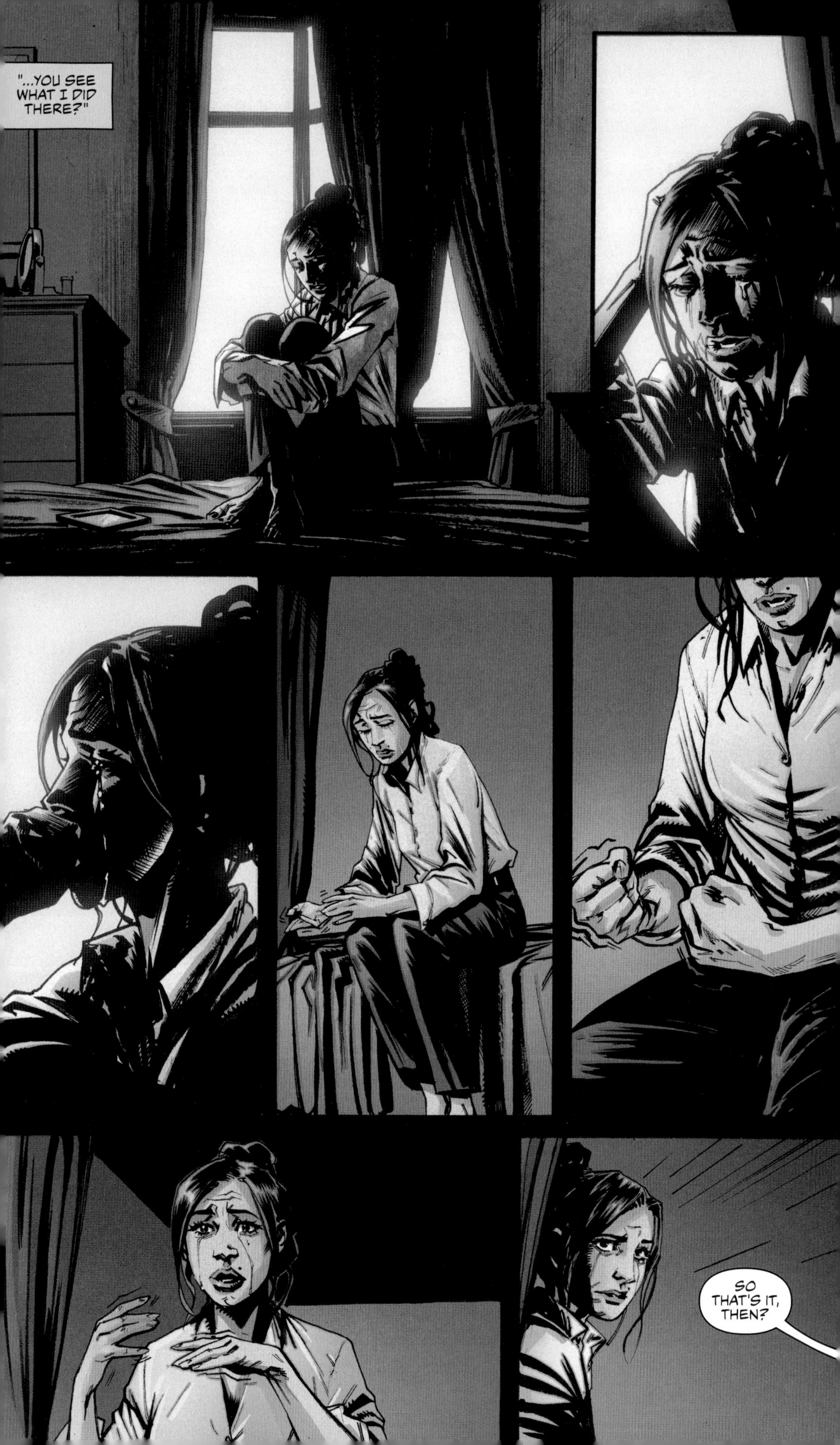
"...YOU SEE WHAT I DID THERE?"
SO THAT'S IT, THEN?

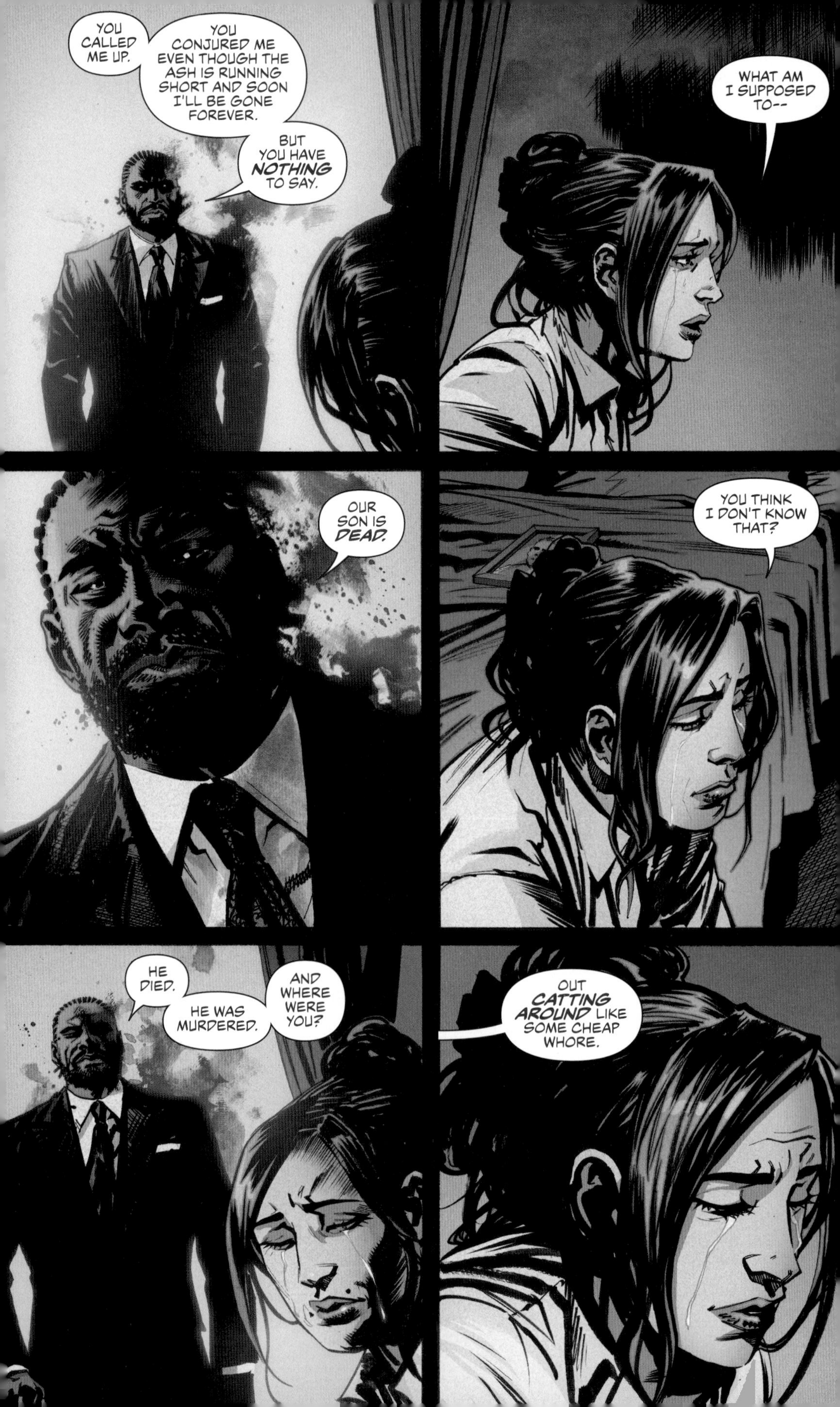

YOU CALLED ME UP.
YOU CONJURED ME EVEN THOUGH THE ASH IS RUNNING SHORT AND SOON I'LL BE GONE FOREVER.
BUT YOU HAVE **NOTHING** TO SAY.
WHAT AM I SUPPOSED TO--
OUR SON IS ***DEAD.***
YOU THINK I DON'T KNOW THAT?
HE DIED.
HE WAS MURDERED.
AND WHERE WERE YOU?
OUT ***CATTING AROUND*** LIKE SOME CHEAP WHORE.

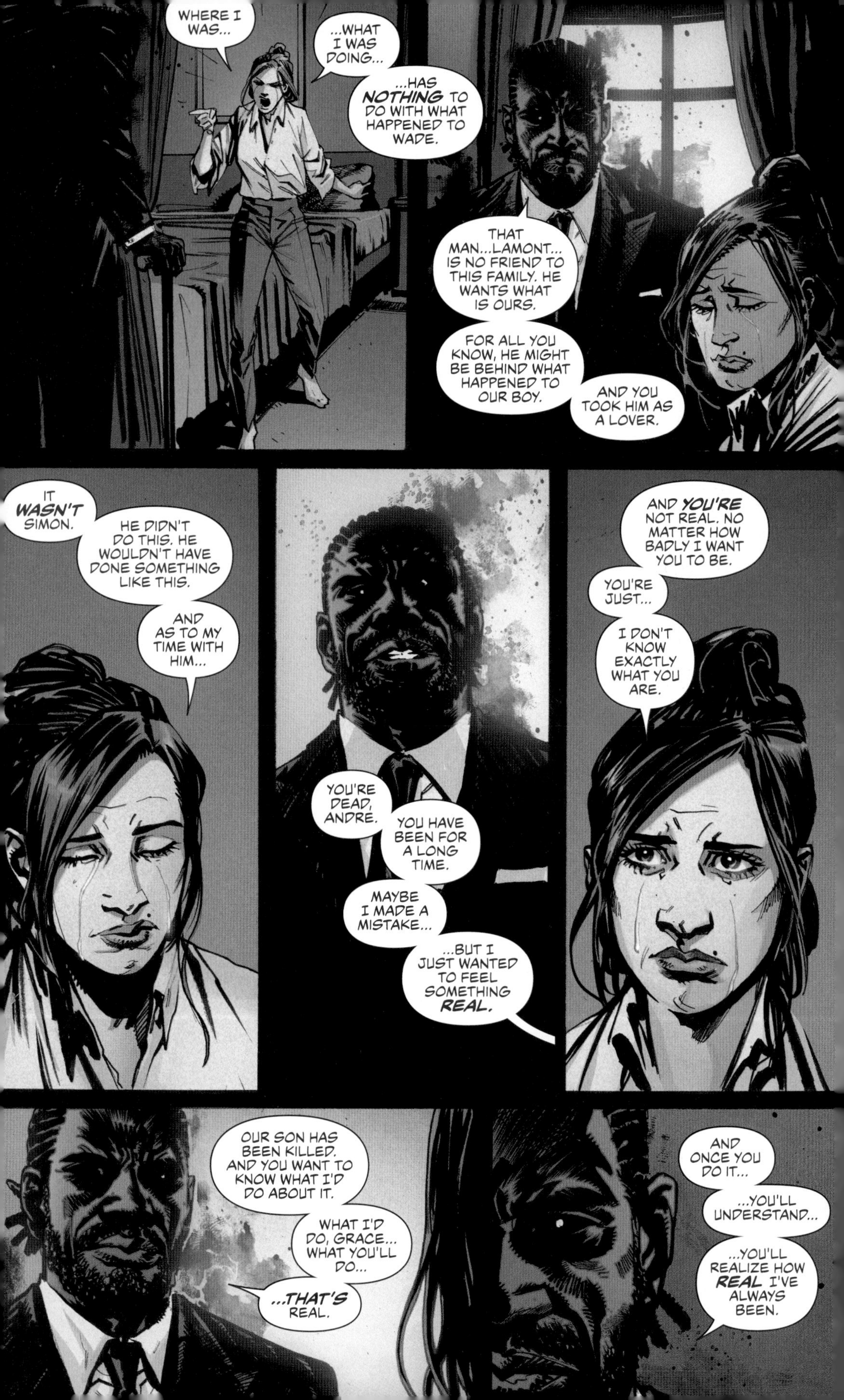
WHERE I WAS...
...WHAT I WAS DOING...
...HAS NOTHING TO DO WITH WHAT HAPPENED TO WADE.
THAT MAN...LAMONT... IS NO FRIEND TO THIS FAMILY. HE WANTS WHAT IS OURS.
FOR ALL YOU KNOW, HE MIGHT BE BEHIND WHAT HAPPENED TO OUR BOY.
AND YOU TOOK HIM AS A LOVER.
IT WASN'T SIMON.
HE DIDN'T DO THIS. HE WOULDN'T HAVE DONE SOMETHING LIKE THIS.
AND AS TO MY TIME WITH HIM...
YOU'RE DEAD, ANDRE.
YOU HAVE BEEN FOR A LONG TIME.
MAYBE I MADE A MISTAKE...
...BUT I JUST WANTED TO FEEL SOMETHING REAL.
AND YOU'RE NOT REAL. NO MATTER HOW BADLY I WANT YOU TO BE.
YOU'RE JUST...
I DON'T KNOW EXACTLY WHAT YOU ARE.
OUR SON HAS BEEN KILLED. AND YOU WANT TO KNOW WHAT I'D DO ABOUT IT.
WHAT I'D DO, GRACE... WHAT YOU'LL DO...
...THAT'S REAL.
AND ONCE YOU DO IT...
...YOU'LL UNDERSTAND...
...YOU'LL REALIZE HOW REAL I'VE ALWAYS BEEN.

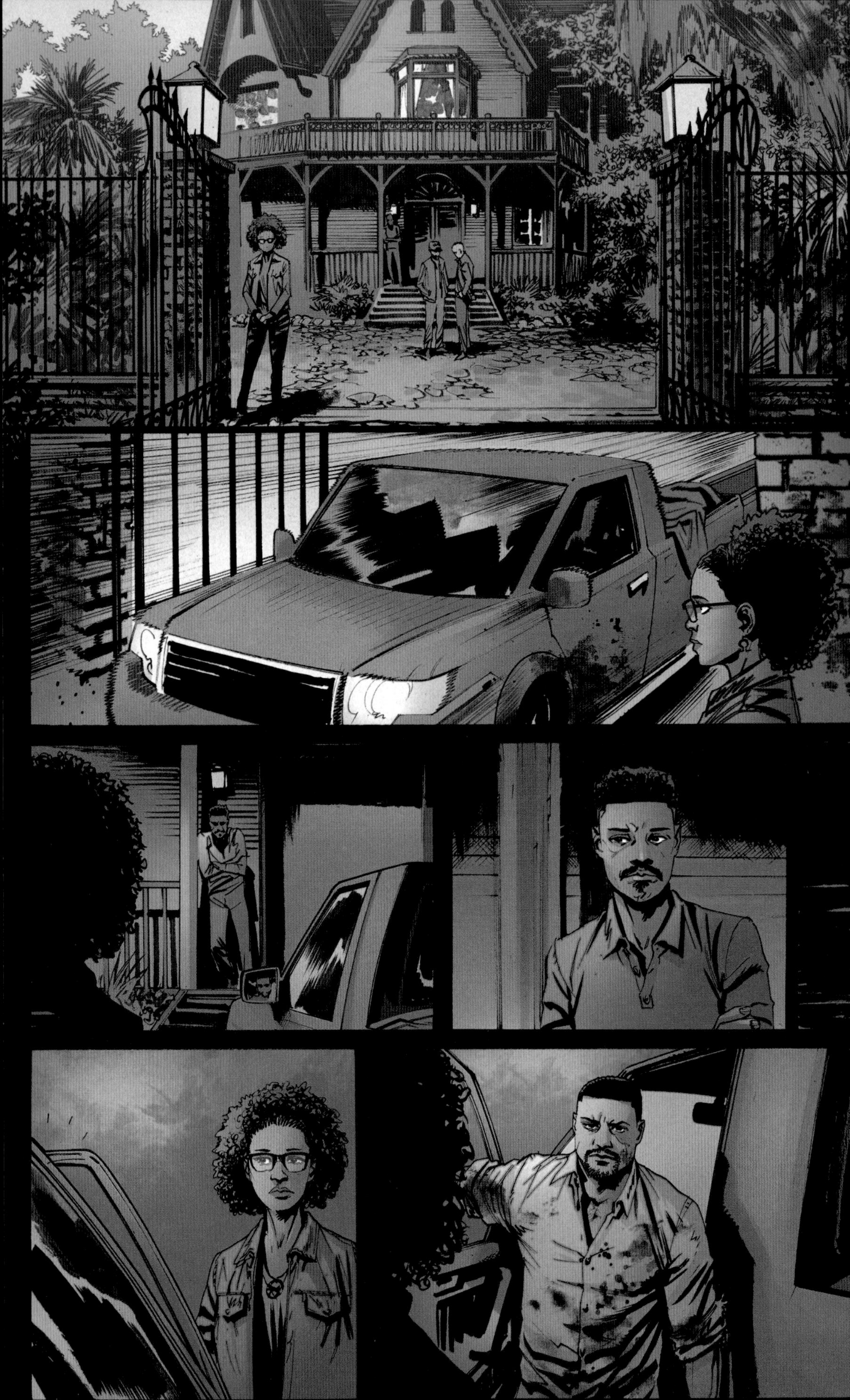

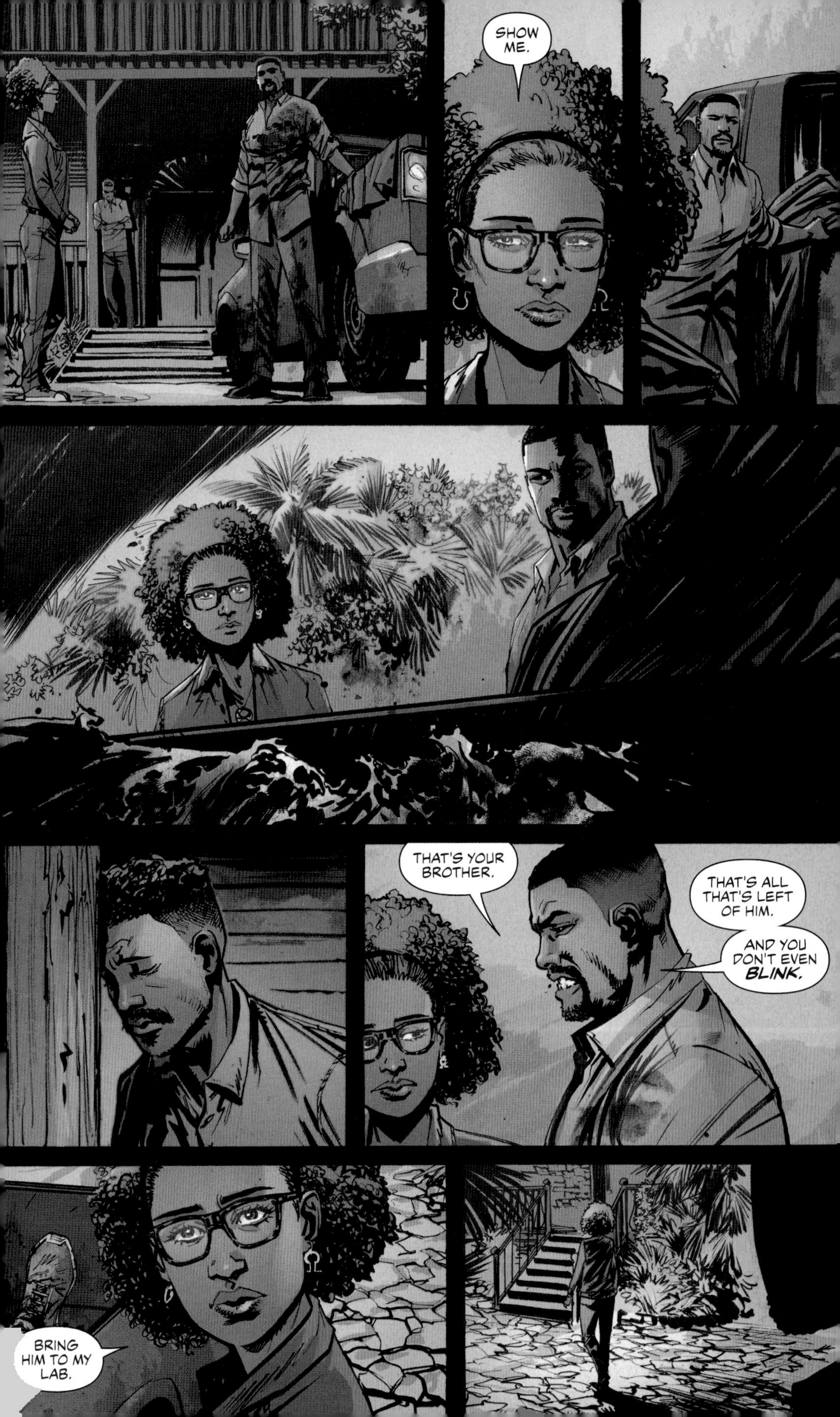

SHOW ME.
THAT'S YOUR BROTHER.
THAT'S ALL THAT'S LEFT OF HIM.
AND YOU DON'T EVEN *BLINK.*
BRING HIM TO MY LAB.

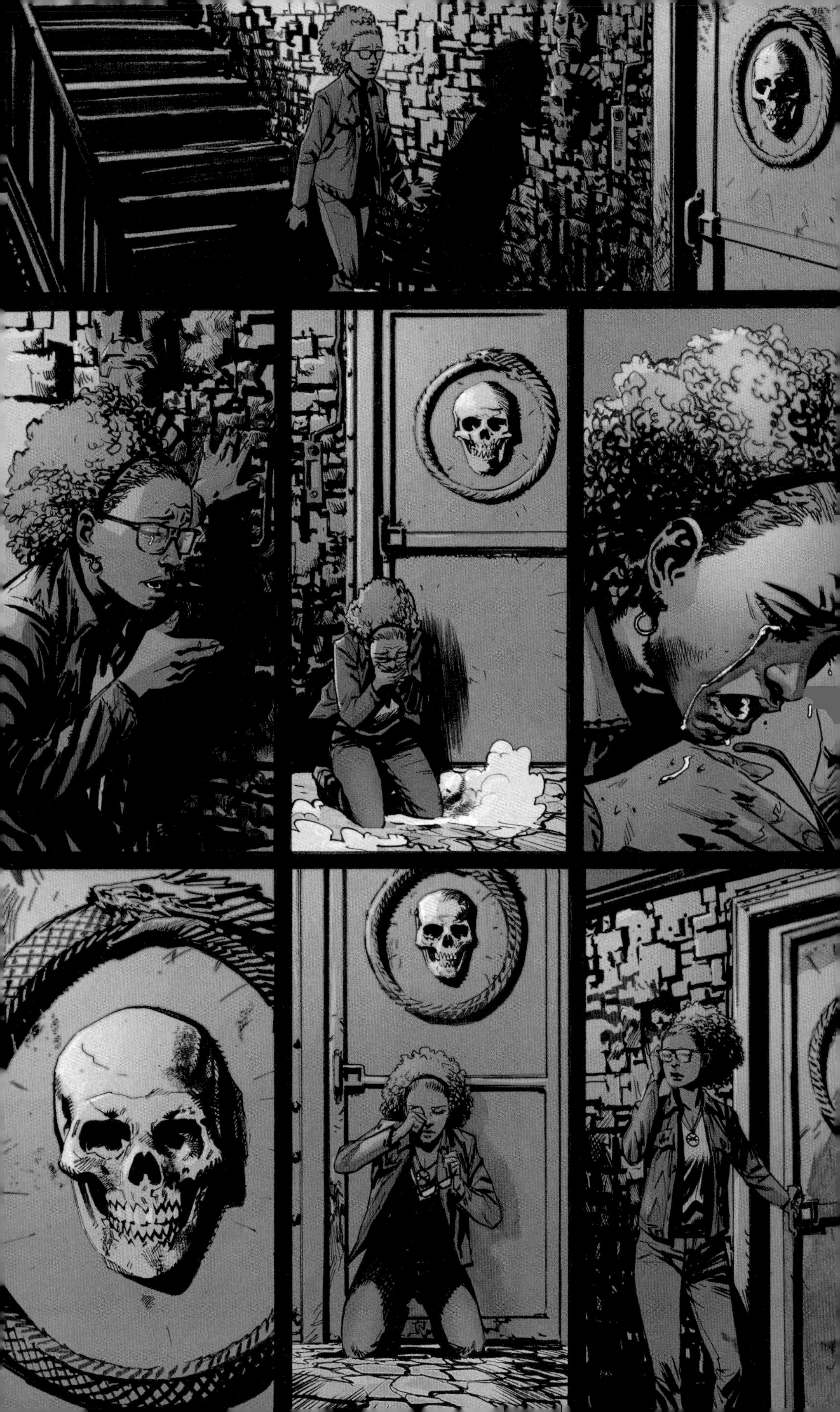

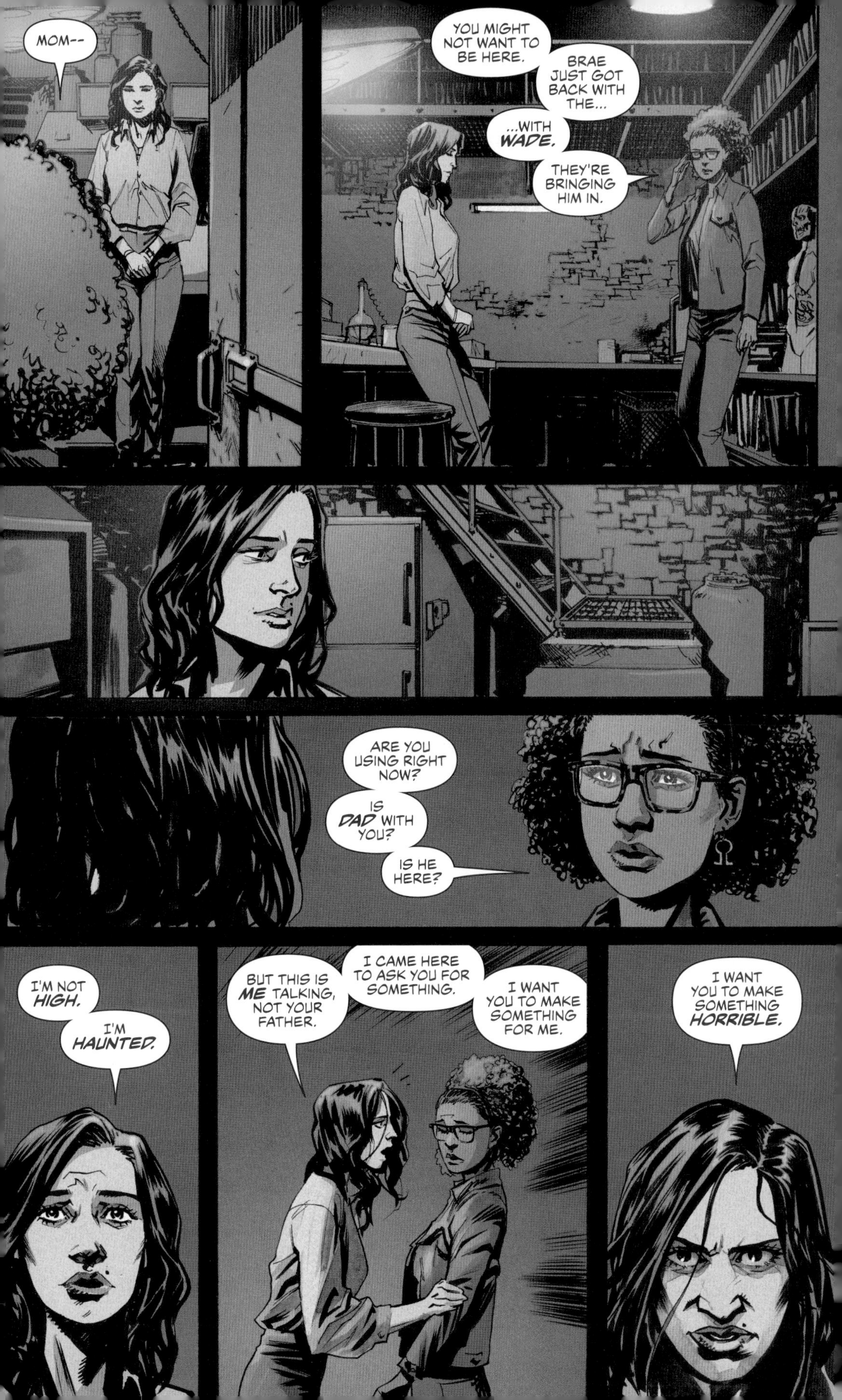
MOM--
YOU MIGHT NOT WANT TO BE HERE.
BRAE JUST GOT BACK WITH THE...
...WITH WADE.
THEY'RE BRINGING HIM IN.
ARE YOU USING RIGHT NOW?
IS DAD WITH YOU?
IS HE HERE?
I'M NOT HIGH.
I'M HAUNTED.
BUT THIS IS ME TALKING, NOT YOUR FATHER.
I CAME HERE TO ASK YOU FOR SOMETHING.
I WANT YOU TO MAKE SOMETHING FOR ME.
I WANT YOU TO MAKE SOMETHING HORRIBLE.

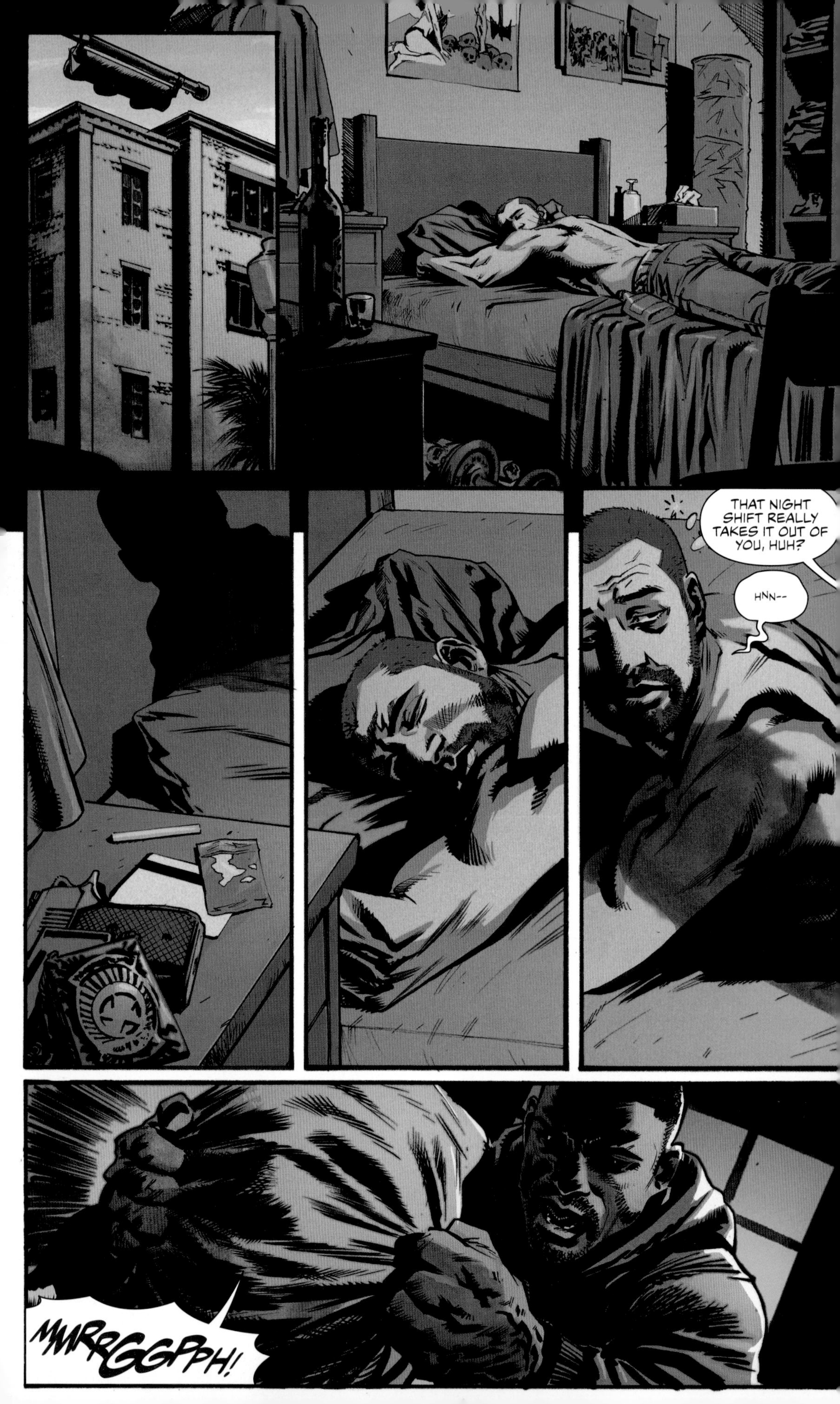
THAT NIGHT SHIFT REALLY TAKES IT OUT OF YOU, HUH?
HNN--
MMRRGGPPH!

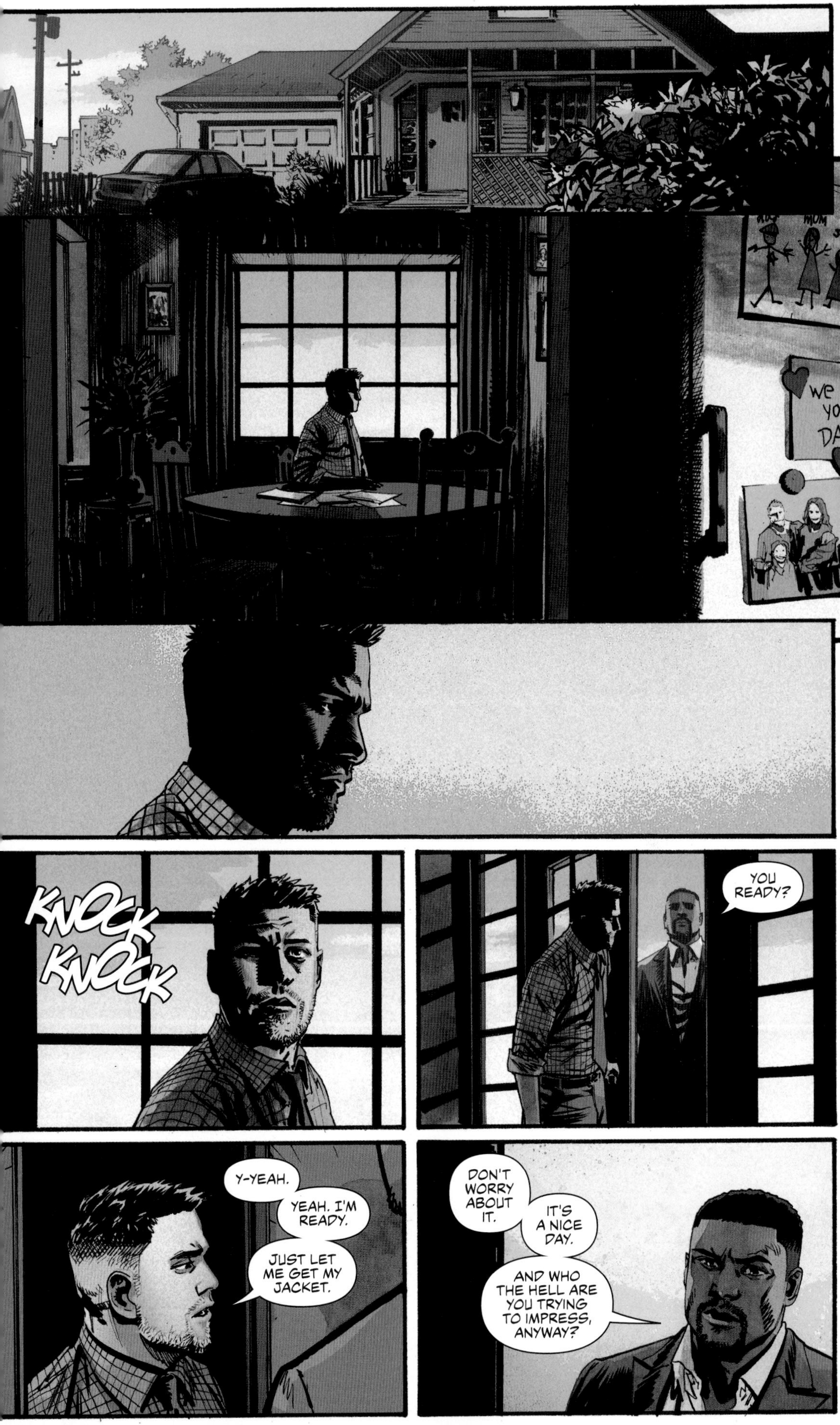
KNOCK KNOCK
YOU READY?
Y-YEAH.
YEAH. I'M READY.
JUST LET ME GET MY JACKET.
DON'T WORRY ABOUT IT.
IT'S A NICE DAY.
AND WHO THE HELL ARE YOU TRYING TO IMPRESS, ANYWAY?

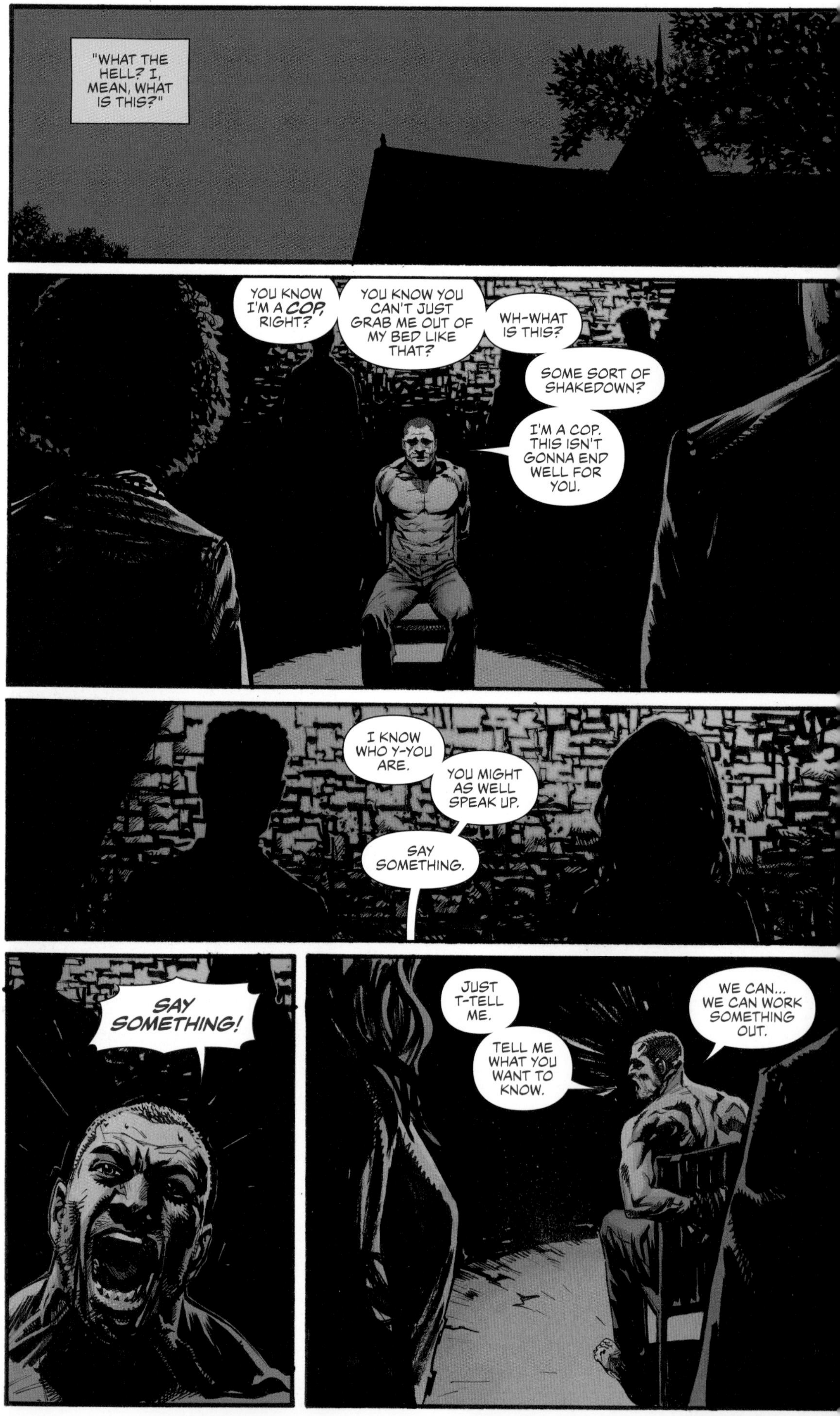
"WHAT THE HELL? I, MEAN, WHAT IS THIS?"
YOU KNOW I'M A COP, RIGHT?
YOU KNOW YOU CAN'T JUST GRAB ME OUT OF MY BED LIKE THAT?
WH-WHAT IS THIS?
SOME SORT OF SHAKEDOWN?
I'M A COP. THIS ISN'T GONNA END WELL FOR YOU.
I KNOW WHO Y-YOU ARE.
YOU MIGHT AS WELL SPEAK UP.
SAY SOMETHING.
SAY SOMETHING!
JUST T-TELL ME.
TELL ME WHAT YOU WANT TO KNOW.
WE CAN... WE CAN WORK SOMETHING OUT.

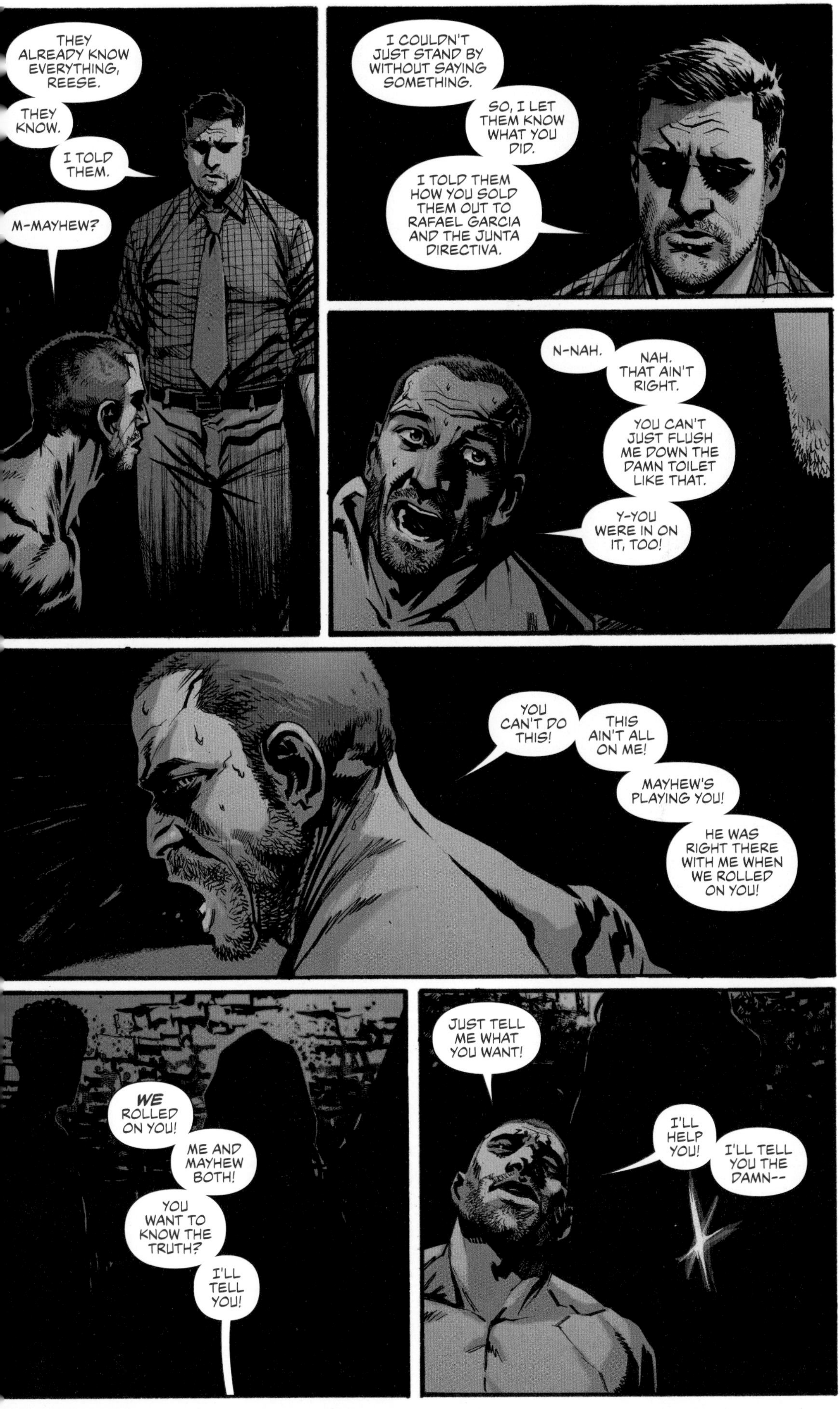

THEY ALREADY KNOW EVERYTHING, REESE.
THEY KNOW.
I TOLD THEM.
M-MAYHEW?
I COULDN'T JUST STAND BY WITHOUT SAYING SOMETHING.
SO, I LET THEM KNOW WHAT YOU DID.
I TOLD THEM HOW YOU SOLD THEM OUT TO RAFAEL GARCIA AND THE JUNTA DIRECTIVA.
N-NAH.
NAH. THAT AIN'T RIGHT.
YOU CAN'T JUST FLUSH ME DOWN THE DAMN TOILET LIKE THAT.
Y-YOU WERE IN ON IT, TOO!
YOU CAN'T DO THIS!
THIS AIN'T ALL ON ME!
MAYHEW'S PLAYING YOU!
HE WAS RIGHT THERE WITH ME WHEN WE ROLLED ON YOU!
WE ROLLED ON YOU!
ME AND MAYHEW BOTH!
YOU WANT TO KNOW THE TRUTH?
I'LL TELL YOU!
JUST TELL ME WHAT YOU WANT!
I'LL HELP YOU!
I'LL TELL YOU THE DAMN--

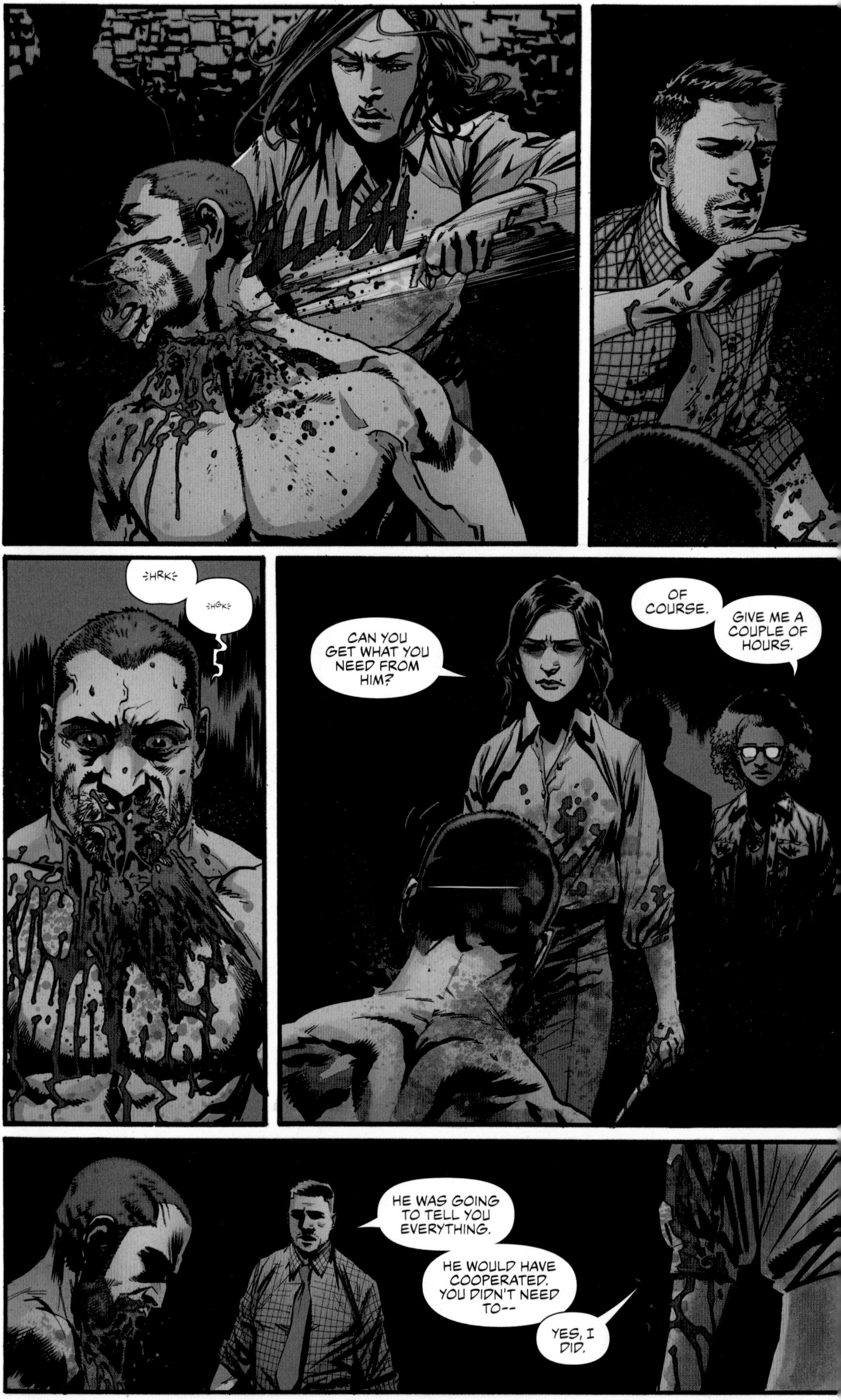
SHLUSH
HRK
HGK
CAN YOU GET WHAT YOU NEED FROM HIM?
OF COURSE.
GIVE ME A COUPLE OF HOURS.
HE WAS GOING TO TELL YOU EVERYTHING.
HE WOULD HAVE COOPERATED. YOU DIDN'T NEED TO--
YES, I DID.

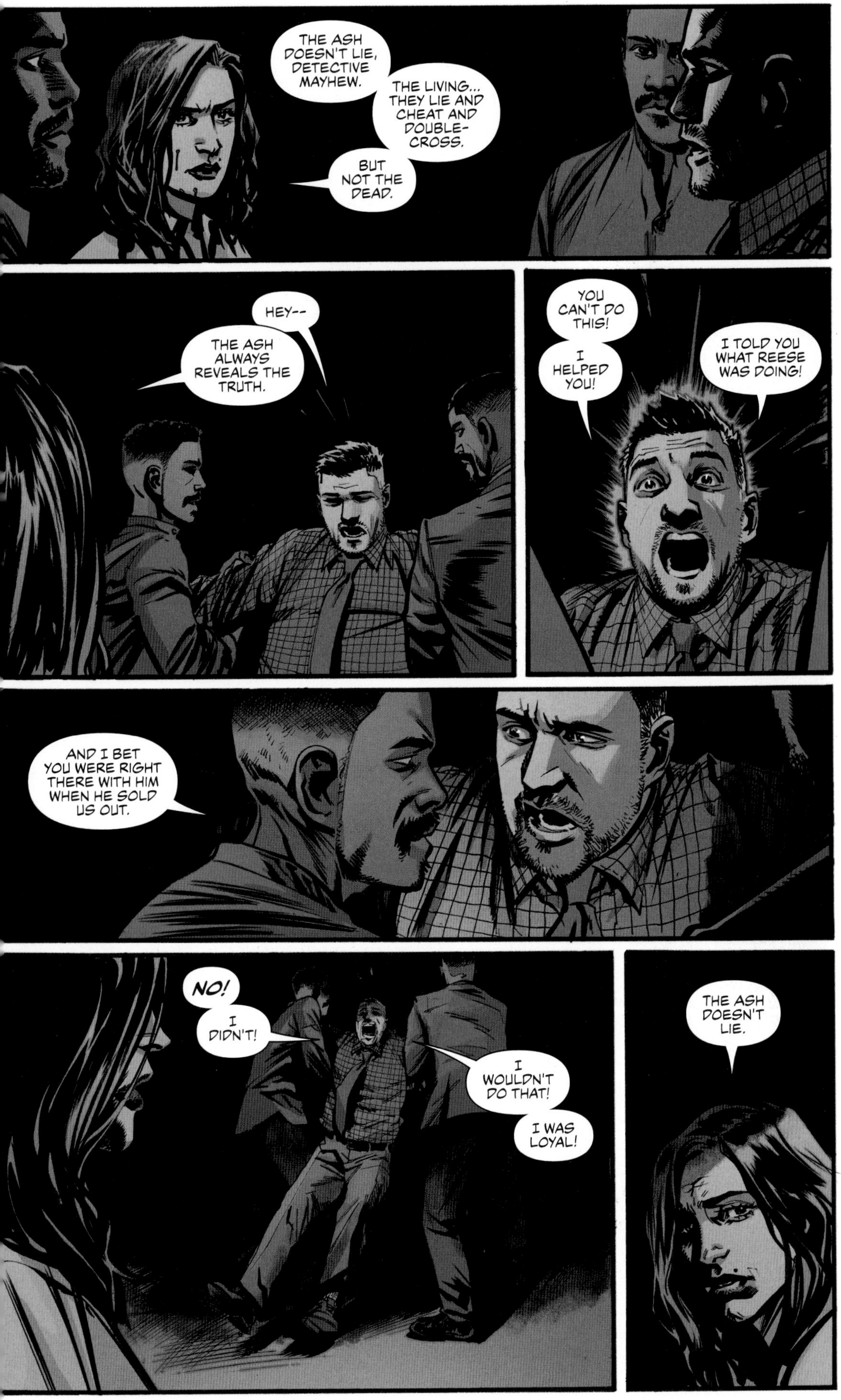
THE ASH DOESN'T LIE, DETECTIVE MAYHEW.
THE LIVING... THEY LIE AND CHEAT AND DOUBLE-CROSS.
BUT NOT THE DEAD.
HEY--
THE ASH ALWAYS REVEALS THE TRUTH.
YOU CAN'T DO THIS!
I HELPED YOU!
I TOLD YOU WHAT REESE WAS DOING!
AND I BET YOU WERE RIGHT THERE WITH HIM WHEN HE SOLD US OUT.
NO!
I DIDN'T!
I WOULDN'T DO THAT!
I WAS LOYAL!
THE ASH DOESN'T LIE.

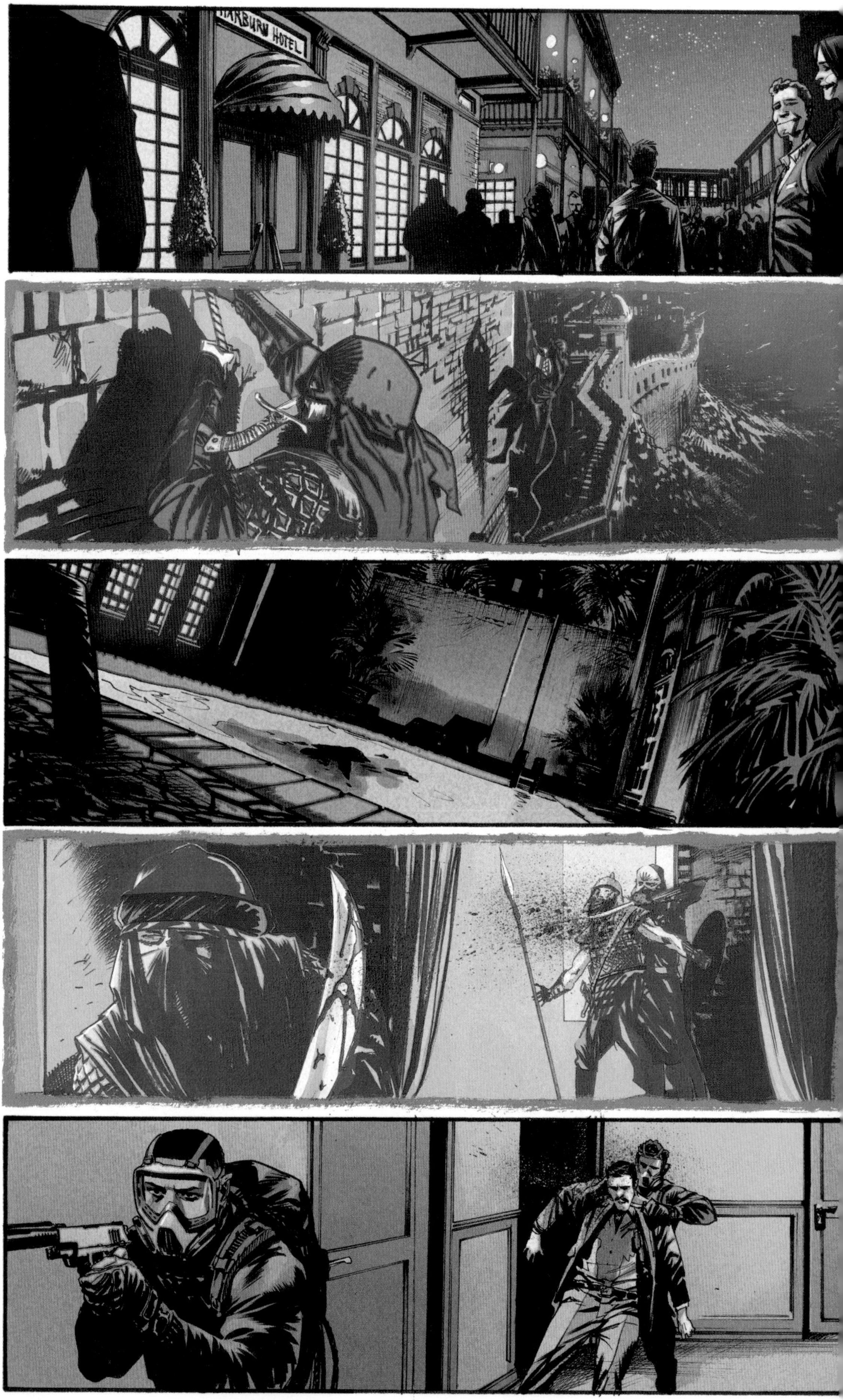

ARBURY HOTEL

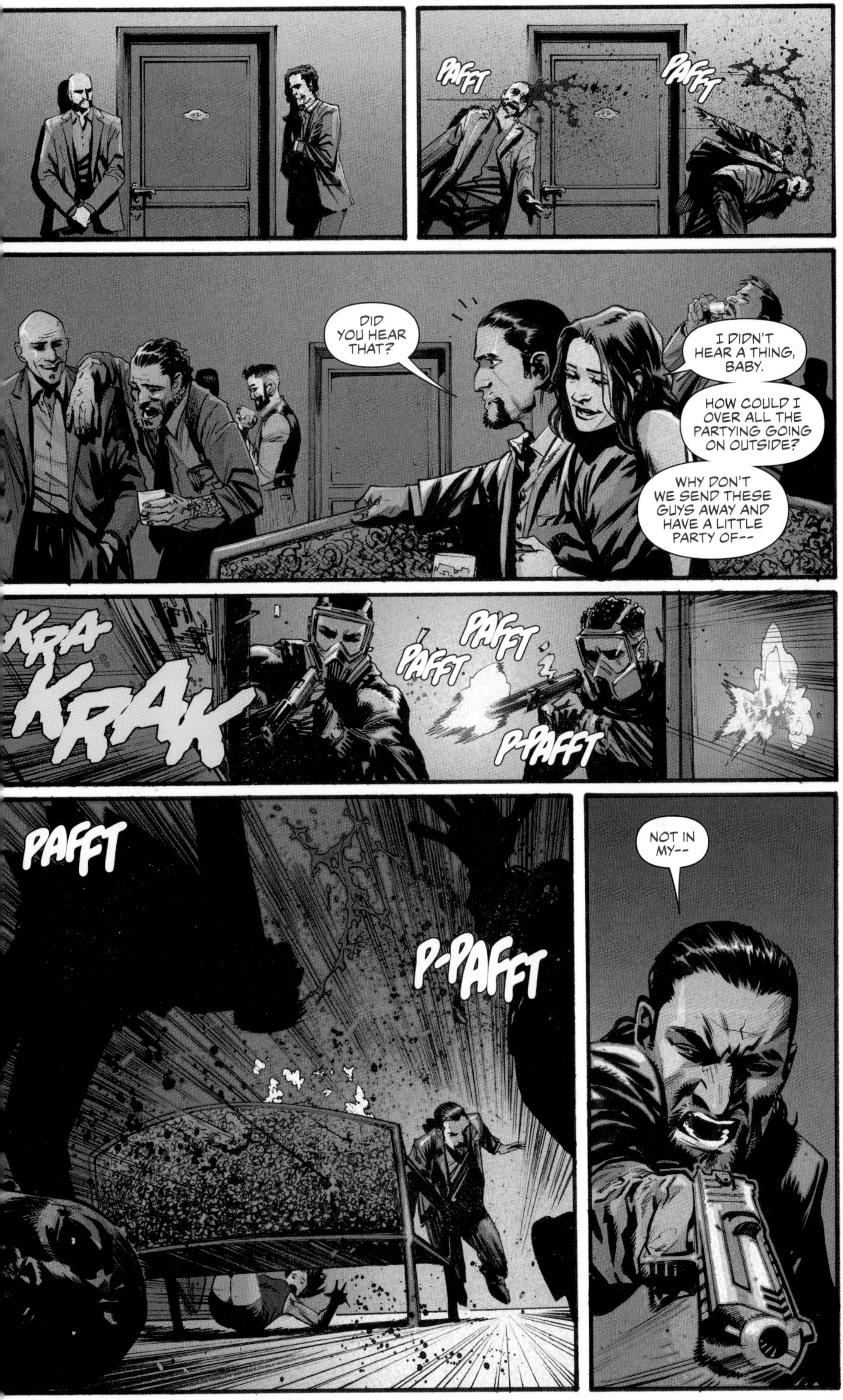
PAFFT
PAFFT
DID YOU HEAR THAT?
I DIDN'T HEAR A THING, BABY.
HOW COULD I OVER ALL THE PARTYING GOING ON OUTSIDE?
WHY DON'T WE SEND THESE GUYS AWAY AND HAVE A LITTLE PARTY OF--
KRA
KRAK
PAFFT
PAFFT
P-PAFFT
PAFFT
P-PAFFT
NOT IN MY--

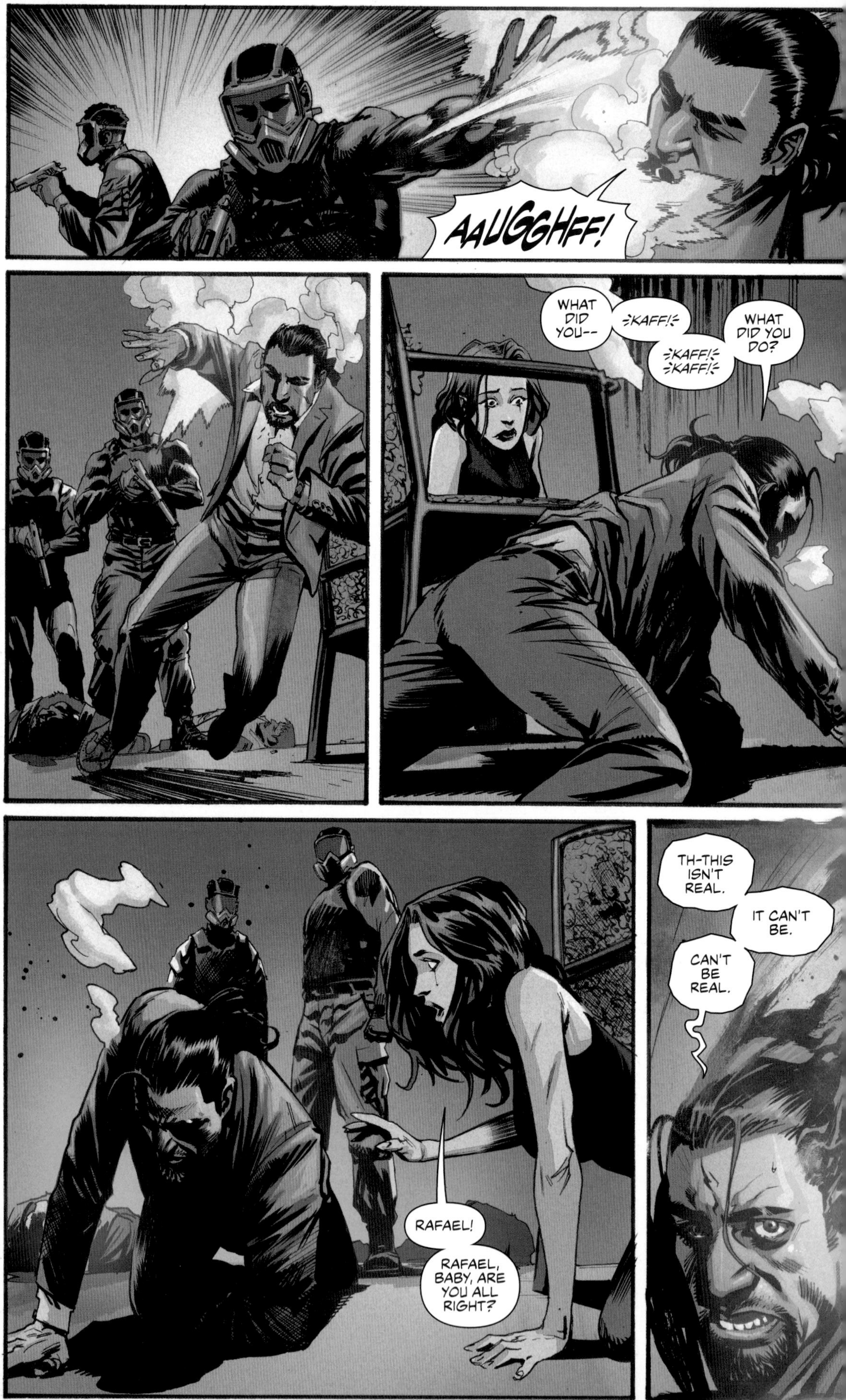
AAUGGHFF!
WHAT DID YOU--
-KAFF!-
-KAFF!- -KAFF!-
WHAT DID YOU DO?
RAFAEL!
RAFAEL, BABY, ARE YOU ALL RIGHT?
TH-THIS ISN'T REAL.
IT CAN'T BE.
CAN'T BE REAL.

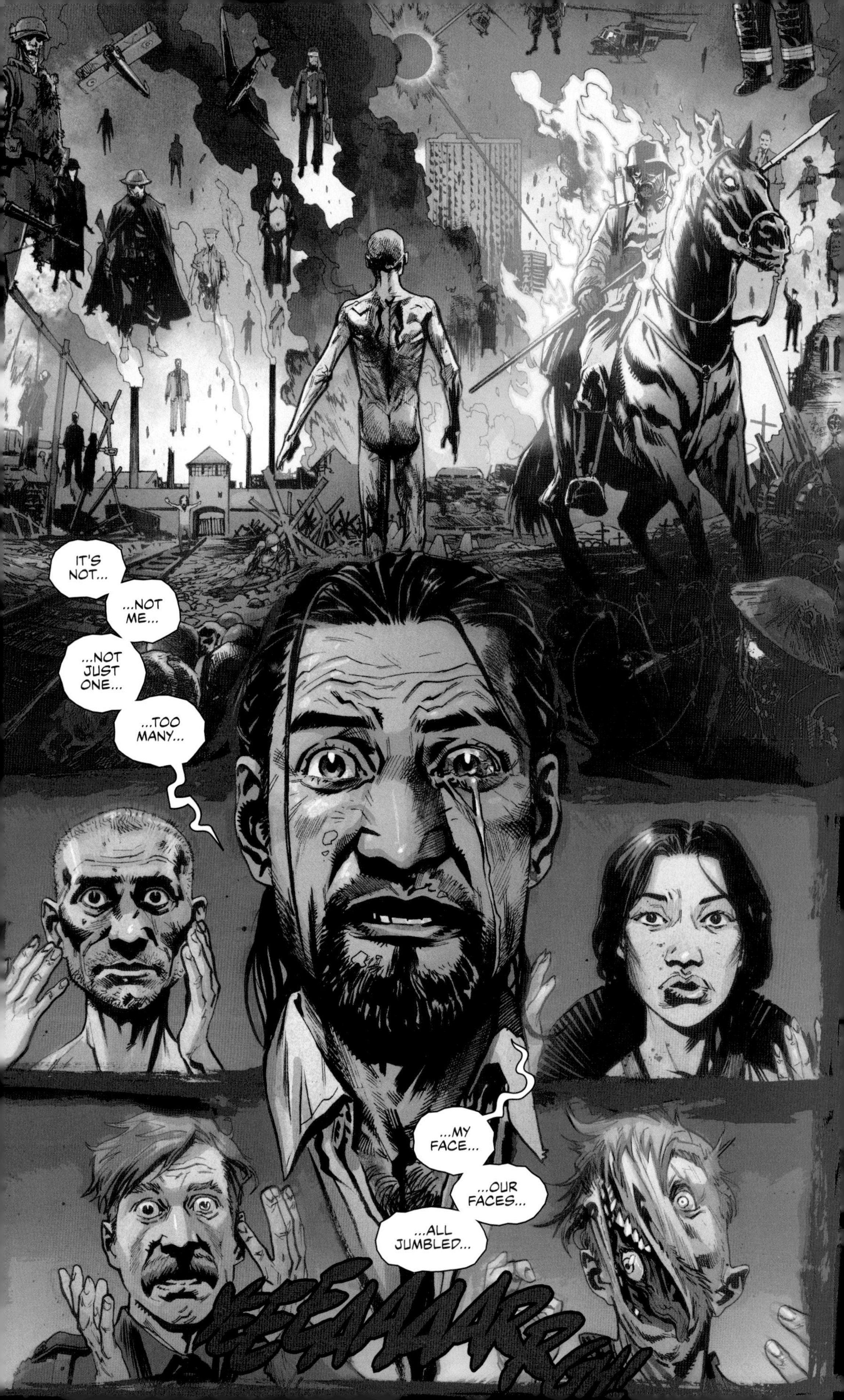
IT'S NOT...
...NOT ME...
...NOT JUST ONE...
...TOO MANY...
...MY FACE...
...OUR FACES...
...ALL JUMBLED...

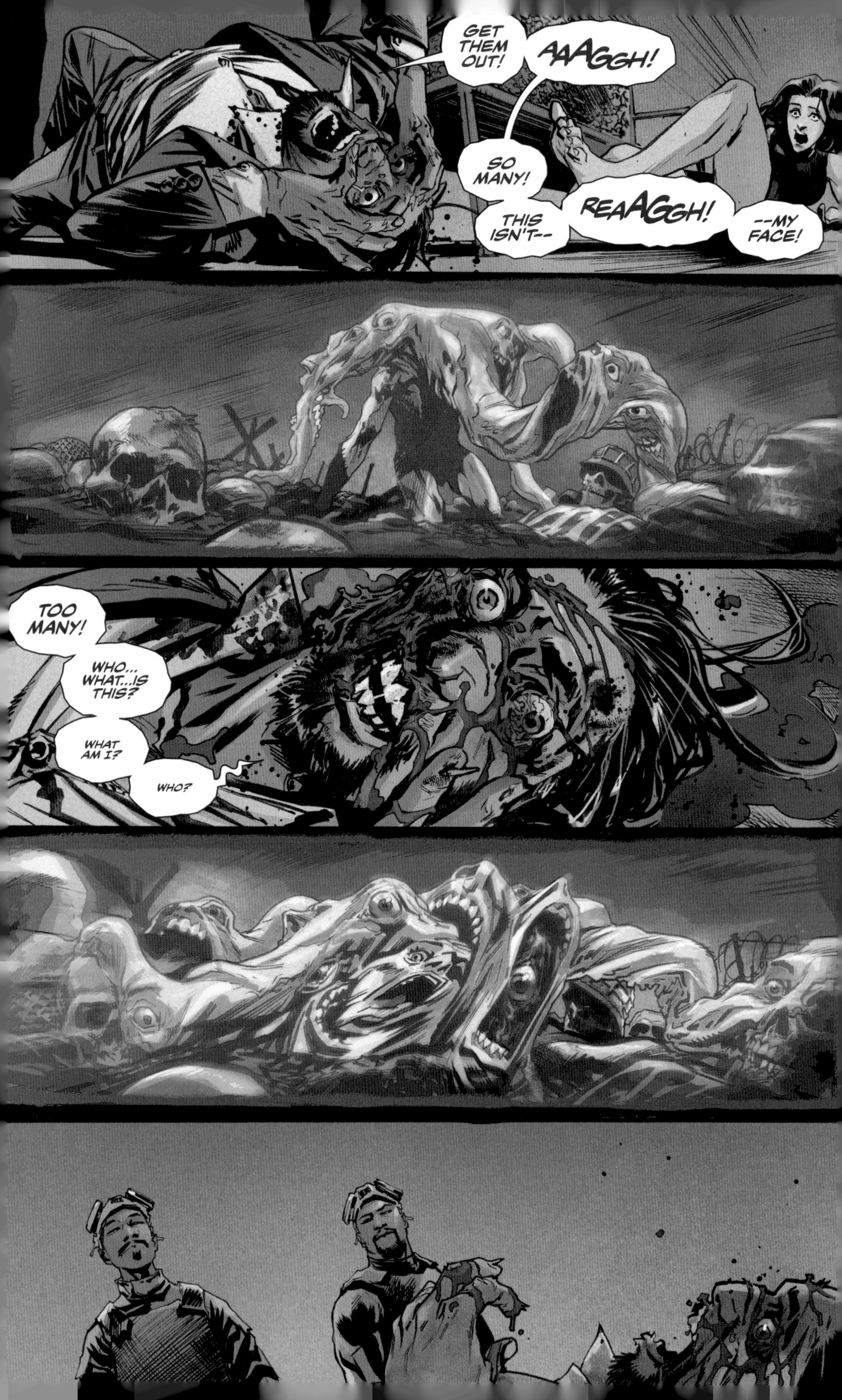
GET THEM OUT!
AAAGGH!
SO MANY!
THIS ISN'T--
REAAGGH!
--MY FACE!
TOO MANY!
WHO... WHAT...IS THIS?
WHAT AM I?
WHO?

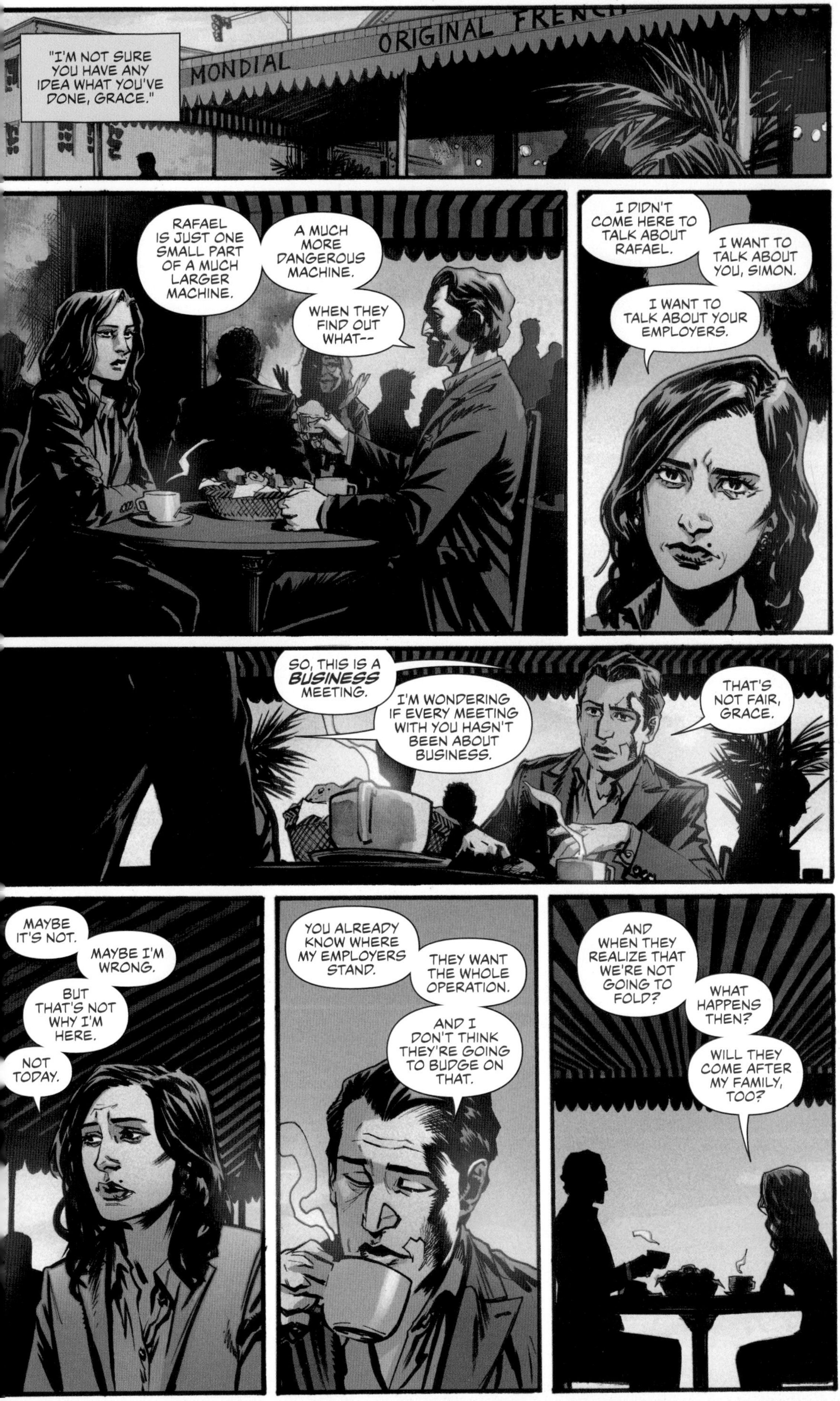

MONDIAL
ORIGINAL FRENCH
"I'M NOT SURE YOU HAVE ANY IDEA WHAT YOU'VE DONE, GRACE."
RAFAEL IS JUST ONE SMALL PART OF A MUCH LARGER MACHINE.
A MUCH MORE DANGEROUS MACHINE.
WHEN THEY FIND OUT WHAT--
I DIDN'T COME HERE TO TALK ABOUT RAFAEL.
I WANT TO TALK ABOUT YOU, SIMON.
I WANT TO TALK ABOUT YOUR EMPLOYERS.
SO, THIS IS A BUSINESS MEETING.
I'M WONDERING IF EVERY MEETING WITH YOU HASN'T BEEN ABOUT BUSINESS.
THAT'S NOT FAIR, GRACE.
MAYBE IT'S NOT.
MAYBE I'M WRONG.
BUT THAT'S NOT WHY I'M HERE.
NOT TODAY.
YOU ALREADY KNOW WHERE MY EMPLOYERS STAND.
THEY WANT THE WHOLE OPERATION.
AND I DON'T THINK THEY'RE GOING TO BUDGE ON THAT.
AND WHEN THEY REALIZE THAT WE'RE NOT GOING TO FOLD?
WHAT HAPPENS THEN?
WILL THEY COME AFTER MY FAMILY, TOO?

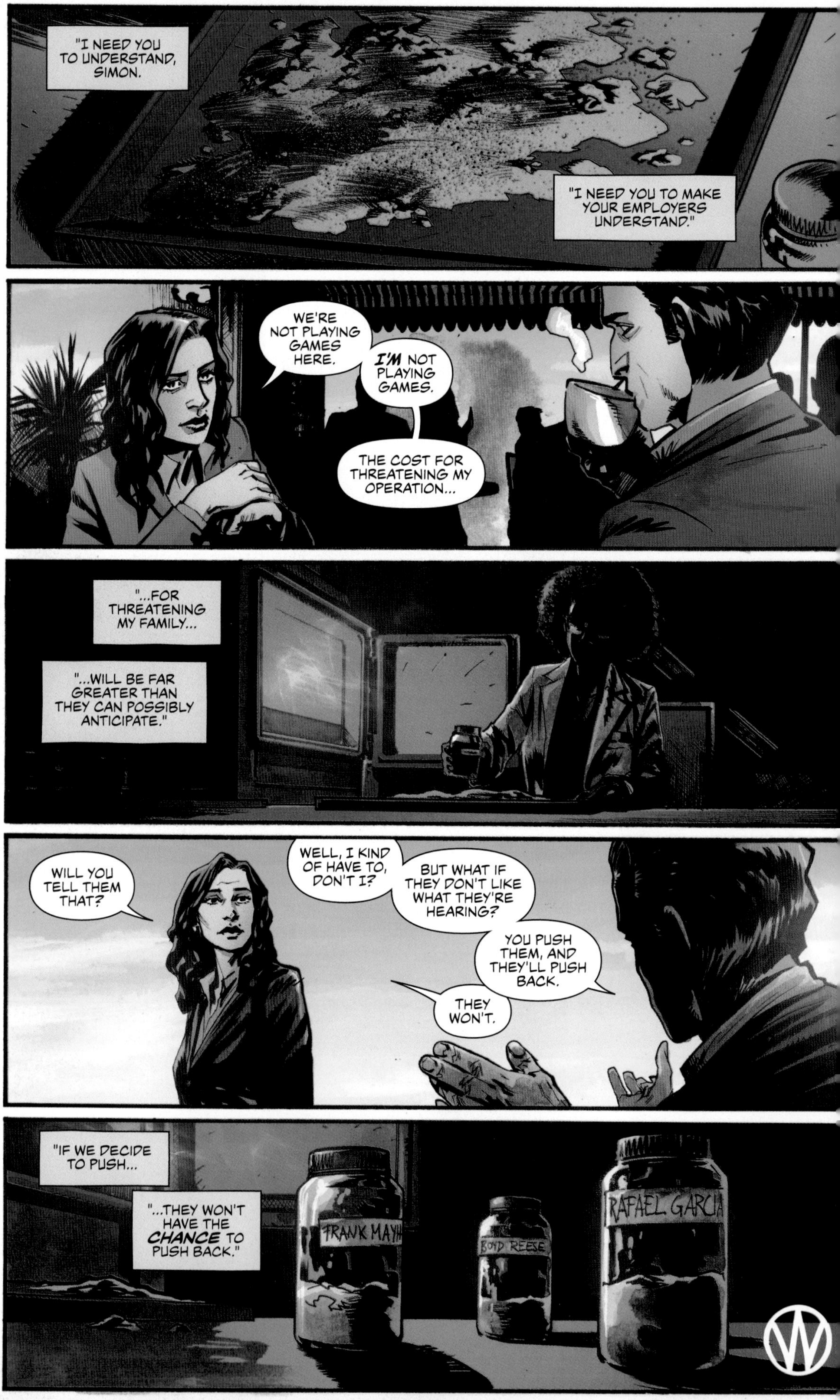

"I NEED YOU TO UNDERSTAND, SIMON.
"I NEED YOU TO MAKE YOUR EMPLOYERS UNDERSTAND."
WE'RE NOT PLAYING GAMES HERE.
I'M NOT PLAYING GAMES.
THE COST FOR THREATENING MY OPERATION...
"...FOR THREATENING MY FAMILY...
"...WILL BE FAR GREATER THAN THEY CAN POSSIBLY ANTICIPATE."
WILL YOU TELL THEM THAT?
WELL, I KIND OF HAVE TO, DON'T I?
BUT WHAT IF THEY DON'T LIKE WHAT THEY'RE HEARING?
YOU PUSH THEM, AND THEY'LL PUSH BACK.
THEY WON'T.
"IF WE DECIDE TO PUSH...
"...THEY WON'T HAVE THE CHANCE TO PUSH BACK."
FRANK MAYH
BOYD REESE
RAFAEL GARCIA

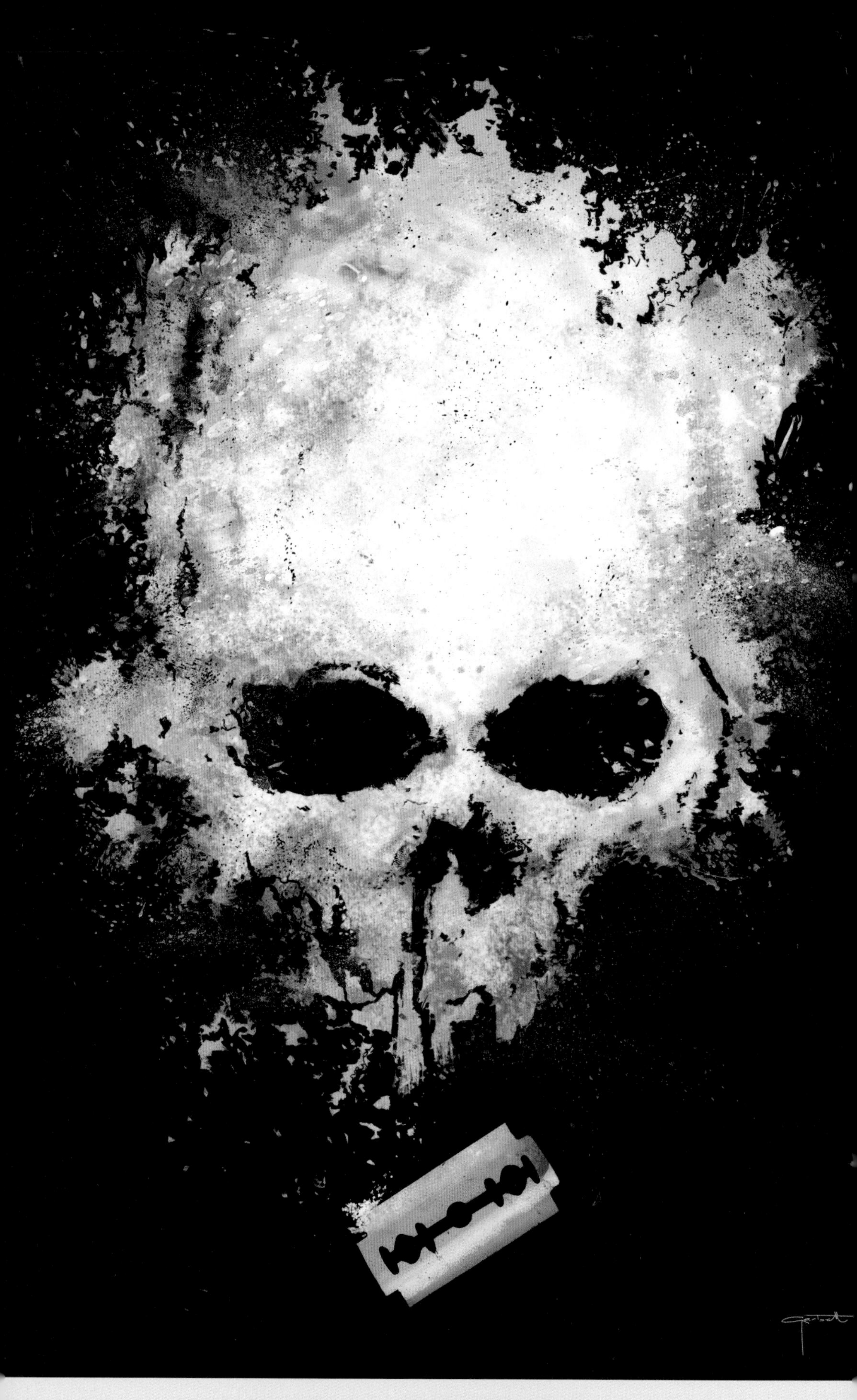

Issue One Cover by **LEE GARBETT**

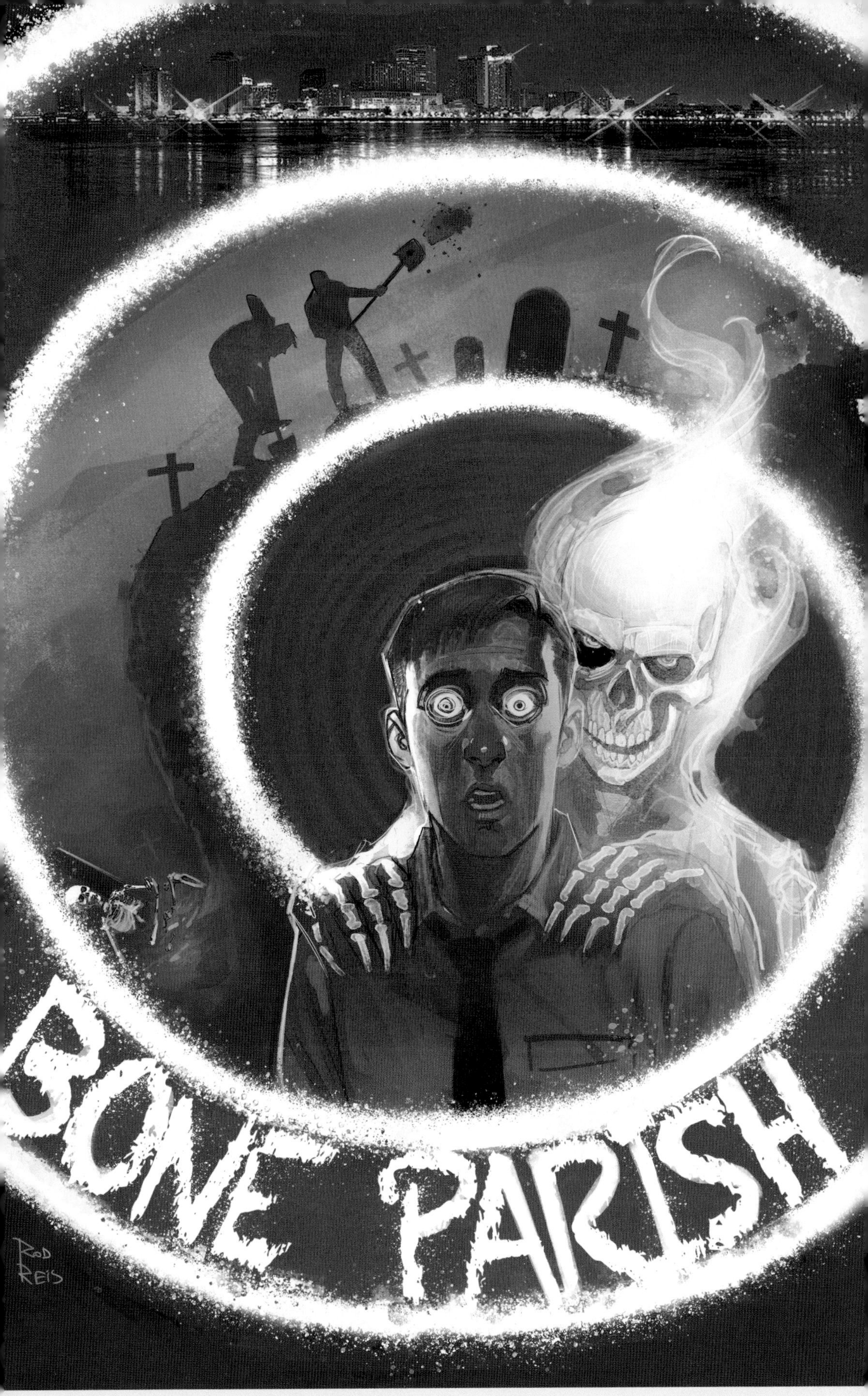
BONE PARISH
ROD REIS

Issue One Cover by **ROD REIS**

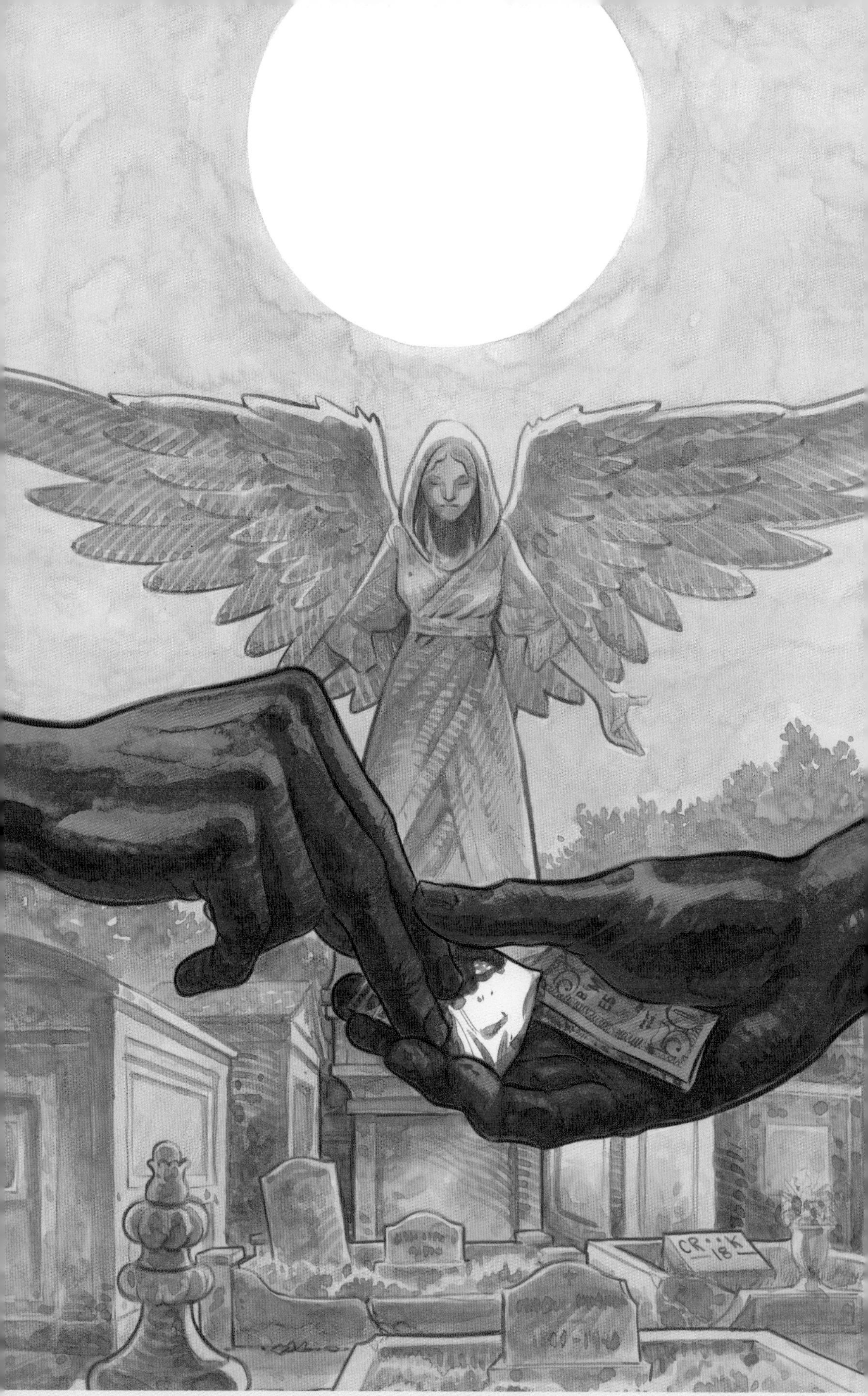
CROOK 18

Issue One Cover by **TYLER CROOK**

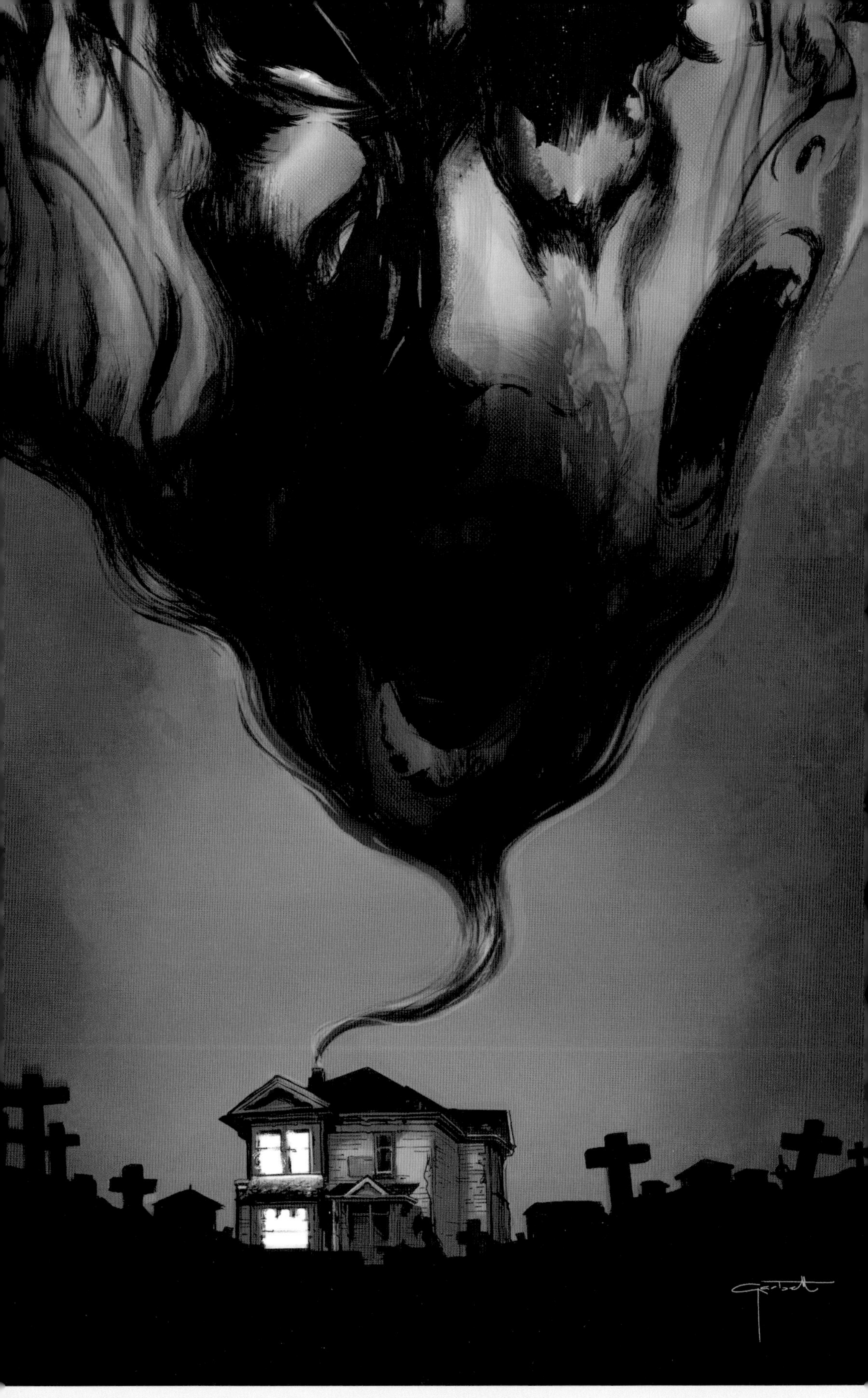

Issue Two Cover by **LEE GARBETT**

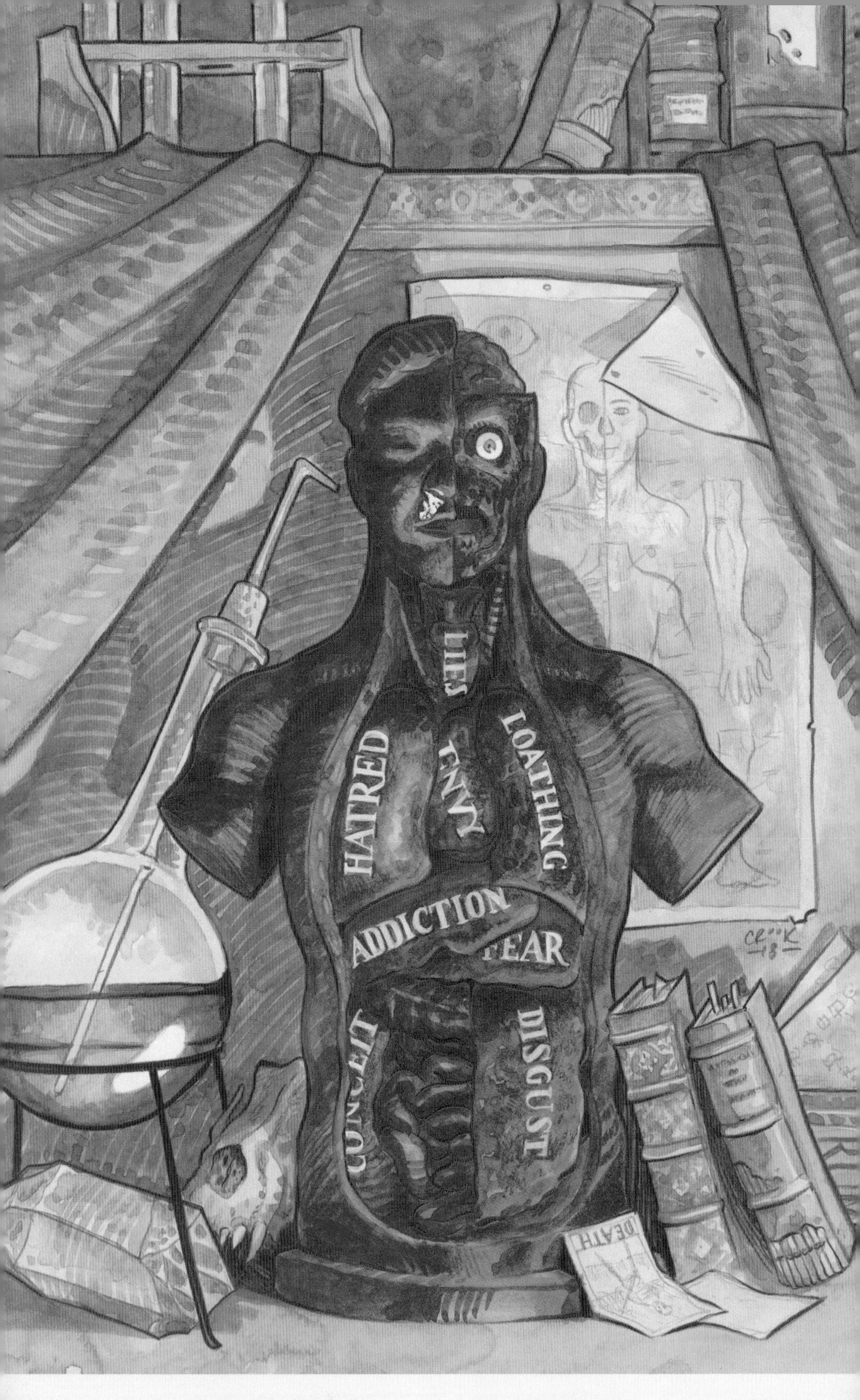
LIES
HATRED
ENVY
LOATHING
ADDICTION
FEAR
CONCEIT
DISGUST
DEATH

Issue Two Cover by **TYLER CROOK**

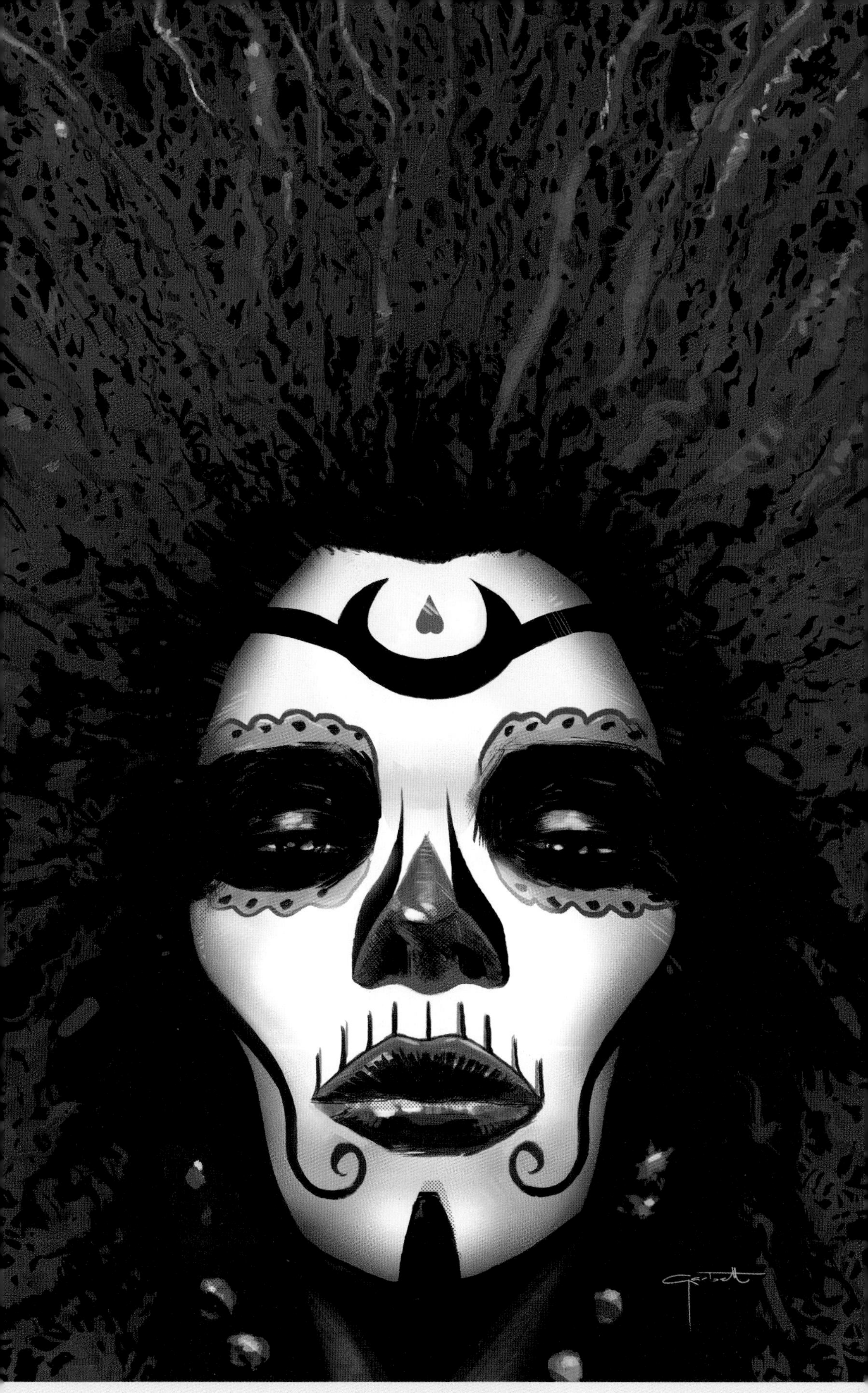

Issue Three Cover by **LEE GARBETT**

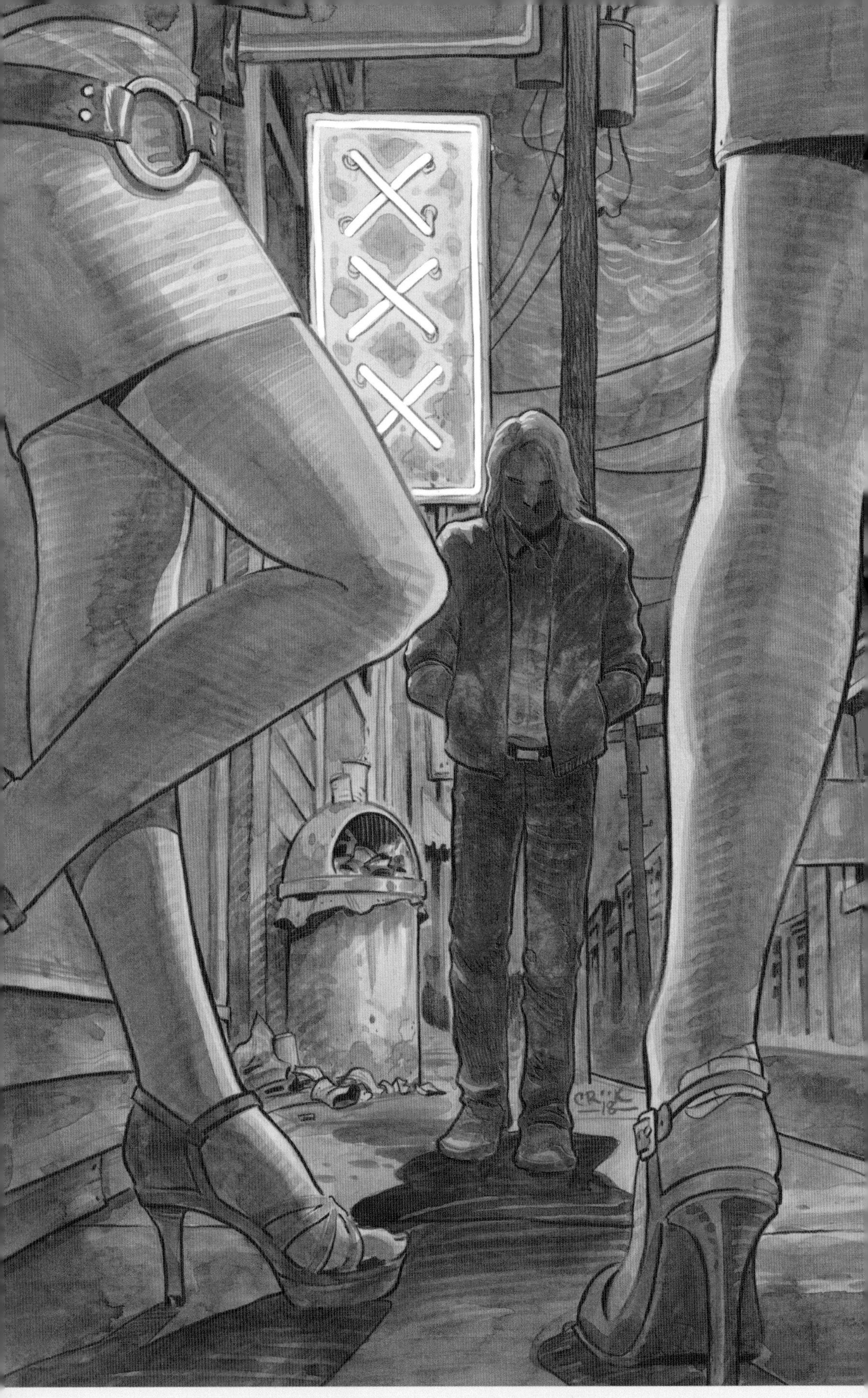

Issue Three Cover by **TYLER CROOK**

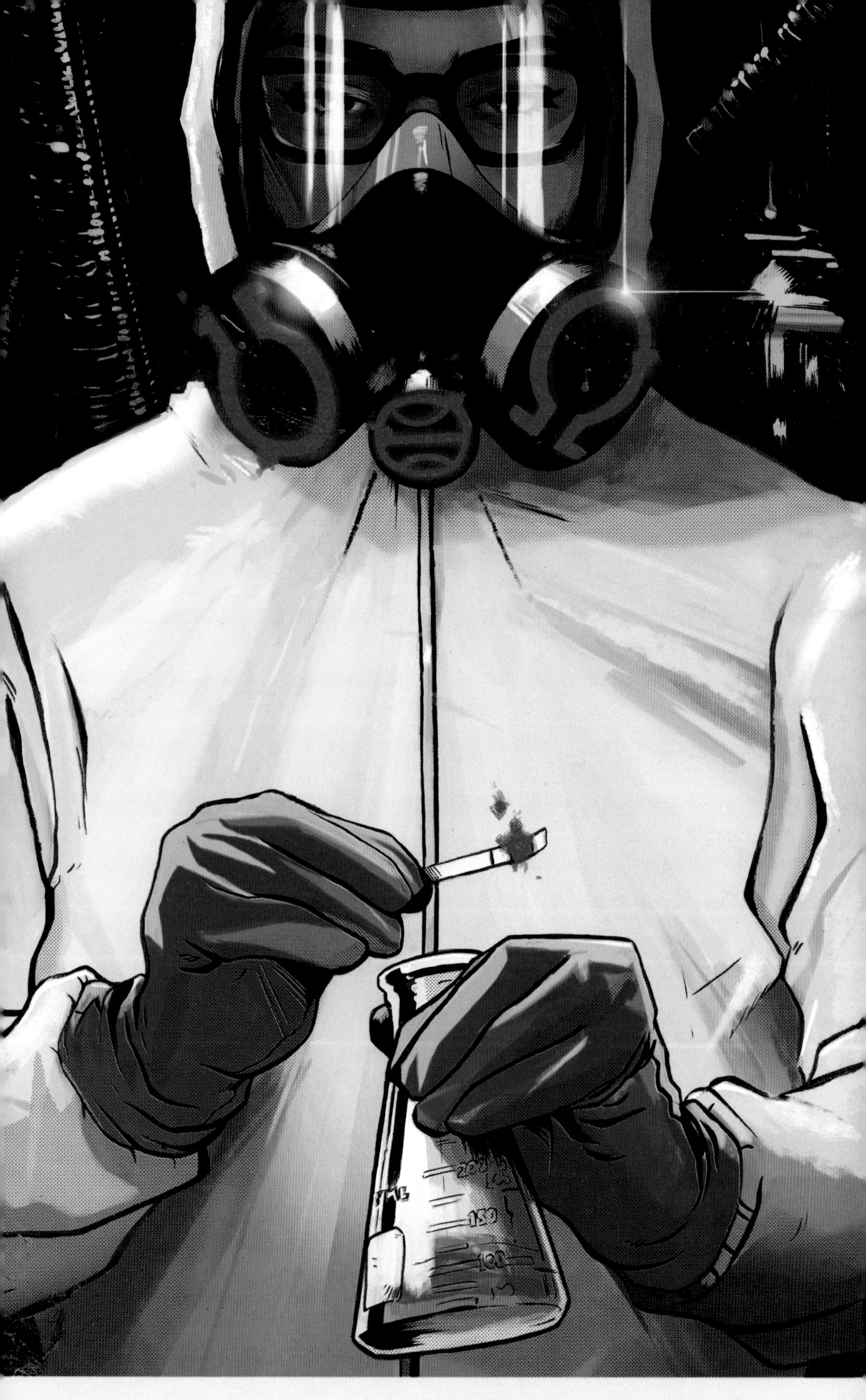

200
150
100

Issue Four Cover by **LEE GARBETT**

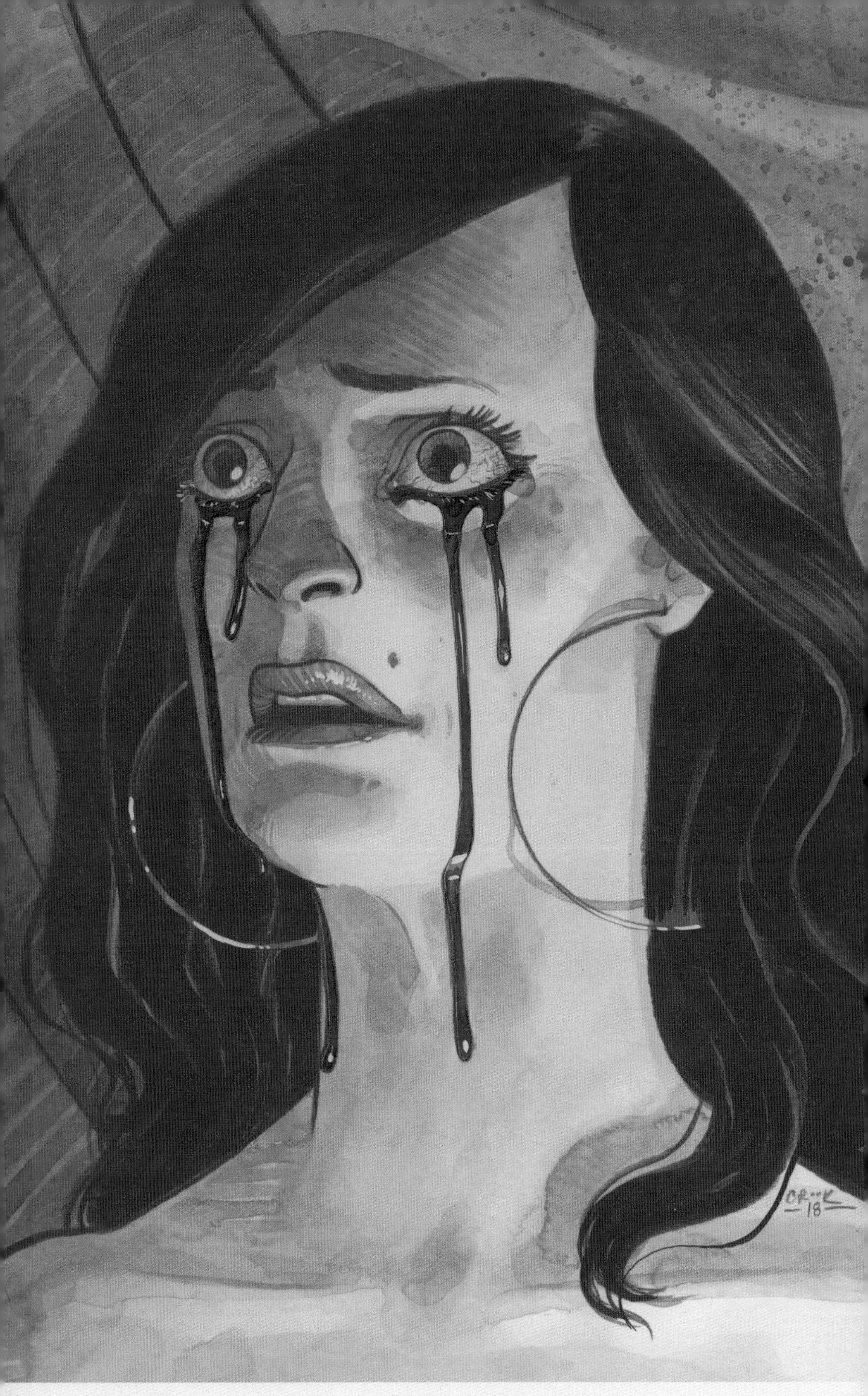

Issue Four Cover by **TYLER CROOK**

CULLEN BUNN

Cullen Bunn writes graphic novels, comic books, short fiction, and novels. He has written *The Sixth Gun*, *The Damned*, *Helheim*, and *The Tooth* for Oni Press; *Harrow County* for Dark Horse; *The Empty Man*, *The Unsound*, and *Bone Parish* for BOOM! Studios; *Dark Ark*, *Unholy Grail*, and *Brothers Dracul* for AfterShock Comics; and *Regression* and *Cold Spots* for Image Comics. He also writes titles such as *Asgardians of the Galaxy* and numerous *Deadpool* series for Marvel Comics.

JONAS SCHARF

As a kid, young **Jonas Scharf** fell in love with comics and drawing and, being the daydreamer that he was, decided he would one day be a comic book artist. After doing the reasonable thing for a while, getting a solid education and a bachelor's degree, he decided it was time to do the unreasonable thing and pursued a career in comics. In 2016, shortly after his graduation, he was offered his first book and hasn't stopped drawing since. So far he is mostly known for his work on titles like *Warlords of Appalachia*, *War for the Planet of the Apes*, and *Mighty Morphin Power Rangers* for BOOM! Studios. Other works include illustrations for the crowdfunded horror series *Blood and Gourd* and *House of Waxwork* for Waxwork Comics.

ALEX GUIMARÃES

Alex Guimarães is a colorist from Brazil. He has been working in comics since 2000, with publishers like Dynamite, DC Comics, 2000 AD, and many others. He started working with BOOM! Studios two years ago, and has had a lot of fun with the variety of projects and characters, from *Planet of the Apes* to *Bill & Ted*. He considers *Bone Parish* a career highlight and his best work so far. In addition to *Bone Parish*, he is also currently working on *Invaders* for Marvel Comics.

ED DUKESHIRE

Born in Seoul, Korea, **Ed Dukeshire** is a graphic artist and Harvey-nominated comic book letterer who has worked in the biz since 2001. He has lettered titles from mainstream to creator-owned favorites. He also owns and operates the Digital Webbing website, a gathering place for comic creators. And you may even catch him playing video games once in a while.

DISCOVER
THRILLING NEW TALES

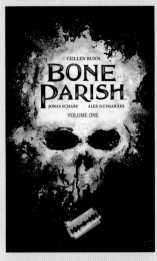

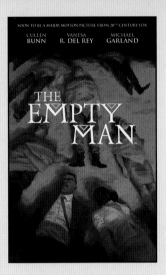

Bone Parish
Cullen Bunn, Jonas Scharf
Volume 1
978-1-68415-354-1 | $14.99
Volume 2
978-1-68415-425-8 | $14.99

The Empty Man
Cullen Bunn, Vanesa R. Del Rey
978-1-60886-720-2 | $19.99

The Empty Man: Recurrence
Cullen Bunn, Jesús Hervás
978-1-68415-356-5 | $14.99

The Unsound
Cullen Bunn, Jack T. Cole
978-1-68415-178-3 | $19.99

War for the Planet of the Apes
David F. Walker, Jonas Scharf
978-1-68415-213-1 | $14.99

Warlords of Appalachia
Phillip Kennedy Johnson, Jonas Scharf
978-1-68415-000-7 | $19.99

Abbott
Saladin Ahmed, Sami Kivelä
978-1-68415-245-2 | $17.99

Black Badge
Matt Kindt, Tyler Jenkins, Hilary Jenkins
Volume 1
978-1-68415-353-4 | $29.99

Victor LaValle's Destroyer
Victor LaValle, Dietrich Smith
978-168415-055-7 | $19.99

AVAILABLE AT YOUR LOCAL COMICS SHOP AND BOOKSTORE
To find a comics shop in your area, visit www.comicshoplocator.com
WWW.BOOM-STUDIOS.COM